Early Islamic Iran

This Volume is dedicated to

Oleg Grabar

and

Iraj Afsha

Already available in *The Idea of Iran* series

Birth of the Persian Empire, Vol. 1
Edited by Vesta Sarkhosh Curtis (British Museum) and Sarah Stewart (SOAS, London).
ISBN: 978–1–84511–062–5

The Age of the Parthians, Vol. 2
Edited by Vesta Sarkhosh Curtis (British Museum) and Sarah Stewart (SOAS, London).
ISBN: 978–1–84511–406–0

The Sasanian Era, Vol. 3
Edited by Vesta Sarkhosh Curtis (British Museum) and Sarah Stewart (SOAS, London).
ISBN: 978–1–84511–690–3

The Rise of Islam, Vol. 4
Edited by Vesta Sarkhosh Curtis (British Museum) and Sarah Stewart (SOAS, London).
ISBN: 978–1–84511–691–0

Early Islamic Iran

The Idea of Iran

Volume V

Edited By

Edmund Herzig
and
Sarah Stewart

in association with The London Middle East Institute at SOAS
and
The Faculty of Oriental Studies, University of Oxford

Supported by the Soudavar Memorial Foundation

LONDON · NEW YORK

Published in 2012 by I.B.Tauris & Co Ltd
6 Salem Road, London W2 4BU
175 Fifth Avenue, New York NY 10010
www.ibtauris.com

Distributed in the United States and Canada Exclusively
by Palgrave Macmillan
175 Fifth Avenue, New York NY 10010

The Idea of Iran Vol. 5

ISBN 978 1 78076 061 2

A full CIP record for this book is available from the British Library
A full CIP record is available from the Library of Congress

Library of Congress Catalogue Card Number: available

Typeset by P. Fozooni

Printed and bound by CPI group (UK) Ltd, Croydon, CRO 4YY
from camera-ready copy edited and supplied by the editors

Contents

Illustrations

Acknowledgements

The Editors would like to thank the Trustees of the Soudavar Memorial Foundation for their continued support of *The Idea of Iran* symposia and publication of the proceedings. Mrs Soudavar-Farmanfarmaian remains very much involved with the planning of each event and we are grateful as always for her ideas and advice.

This volume combines the contributions of speakers from two symposia (2009/10) and, once again, we are indebted to Dr Parvis Fozooni for his dedication, eye for detail and expertise in formatting and typesetting the papers. Thanks are also due to Louise Hosking for her patience and the time that she has devoted to copy-editing and liaising with authors.

We would like to thank Iradj Bagherzade, Alex Wright and staff at I.B.Tauris for their help in producing the publication.

Finally, our thanks go to the authors for their excellent contributions.

Foreword

Edmund Herzig
(The Faculty of Oriental Studies, University of Oxford)

and

Sarah Stewart
(The London Middle East Institute at SOAS)

The chapters in this volume are based on papers presented at two symposia in *The Idea of Iran* series held in London in 2009 and 2010 and both dealing with the early Islamic period in Iranian history. Many questions about this period remain debated and in some cases controversial: how did the population of the Iranian Empire react to the Muslim conquest? How rapidly were existing elites reconciled and assimilated into the new status quo? What was the character and the pace of the process of conversion from Mazdaism/Zoroastrianism to Islam, and how did the remaining Mazdaians respond to the Islamic challenge? How much survived of the pre-existing Iranian cultural traditions, in literature, art and architecture, and in social and political practices, and what transformations did these undergo as they re-emerged in Islamic garb in the Abbasid caliphate and the capitals of the 'independent' Iranian dynasties of the Tahirids, Saffarids, Samanids and Buyids? And last, but by no means least, why did the new Persian language emerge when it did, where it did and in the way that it did, whereas in most of the rest of the Islamic empire the languages that had been current prior to the coming of Islam were entirely displaced by Arabic as the written language of Muslims? The chapters gathered in this volume address a range of subjects in the political, cultural and religious history of this period, shedding light on these and other questions and allowing us to achieve a more nuanced understanding of the political, artistics, religious and literary developments of this crucial era.

Note on Transliteration

The chapters in this volume do not follow a uniform transliteration system. This approach was adopted primarily because of the linguistic nature of the source base for Persian/Iranian studies in the early Islamic period. The chapters use a wide range of sources in different languages (principally, but by no means exclusively, Arabic, New Persian and Middle Persian) and the transliteration system that was most appropriate for one chapter would not have been suitable for another.

A further word is needed on the transliteration of Arabic script languages (Arabic and Persian). In this respect also, the authors of individual chapters have adopted the system that they consider appropriate. In the interest of readability, the editors have favoured systems that are relatively light in the use of accents and diacritics. In most chapters, there are no diacritics on consonants, but long and short vowels are distinguished by the use of macrons. Chapters that rely more heavily on Persian sources have generally used 'a', 'e' and 'o' for the short vowels, and 'ā', 'i' and 'u' for the long vowels, whereas chapters that rely mainly on Arabic sources have tended to prefer 'a', 'i' and 'u' for the short vowels and 'ā', 'ī' and 'ū' for the long vowels. In the index we have preferred the Persian spellings, but have provided a cross reference from the Arabic spelling as required.

1

The Samanids: The First Islamic Dynasty of Central Asia

Luke Treadwell
(Khalili Research Centre and Ashmolean Museum)

E ach one of the chapters in this volume, for all the rich diversity of their subject matters, touches upon a common theme: the impact of pre-Islamic Persian concepts and world-views, which survived the shock of the Arab conquests and nurtured the cultural synthesis that dominated pre-Mongol Iran. The long reach of the ancient past can be seen in many different ways; the persistence of spoken Persian as the *lingua franca* of eastern Iran; the ceremonial of caliphal and royal courts; the genealogies of Sasanian emperors which maintained a powerful grip on the imaginations of poets and rulers alike. Even the commonplace objects of everyday life – like the silver *dirham* which in its size, dimensions and fabric, was the direct descendant of the Sasanian *drachm* – all testify to the enduring quality of Persian culture. The idea of Iran, to borrow the title of this book, was omnipresent throughout the early Islamic east.

The Samanid rulers of the Mashriq who in the tenth century governed a huge swathe of territory stretching from modern-day Tehran to Uzkand in the Farghana valley, a distance that took two months to cover on horseback, hold a special place in the historical consciousness of the Iranian world.[1] They were not only the last royal house of Iranian extraction to rule eastern Iran before the Turkish invasions changed the demography of the Islamic world for ever, but also the patrons of a literary renaissance which challenged the monopoly that Arabic had exerted on high culture. Under their patronage the earliest canon of New Persian poetry and prose literature was produced, triggering a huge output of Persian writing in subsequent centuries and laying the foundations of modern Persian literature. It was the Samanid world where the first *Shahnama* was written, where Rudaki sang his odes and where the contemporary classics of Arabic scholarship were translated into Persian.

But the dearth of information which blights attempts to reconstruct the political and social history of eastern Iran in the ninth and tenth centuries and which has blurred our perception of all the contemporary ruling houses (Taherids, Saffarids, Samanids) has affected the Samanids more than most.

Samanid history is told by outsiders and lacks a coherent and consistent central narrative, such as that which Miskawayh wrote for the Iraqi Buyids. For this reason, it is not surprising that Samanid patronage of letters has acquired such a central importance in the common perception of the dynasty. Open any general survey of the period (such as the *Cambridge History of Iran* or the *Encyclopaedia of Islam*) and you will find extensive discussions of language and cultural patronage but only a few pages on the political history of the dynasty, the administration of the state and court life. All histories require a narrative structure in order to make sense to their readers: in the Samanid case, the long gaps in the narrative have been silently closed and the absence of easily grasped central themes covered up by reference to the Samanids' service to the caliphate and their role as literary patrons, both features which contemporary writers found to be lacking in the courts of their Saffarid and Buyid rivals. Medieval historians were fond of exemplary history and liked to sharpen contrasts between rival dynasties in order to be able to present history as allegory. The image of the Samanids as loyal vassals of the caliph, defenders of the Turkish frontier and rulers of a land of plenty, quickly become fused with a nostalgic sense of loss in the wake of the Turkish invasions of the late tenth century, making the Samanid era a golden age of Persian achievement. But this unwieldy fusion of cultural progress and historical moment is deceptive. In fact, a reappraisal of the formative period of Samanid rule (205–287 AH / 820–900 CE), which makes use of the evidence provided by Russian archaeologists and numismatists and carefully reviews the textual sources, reminds us that the Samanids were of Central Asian origin, that their orientation as rulers was directed towards the steppe rather than the Iranian plateau and that the shape and structure of the early Samanid polity in Transoxiana cast an enduring shadow over their history.

Maps of course can be just as misleading as texts. Let us begin by looking at the Samanid territories from a fresh perspective, not as the eastern fringe of the Iranian world, but as the western terminus of the Central Asian Silk Route. This was the domain of the former Sogdian city states – Samarqand, Bukhara, Kish and Nakhshab – which three centuries before the Muslim conquests had traded silk, musk and precious metals between China and Byzantium, bringing to the area the great wealth which attracted the attention of the Umayyad caliphs.

This region was a vast open steppe zone in which tribal confederations, not city states, held the upper hand. It lay between the great empires of Late Antiquity, quite distinct in its social, political and cultural configuration from the lands to the south of the Oxus river. Transoxiana's topography is a crucial determinant of its history. Its eastern border with the steppe is unprotected by any physical barrier more imposing than the Jaxartes river (Syr Darya) and its tributaries. The Zarafshan valley, the spine of the urban zone of Sogd, was constantly exposed to attack from the steppe tribes, a factor which constrained the expansion of caliphal authority beyond the walls of the garrison city and rendered caliphal control of the region extremely precarious.

Here I will summarize some aspects of early Samanid history that have been neglected in the standard accounts of the period. Most medieval historians date the beginning of Samanid rule to either 260 / 873 or 280 / 893, the first date being that in which Isma'il Samani occupied Bukhara, the second the year in which he conquered the city of Taraz and expelled the Turkish khan. But the numismatic evidence reminds us that the Samanids were appointed to the region as Abbasid governors at the very beginning of the ninth century. I will begin with a reconstruction of the family's origins and the circumstances of their appointment to the governorship of Samarqand. I will then briefly describe their conquest of Transoxiana and the measures they took to consolidate the new frontier and protect the trade routes which sustained their prosperity. I will complete this survey with a few remarks on the tenth-century history of the dynasty. In conclusion I will turn to the question of the so-called Persian 'renaissance' and examine the linguistic and political background to the literary production of the court in the reigns of Nasr b. Ahmad (301–331 / 913–942) and his grandson Mansur b. Nuh (350–365 / 961–975). My argument is twofold: first, that the key to understanding their history, both their precipitate rise to power in Transoxiana in the early ninth century and the slow erosion of their control over the Mashriq in the late tenth century, lies in their role as Central Asian, rather than Iranian, rulers and secondly, that the linguistic preconditions for the cultural renaissance for which the dynasty is celebrated were already well established before the Samanids arrived in the region.

Early Samanid History

Samarqand, Balkh, Tirmidh and the mountains of Tajikistan have all been suggested as the location of the Samanids' homeland.[2] However, three of the four tenth-century texts which allude to their origins, all of them written during the Samanid period and thus worthy of close attention, state that Samankhoda, the Samanids' ancestor, was the *dehqan* of a village in the Balkh region.[3] Of these sources, Farghani, whose informant was a man from Bukhara, gives an intriguing clue that allows us to locate their homeland accurately and offers some tantalising information about the social milieu from which they emerged. Here is Yaqut al-Hamawi's version of Farghani's statement: *wa qāla al-farghānī anna asla-hum min sāmān wa hiya qarya min qurā balkh min al-bahārima* ('Farghani said that they originated from the village of Saman, one of the villages of Balkh which was *min al-bahārima*').[4] This last phrase is puzzling and yields no obvious meaning in Arabic. However, in the later anonymous history of Balkh, the *Faza'el-e Balkh,* we find the Balkhi toponym *bahār durra,* itself possibly a corruption of the phrase *bahār diza* (the castle monastery).[5] We learn from the same source that this toponym was the royal

district of Balkh, in which was located the castle of the last of the northern
Hephthalite rulers, Tarkhan Nizak, who was executed by Qutayba b. Muslim in
91 / 709, just three years before Qutayba conquered Bukhara.[6]

The idea that Samankhoda originated from a Hephthalite princely milieu fits
well with the early history of the family and the sketchy record of their
appointment to high office. Unlike their Taherid overlords, the family only
emerged into the light of history during the early years of Ma'mun's reign,
when the caliph was resident in Marv.[7] Ma'mun himself was the son of a
Badghisi slave girl, and was criticized for surrounding himself with his
maternal relatives.[8] As noblemen of Tokhari origin, from the same region as the
caliph's mother's family, the grandsons of Samankhoda were probably at home
among the caliph's closest circle. They were also well qualified to serve as
governors of Transoxiana, the troublesome region to the north of the Oxus river
which had only recently rebelled against the Abbasids under the leadership of
Rafi' b. Layth. On the one hand, they were products of the regional culture of
western Central Asia, but on the other they were socially and politically distinct
from their Sogdian neighbours with whom they shared neither language nor
political allegiances. They presented Ma'mun with a combination of noble
status, local knowledge and foreign origins which, as events were to show, they
utilized effectively in order to stabilize the turbulent region of Transoxiana and
secure its borders.

Another intriguing clue which indicates a possible Bactrian origin for the
Samanids comes to us from a different kind of evidence. The Samanid amir
Mansur b. Nuh, who famously commissioned the translation of Tabari's works
into Persian, produced a figured medallion in Bukhara in 358 AH. This
medallion, a special donative coin which was probably intended for distribution
to Samanid courtiers during the Nawruz festivities, shows on the left-hand side
the profile bust of an imposing royal figure, which is quite dissimilar, both in
its physical features and its regalia, to the Sasanian imperial iconography
favoured by Buyid courtly culture. The royal figure on Mansur's medallion
does, however, display a marked resemblance to some silver coins struck by the
Hephthalite rulers of Bactria in the sixth and seventh centuries CE. The wings
above the crown, and particularly the profile bust with its arresting facial
features – prominent nose, heavy-lidded eye, receding chin – are shared by both
images. These correspondences suggest that the designer of the Bukharan
medallion had a Hephthalite coin of the Nizak Malik type as his model, and
this, in turn, raises the question of the intention behind his selection of that
model. Did the Samanid ruler who commissioned the piece mean to
acknowledge a connection with the Hephthalite royal line with which his
ancestors were affiliated? The question remains open, but the numismatic
evidence is compelling, particularly since there were other models of royal
portraiture of which the designer must surely have been aware, but which he
consciously rejected in favour of the Hephthalite model.[9]

Turning now to the early history of the state, Nuh b. Asad, the first governor of Samarqand, was appointed to the post in 205 / 820 and spent the two decades of his governorship overseeing the eastward expansion of the frontier with the steppe. Shortly after his arrival, the rulers of the mountainous province of Ushrusana to the east of Samarqand converted to Islam; a decade later the provinces of Farghana and Shash were conquered with the help of a Taherid army and the process of expansion into the steppe lands began in earnest.[10] In 225 / 839, the city of Isfiyab on the Jaxartes river was taken by Muslim arms and in 260 / 873, in the wake of the collapse of Taherid authority in Khorasan, Bukhara was incorporated into the Samanid state, at which point the Samanids became the governors of the whole of Transoxiana.[11] It was only in 287 / 900, more than eighty years after Nuh b. Asad had arrived in Samarqand, that Samanid armies occupied Khorasan in the wake of Isma'il Samani's defeat of the Saffarid ruler, Amr b. Layth, at the battle of Balkh. Thereafter the Samanids ruled eastern Iran for a further century before the Qarakhanid Turks invaded Transoxiana and reclaimed the region for the steppe in the 380s / 990s. Throughout the course of this century, however, the Samanids kept the seat of government in Bukhara and never established a court in Nishapur, choosing instead to delegate authority over Khorasan to a governor.

How did the Samanids consolidate their gains in Transoxiana? They built physical structures (*ribats*) which allowed them to monitor and regulate human traffic across their frontiers and to concentrate military resources in sensitive areas, and they invested social capital in the construction of durable relationships with local princes. They forged strong links with the Muslim urban elites who governed the cities and led the local militias which played such a key role in defending the region against attack from the steppe. *Ribats* were constructed all along the northern fringes of their state: around Isfiyab, where Bukharan, Samarqandi and Nakhshabi militiamen were stationed, in Dizak (western Ushrusana), in Nur (the steppe region to the north of Samarqand) and in Paykand. Further to the west, a line of *ribats* ran along the border between the Ghuzz steppe and the mountainous northern fringes of Jurjan, including large military complexes such as Ribat Farawa which comprised three interlinked forts, one surrounded by a moat, that contained a barracks, stable and an arsenal and had it own water supply. Two more lines of *ribats* were constructed along the western edges of Transoxiana: one extended from Marv to Amul and protected the main east–west route linking Transoxiana to Khorasan and the other from Amul along the course of the Oxus river to Khwarazm.[12]

The Samanids also made efforts to secure the favour of local princes around their periphery, a political process that becomes easier to track in the tenth-century sources, but which must have already begun in the ninth century. These princes included the Khwarazmshah, a very wealthy and powerful ruler whose kingdom lay astride the most profitable trade route of the region, which linked

Transoxiana to the Volga Basin and the northern lands.[13] It was from these forest lands that the most precious commodities (furs and slaves) were sourced. The Samanids also cultivated the petty Turkish princes of the Jaxartes region, who deployed their tribal subjects as frontier guards against the tribesmen of the inner steppe and were given trade and tax concessions as a reward for their compliance.

In Sogd itself, the Samanid rulers cultivated a 'horizontal' style of leadership, in which the boundaries between the amir's household and the leaders of the community were intentionally blurred and the ruler cast himself in the mould of the idealized *ghazi* warrior. Courtly hierarchy was minimized and the Samanid amir made himself accessible to the scholarly class, assiduously attending the funerals of theologians, *muhaddithun* and ascetics. One description of the amir Nuh shows him standing in a muddy grave in his bare feet, lowering the body into the earth with his own hands, while another describes the amir Isma'il Samani attending a regular *majlis* (assembly) with the Hanafi scholars of Samarqand, greeting and conversing with the scholars informally, as if among his equals. Such close ties between the amirs and the urban elite meant that the ruling house could rely for military support not just on its own standing army of slave soldiers, but also on the expertize of the urban miltias, the so-called *muttawwi'a* (or volunteer forces), who manned the frontier *ribat*s and supplied citizen armies for urban defence. These militias were very different from the camp followers and urban underclass who enrolled as volunteers in military campaigns in other regions of the Islamic world. The Samanid militias emerged from a long tradition of urban military service which had sustained the Sogdian city states for centuries. They were well trained, accustomed to bearing arms and fully capable of confronting both tribal invaders and slave soldiers. On one notable occasion, the *muttawwi'a* of Bukhara successfully defended the city against an attacking force of 6,000 slave soldiers who were intent on placing their own candidate on the Samanid throne. [14]

This brief sketch of the Samanid polity in ninth-century Transoxiana stands in sharp contrast to the modalities of government in the province of Khorasan which fell to them in 287 / 900. It is striking that the Samanids never attempted to absorb the lands to the south of the Oxus within their state until forced to do so by the rise of Saffarid power towards the end of the ninth century. That Isma'il's interest lay in the east rather than the west is demonstrated by the first action he took immediately after he was appointed governor of Transoxiana in 280 / 893. In that year he annexed the province of Ushrusana and led a momentous campaign against the city of Talas which resulted in the expulsion of the Turkish Qarluq khan.[15] Once the Saffarid Amr b. Layth had made clear his intention to subjugate Samanid Transoxiana, however, Isma'il was compelled to assemble his forces and confront Amr in Balkh. But even after Khorasan had fallen to him, Isma'il was reluctant to follow the Abbasid caliph's instructions to send his army into the Caspian region and Sistan, the perennially unstable regions to the north and south of Khorasan.

The Samanids in the Tenth Century

After they had assumed control of Khorasan, the Samanid amirs kept their capital in Bukhara and delegated authority over Khorasan to a series of governors. At first they relied mainly on local Khorasani magnates. But in later years, they appointed the Mohtajid princes of Chaghaniyan, and finally, from the middle of the fourth century, their own household slaves, the Simjurids.[16] Although loyal to the royal house in the early years, after a quarter of a century of *de facto* independence, the Simjurids became embroiled in efforts to maintain their authority in Khorasan against the emerging power of the Ghaznavids in the east and their ties with Bukhara were loosened. In the 370s / 980s a dispute over the payment of annual taxes to Bukhara led to a crisis. The Simjurid governor withheld the tribute, sent an insulting message to Bukhara in which he addressed his sovereign as *wali Bokhara* (governor of Bukhara) and called in the Qarakhanids. The power vacuum which opened up in Khorasan with the fall of the Saffarids had dragged the Samanids westwards, but in Khorasan they were unable to replicate their success as lords of the eastern marches. Unlike the other successor dynasties of this period, they formed no power base in the caliphal court and were unable to cultivate strong ties with the *dehqan*s of the Mashriq. They represent a rare phenomenon in Islamic history: a powerful state which emerged and flourished on the periphery, but struggled to find its place within the *Dar al-Islam*.

The course of Samanid history in eastern Iran in the tenth century, which I have described here in very condensed form, was determined by the shape of the polity they had constructed in Transoxiana in the previous century. As Muslim princes of Central Asian origin, they were well equipped to lead the last major campaign of conquest in the early Islamic period, but in doing so they formed a state which was irreversibly orientated towards the north-eastern steppe, in which lay the source of the commercial wealth which sustained them *and* the perennial tribal threat to their continued existence. Most of our sources focus on Samanid relations with their Muslim neighbours to the west and tell us next to nothing about their relations with the steppe. But from the few hints we can retrieve from these sources, it is clear that it was the eastern steppe that constantly preoccupied them throughout the two centuries of their existence as they struggled to maintain a fragile equilibrium with their eastern neighbours. Abu Abdallah al-Jayhani (d. *c*. 313 / 925), wazir of Nasr b. Ahmad Samani and the well-known author of the famous lost geography in the *masalik* genre, agreed to the payment of a huge annual tribute in order to keep the steppe powers at bay while he fought to secure the throne of his young protégé.[17] Towards the end of his reign, this same Nasr b. Ahmad concluded a marriage contract with the 'King of China', probably the khan of the Uighur kingdom, and sent an embassy to the city of Sandabil in western China to escort a Uighur princess back to Bukhara as a bride for his son, the heir apparent.[18] The Samanid alliance with the Uighurs must have been intended to create a second (eastern) front against the Samanids' immediate neighbours in the Turkish steppe. In the year 349 / 960, Ibn al-Athir remarks cryptically that 200,000 Turkish tents converted to Islam.[19] Conversion on such a scale must have signalled a significant improvement in relations with the steppe but our sources throw no light on its consequences and tell us next to nothing about the steppe in the three decades before the Qarakhanid invasion.

The Samanid Literary 'Renaissance'

And so we return to the point at which I began this discussion. As noted above, the political history of the early Samanid state is fairly obscure and the Samanids are celebrated, above all, for reviving Persian literary culture. Nasr b. Ahmad Samani patronized great figures in the Persian poetic pantheon, such as Rudaki and Daqiqi, who composed lyrical panegyrics in his praise, as well as epic poems which retold the ancient tales of Persian kings in the language known as Dari, or New Persian. The Samanids also commissioned Persian prose compositions, including translations of classics of Arabic literature, both popular works like the animal fables known as *Kalila wa Dimna* and substantial works of scholarship, such as Bal'ami's translations of Tabari's *Ta'rikh* and *Tafsir*. Royal patronage, both in Samanid and lesser princely courts, is seen in traditional accounts as the main impetus behind the revival of a tradition of literature which had long been suppressed under the pressure of the Arab yoke. Here, not being a specialist in these matters, I will confine my remarks to a few simple comments. First, New Persian, the language in which Samanid literature was composed, was by no means a low-status vernacular struggling to survive the overwhelming success of Arabic in eastern Iran in the eighth and ninth centuries. As Fragner has recently reminded us, far from being restricted to everyday use at a popular level, Persian was written down for commercial, religious and practical purposes, in various different scripts, including Hebrew, Syriac and Manichaean.[20] The eighth-century Judeo-Persian fragment from Dandan Uiliq, in the Tarim Basin, forms just one small reminder of what must have been a common practice in a commercial zone where Persian played the role of a *lingua franca* long before the Samanids appeared on the scene.

Secondly, the use of Persian in Transoxiana was given considerable impetus by the arrival of Persian-speaking Muslim soldiers in the armies of Qutabya b. Muslim, who were billeted in the garrison cities of Bukhara and Samarqand and communicated with their Sogdian converts in this language. In an extraordinary passage in Narshakhi's *Tarikh-e Bokhara,* the author gives a description of Friday prayers in Qutabya's newly-constructed mosque in Bukhara. He tells us that while the Sogdian converts were given instructions to stand up and prostrate themselves in their own language, the prayers they heard were conducted in Persian.[21] Although Arabic was the language of the revealed scripture and religious scholarship, Hanafi scholars of Transoxiana continued to permit the use of Persian in worship for Muslims who lacked knowledge of Arabic. This we know from the statements of the eleventh-century scholar Sarakhsi and the vitriolic attacks directed against this practice by the Hanafis' Shafi'i rivals.[22]

Thirdly, Persian was undoubtedly the language of the royal chancery in several of the Persian successor states. This was true of the Saffarid administration as it was of the Samanid: Muqaddasi tells us that the royal correspondence of the Samanid court was written in Persian as were the petitions that were addressed to the king.[23] The use of Arabic script for writing Persian must have added to its prestige and facilitated a rapid rise in use of the language.

These observations lead me to suggest that Persian had already begun to acquire the status of a 'high' language some time before Rudaki sang his odes. Given the elevated status of Persian, it is no surprise that the Samanids wanted to encourage its use at their court and to sponsor Persian prose and poetry. Current views on the reception of early Persian literature are perhaps too much in thrall to the strident protests of Biruni, Tha'alibi and their ilk, the arch-conservatives in matters linguistic who proclaimed that 'Persian is only fit for telling bedtime stories'.[24] My impression is that Biruni and others represented a small but vocal minority, whose noisy protestations have been amplified by their literary reputation. In reality, there was probably less resistance to the use of Persian as a language of high culture and scholarship than they lead us to believe. The fundamental changes in the status of Persian language that supplied the preconditions for the outburst of literary creativity which characterized the Samanid world had occurred long before the Samanids arrived on the scene.

The Samanids, princes from a cultural tradition which lay on the very outer fringes of the Persian mainstream, capitalized on the rapidly growing self-confidence of their Persian-speaking subjects to proclaim themselves the kings of Ajam. The political goals which underlay the greatest monuments of the Samanid translation movement, the translation of Tabari's *Ta'rikh* and *Tafsir*, have been overlooked in favour of the broader cultural aims because the political history of the Samanid court has itself not yet been thoroughly investigated. Let me conclude with a few remarks on Bal'ami's translation of Tabari's *Ta'rikh* to illustrate this point. Several commentators have noted that the contents of Bal'ami's work differ radically from the Arabic original and lack entirely the technical apparatus in the form of lists of transmitters of individual reports (the *isnad*s) which are found in Tabari. In the Arabic preface to his work, Bal'ami tells his reader that the king Mansur b. Nuh, having derived great benefit from reading the Arabic text, ordered him to simplify and shorten the text so that his Persophone subjects should be able to read and understand it. The Persian *Tafsir*, a translation undertaken by a group of Hanafi scholars, also shows signs of a radical simplification of the original.

Modern scholars have given different explanations of the intention behind the translations. Meisami suggests that Bal'ami introduced revisions to the history that were designed to promote a vision of the Samanids as the heirs of a glorious Persian imperial past, while Daniel believes Bal'ami's version was intended to serve as a warning to all who challenged Hanafi orthodoxy.[25] A recent study by Peacock rejects both views in favour of a less sceptical appraisal of Bal'ami's intentions which underlines the Samanid commitment to orthodox Islam, as a source of legitimation which offered the dynasty an identity that distinguished it from the impious Buyids to the west and the newly converted steppe Turkish confederation to the east.[26] All three scholars construct their explanations for the translations from the general context of Samanid political history, to the extent that it is recoverable from the meagre sources that are available to us. But it is also helpful to recall the immediate political context of both translation projects.

The translation of the history was commissioned in 352 / 963, just two years after Mansur b. Nuh had usurped the Samanid throne, deposing the heir who had succeeded his brother Abd al-Malik (d. 350 / 961) and contravening the succession arrangements laid down by his father, Nuh b. Nasr.[27] The mastermind behind the *coup* which brought him to power was the Spanish eunuch Fa'iq al-Andalusi, Mansur's mentor and chamberlain. Once installed as the dominant political figure at court, Fa'iq maintained control of the levers of power in the Samanid state for the next quarter-century. As the preface tells us, it was Fa'iq who conveyed the order to translate the history to Bal'ami, with the intention no doubt of bringing lustre to the reign of an illegitimate king. The royal patronage of these translations was an act of political opportunism which capitalized on the status of Persian as the *lingua franca* by boldly challenging the monopoly which Arabic had hitherto exercised upon religious scholarship. The coherence of the translated texts appears to have suffered considerably from the pressure exerted on the translators by their political masters. The excision of so much material from Tabari's original robs the text of its underlying structure, while the introduction of fresh material in Bal'ami's version speaks of a poorly regulated process of integrating information from new sources. As for the Persian *Tafsir*, this is an extraordinary *mélange* of texts which bears little relation to the original and whose form and content has puzzled commentators ever since its creation. The confused and garbled state of the text is so marked that it looks like a bungled job, one which would never have been approved by the group of erudite editors who were commissioned to carry it out.[28] Deficiencies in both texts can best be explained by the absence of a carefully planned structure for the works – a feature that was not a priority for a project that was driven by a political rather than a literary agenda – and the pressing need for rapid completion to a timetable laid down by the authors' political masters.

The aim of the translations was, as Peacock notes, to cast the Samanid amirs as the righteous defenders of Sunnism. But the decision to put both works into Persian was, first, a means of humbling the scholarly class by enforcing their obedience to the king's will and, secondly, a way of demonstrating, through a commission of unparalleled scope and ambition, that the Samanids were qualified to claim the title of 'kings of Ajam', the rulers of an eastern Iranian Persophone world where Persian had long been dominant as the common language of communication. The Samanids had clung stubbornly to the geographical periphery because their social and economic capital was concentrated on the border with the steppe. Samanid court culture was also marginal to the mainstream. The figural medallion cast by Mansur b. Nuh, just six years after Bal'ami began work on the *Tarikh*, shows a royal figure which resembles the Hephthalite ruler of Tokharistan, the Samanids' region of origin. It hints at the survival of a form of regional self-identity at the Samanid court which placed the dynasty far from the mainstream tradition of Persian kingship to which their contemporary rivals ascribed their claims to rule. Geography and genealogy both underline the dynasty's Central Asian background and reinforce their marginality to Persian heritage. It is no wonder that the Samanids, of all the successor states, were such enthusiastic promoters of Persian language and literary culture. As rulers of a diverse frontier zone, where numerous dialects and indigenous social identities survived at local level, the Samanids faced an urgent need to create a common culture based on the language which Qutayba b. Muslim's soldiers brought to Bukhara.

Notes:

1. For the time taken to cover the distance between Rayy (Tehran) and Uzkand, via Nishapur, Amul, Bukhara and Samarqand, see Abū Ishāq Ibrāhīm b. Muhammad al-Istakhrī, *Kitāb masālik al-mamālik,* ed. by M.J. de Goeje (Lugduni Batavorum, 1870), 215f, 282, 284 and 334f.
2. See Muhammad b. Ahmad al-Muqaddasī, *Ahsan al-taqāsim fī ma'rifat al-aqālīm* (Bibliotheca geographorum arabicorum), vol. 3, ed. by M.J. de Goeje (Leiden, 1906) (Samarqand); Yāqūt al-Hamawī, *Mu'jam al-buldān,* vol. 3 (Beirut, 1957) (citing Farghānī); Hamza Isfahānī, *Ta'rikh sinī mulūk al-'ard wa 'l-anbiyā',* ed. by I.M.E. Gottwald (Petropolis, 1922); Mohammad b. Ja'far Narshakhī, *Tarikh-e Bokhara*, ed. by Razavi (Tehran, 1351 AH) as well as several later authors (Balkh); the twentieth-century scholar, G. Lüling suggests Suman (*sumān*), 200 km north east of Tirmidh, G. Lüling 'Ein anderer Avicenna', *ZDMG Supplement III,* 1 (XIX. Deutscher Orientalistentag), ed. by W. Voigt (1977), 496–503; while Semenov (1954) presents evidence that the Samanids originated from Farghana but settled in the environs of Tirmidh, A.A. Semenov, 'K voprosu o proiskhozhdenii Samanidov', *Sbornik statei, posviashchennykh istorii i kul'turi perioda formirovaniia tadzhikskogo naroda i ego gosudarstvennosti* (Trudy akademii nauk Tadzhikskoi SSR), vol. 27, Stalinabad (1954), 3–11.
3. See previous note for Yāqūt, Hamza Isfahānī and Narshakhī.
4. Yāqūt, vol. 3, 173.
5. I am grateful to Nicholas Sims-Williams for this suggestion.
6. *Fazā'el-e Balkh,* anon. (Tehran, 1350), 31–2.
7. In contrast to the early Taherids, neither Samankhoda nor any of his sons appears in any of the chronicles which recount the events of the revolution.
8. Al-Jahshiyarī, *Kitāb al-wuzarā'* (Cairo, Maktaba Mustafa al-Halabi, 1938), 278.
9. The Bukharkhuda *drachm*, an ancient coin type which followed a fifth-century Sasanian prototype, had circulated in pre-Islamic Transoxiana and was still in circulation in Samanid times (see W.L. Treadwell, 'The Monetary History of the Bukharkhuda Drachm ('Black Dirham') in Samanid Transoxania (204–395 / 819–1005)', *Coinage and History in the Seventh Century Near East*, Supplement to the Oriental Numismatic Society Journal, no. 193 (Autumn 2007), 25–40.
10. Farghana and Shash were conquered with the aid of a Taherid army in 212 / 827 see Najm al-Dīn Umar b. Muhammad al-Nasafī, *al-Qand fī dhikr ulamā' Samarqand,* ed. by Y. al-Hādī (Tehran, 1999), 276. For the first Samanid copper coin struck in Shash (in 214 / 829), see E.A. Davidovich, 'Vtoraia moneta Samanida Nukha b. Asada', *Epigrafika Vostoka*, 9, (1954), 38–9.
11. Abu Sa'd Abd al-Karīm b. Muhammad Sam'āni, *Kitāb al-ansāb,* vol. 7 (Hyderabad, 1992), 26 (capture of Isfiyab).
12. References to the construction of *ribat*s are scattered throughout the primary sources: see for example, Istakhrī, 327 (Dizak); Muqaddasī, 320 and Abū Sa'd Abd al-Karīm b. Muhammad Sam'āni, *Kitāb al-ansāb,* vol. 10, (Hyderabad, 1979), 166 (Ribāt Farāwa).
13. See M.N. Fedorov, 'The Khwarazmshahs of the Banū 'Irāq (fourth/tenth century)', *Iran,* 38 (2000), 71–5.
14. For Samanid relations with local elites and their military policies, see J. Paul, 'The Histories of Samarqand', *Studia Iranica,* 22 (1993), 69–92 and D.G. Tor, 'The Islamization of Central Asia in the Samanid Era and the Reshaping of the Muslim World', *BSOAS,* 72/3, (2009). For the Bukharan volunteers' successful defence of

the city against the slave soldiers, see W.L. Treadwell, 'Ibn Zafir al-Azdi's Account of the Murder of Ahmad b. Isma'il al-Samani and the Succession of his Son Nasr' in *Studies in Honour of Clifford Edmund Bosworth,* vol. 2, (Leiden: Brill, 2000), 397–419.

15. For the most detailed summary of the conquest of Taraz see O. Pritsak, 'Von den Karluk zu den Karachaniden', *ZDMG*, 101 (1951), 270–300. (288–90).

16. For the Mohtajids, see C.E. Bosworth, 'The Rulers of Chaghāniyān in Early Islamic Times', *Iran*, 19, (1981), 1–20: for the Simjurids, see Luke Treadwell, 'Simjurids', *Encyclopaedia Iranica* (online).

17. See Rashīd Ibn al-Zubayr, *Kitāb al-dhakhā'ir wa 'l-tuhaf,* ed. by M. Hamīd Allāh, (Kuwait, 1959), 140 (tribute) and C.E. Bosworth, 'An Alleged Embassy from the Emperor of China to the Amir Nasr b. Ahmad: A Contribution to Samanid Military History', in *Yad-nameh-ye irani-ye Minorsky,* ed. by M. Minovi and I. Afshar (Tehran, 1969), 17–29.

18. Abu Dulaf's account is most conveniently found in Yāqūt's recension (Yāqūt, vol. 3, 445–58).

19. Ibn al-Athīr, *al-Kāmil fī al-ta'rīkh*, vol. 8, ed. by C.J. Tornberg, (reprint Beirut, 1966), 532.

20. B. Fragner, 'Das Persische als Hegemonialsprache in der islamischen Geschichte' in *Turkic-Iranian Contact Areas: Historical and Linguistic Aspects*, ed. by L. Johanson and C. Bulut (Wiesbaden: Harrassowitz, 2006), 39–48.

21. Narshakhī, 67.

22. Muhammad b. Ahmad Sarakhsī, *Kitāb al-mabsūt*, vol. 1, ed. by M.R. al-Hanafī, (Cairo, 1324 AH), 36f; Abū al-Ma'ālī Juwaynī, *Mughīth al-khalq,* quoted in Ibn Khallikān, *Wafayāt al-a'yān,* vol. 4, ed. by M. Abd al-Hamīd, (Cairo, 1948), 267.

23. Muqaddasī, 335.

24. See L. Richter-Bernberg, 'Linguistic Shu'ūbīya and Early Neo-Persian Prose', *JAOS*, 94/1 (1974), 55–64.

25. J.S. Meisami, *Persian Historiography to the End of the Twelfth Century,* (Edinburgh: Edinburgh University Press, 1999), 29–37; Daniel cited by Meisami, 35.

26. A.C.S. Peacock, *Mediaeval Islamic Historiography and Political Legitimacy: Bal'ami's Tārīkhnāma*, (London: Routledge, 2007), 170.

27. The identity of Abd al-Malik's immediate successor is not clear: Muqaddasī tells us that it was Abd al-Malik's son, but Gardizi's text suggests that it was Abd al-Malik's brother, Nasr b. Nuh (Muqaddasī, 337; Gardizi, *Zayn al-akhbār,* ed. by Habībī (Tehran, 1347 AH), 159.

28. See A. Azarnush 'Āyā tarjuma-ye tafsir-e Tabari be-rāsti tarjuma-ye tafsir-e Tabarī ast?' in *Yeki qatra bārān (Jashnnāma-ye Ostād Doktor Abbās Zaryāb Kho'i),* ed. by A. Tafazzoli (Tehran, 1370 AH), 551–60 for the argument that the Samanid *Tafsir* was not intended to be a translation of Tabari's work.

2

The Good, the Bad and the Beautiful: The Survival of Ancient Iranian Ethical Concepts in Persian Popular Narratives of the Islamic Period

Ulrich Marzolph
(Georg-August University, Göttingen)

In the chapter on 'soufys' in his travel report about his 'three years in Asia', French author Arthur Comte de Gobineau, author of *Les Pléiades* (1816–82), tells an entertaining story about one of the sons of the Qajar monarch Fath-ʿAli Shāh.[1] This Qajar prince apparently had a strong inclination for the occult sciences. A particular obsession of his was the search for the philosopher's stone, the alchemist's most powerful requisite whose particular capacity is thought to be the effortless production of gold. In connection with his interests, the prince held a high respect for specialists of occult and mystical knowledge, in particular wandering dervishes. One day, the Comte de Gobineau narrates, the prince was visited by an Indian dervish who – after demonstrating his superior knowledge – informed him in private that he had travelled all the way from Kashmir to Tehran at the command of a supreme being whose orders he was powerless to resist. This person was none other than a *parizādeh*, in other words: one of the daughters of the king of the *pari*s. While the prince was not at all surprised to hear about a human's contact with a being from the realm of the *jinn*, he was amazed and, in fact, fascinated to learn that the *pari* had fallen immortally in love with him and, realizing that she could not resist her passion, wished to unite with him. Meanwhile, the dervish warned the prince that he would have to take special precautions to meet the *pari* since this supreme being was used to being treated with particular delicacy. In fact, her affection might easily turn into wrath if he acted in any way that might offend her. Having no reason to doubt the dervish's report, and being further excited by an exchange of ardent letters expressing their mutual love, the prince, on the advice of the dervish, then went through a full month of fasting and purification. At the end of this period he was to unite with the *pari* in the secluded atmosphere of a private garden pavilion outside the city boundaries.

This garden pavilion had been adorned for the special occasion – as the report says – with magnificent carpets, precious golden and silver vessels, jewellery, costly furniture and beautiful chinaware. Since the meeting was scheduled to take place an hour after sunset, the prince went to prepare himself by taking a bath where, being exhausted, he inadvertently fell asleep. Waking up only when the night had well progressed, he was afraid to have hurt the *pari*'s feelings, who must have left without notifying him. Wandering about the garden compound in despair, he found, however, that not only was the *pari* not there, but also the dervish had left, and with him all the precious goods had disappeared too. Only when some farmers on the way to the city's market found him in the morning did it slowly dawn upon him that he had been deceived by a clever trickster. The story ends by mentioning that Fath-'Ali Shāh was so annoyed about the ridicule that bazaar gossip henceforth attached to his son's adventure that in the end he exiled the prince.

The Comte de Gobineau, nowadays probably best remembered for his infamous essay on the inequality of the human races (1853–5)[2], visited Tehran at the orders of Napoleon III in 1855, and so the mentioned report had already been lingering on in the mind of the people for more than two decades since Fath-'Ali Shāh had died in 1834. The author himself presents the narrative with a certain tone of mockery, taking particular delight in the prince's gullibility. In his general assessment of the events, he moreover makes special mention of what he calls the 'spirit of the Persian nation' as being imbued with an inclination for the marvellous and the fantastic.[3] Additional data from the Qajar period, in particular the high esteem accorded to popular literature, appears to support this impression. For instance, we know that Fath-'Ali Shāh's grandson, the Qajar monarch Nāser al-Din, had a special liking for the fantastic stories of *The Thousand and One Nights* from his childhood onwards.[4] This monarch's fascination eventually resulted in what has unanimously been termed the last outstanding specimen of the art of the book in the Qajar period: the magnificent Persian manuscript translation of the *Nights* in six exuberantly illustrated volumes that is today preserved in the Golestān Palace.[5] And for no other period of Iranian history do we find such a wealth of imaginative and fantastic narrative literature drawing on traditional themes and topics, an output that to a certain extent profited from the introduction of printing, notably lithographic printing, to Iran.[6]

Whether or not de Gobineau's general assessment of the 'spirit of the Persian nation' is correct, the story of the Qajar prince anticipating his marriage with a *pari* indicates that at the dawn of modernity, ancient Iranian concepts – such as the concept of *pari* – reigned supremely in popular belief and, needless to say, to a certain extent persist today. Besides popular belief and practice, often conveniently termed 'superstition' (Persian *khorāfāt*), ancient Iranian characters such as the *pari* also make their appearance in a fair number of popular narratives of the Islamic period, from the Persian national epic,

Ferdowsi's *Shāhnāmeh*, and related secondary epics, via the romantic epics of the Safavid period and the popular literature of the Qajar period up to folk-tales and fairy tales, such as those documented from oral tradition in nineteenth and twentieth-century Iran. Deriving from an ancient Iranian tradition, the concept of what a *pari* is supposed to be has undergone considerable developments over time.[7] As for the *pari*'s image in the popular literature of the Islamic period, its closest analogue is the European fairy, a concept to which it is probably more closely connected than the standard disregard of such a connection in etymological dictionaries suggests. In the popular literature of the Islamic period, the *pari* is a non-human character living in a universe parallel to that inhabited by human beings. The *pari* is endowed with immortality and magical powers, including the ability to fly. Usually, but not necessarily, imagined as a female being, the *pari* is above all the acme of beauty. Given her erotic appeal, nothing could be more desirable for a mortal man than to marry a *pari*, even though *paris* are also known for a certain obsessiveness, quickly changing temper and jealousy – all of these traits of character well known to the Qajar prince.

In this chapter, I therefore propose to take a closer look at some of the Iranian narratives of the Islamic period involving characters that relate to ethical concepts ultimately deriving from pre-Islamic tradition. Rather than enumerating the universe of supernatural creatures that was assessed in Arthur Christensen's 1941 essay on Iranian demonology,[8] my particular interest lies with those characters from popular tradition that metaphorically exemplify the pivotal ethical values of the Good, the Bad and the Beautiful. The allusion of the title of my chapter to Sergio Leone's 1966 spaghetti western *The Good, the Bad, and the Ugly* is probably a little presumptuous. Yet it serves well to outline the main motivating forces for the genesis of a large variety of Persian folk-tales, in particular the epics and modern tales of magic. But before beginning a more detailed discussion of these concepts, allow me to introduce further my topic by presenting a few remarks on the position of story-telling in pre-Islamic Iran.

The art of story-telling is firmly rooted in pre-Islamic Iranian tradition. Ebn al-Nadim, the Baghdad bookseller whose inventory of books available at the end of the tenth century constitutes an invaluable mine of information, informs us – albeit from his Arabic perspective – that the first one who consciously employed narratives was Alexander, the Macedonian emperor who was incorporated into Iranian tradition as an offspring of the Achaemenid dynasty.[9] Alexander is said to have hired professional story-tellers to entertain him at night – probably less as a simple distraction than to keep him alert during periods of recreation. Stories of the heroes of ancient Iran were immortalized in the pre-Islamic chronicle *Khwadāy-nāmag* from which the Persian national epic derives. That these stories were also current in oral tradition prior to the compilation of the *Shāhnāmeh* by Ferdowsi is documented by an often quoted anecdote reported by Ebn Ishāq (died 767), the Prophet Mohammad's biographer.[10] Ebn Ishāq tells us of a certain al-Nadr b. al-Hārith, one of the unbelievers of the Qoraysh, who apparently had commercial relations with Iran. The Prophet had once held a meeting admonishing his listeners and warning the people of what had happened to bygone generations as a result of God's vengeance, after which al-Nadr is said to have claimed that he knew better stories than that, proceeding to tell the people about the kings of ancient Iran, of Rostam and Esfandiyār. As late as the tenth century, Persian poet Monjik Tirmidhi claims to have heard and read 'a thousand times' versions of the tales of the Seven Trials (*haft khān*) and of the Brass Fortress (*dezh-e ru'in*), obviously alluding to the exploits of Esfandiyār.[11] In a similar vein, the verse of the early eleventh-century Persian poet Farrokhi alludes to the tales of Rostam, the quintessential hero of the Iranian epic tradition.[12]

As an aside, it is interesting to note that the passages quoted from the Persian poets refer to the epic tales as being incorporated in the Persian book *Hazār afsān*, a book that by virtue of the testimonies of both Ebn al-Nadim and the tenth-century Arab historian al-Mas'udi is unanimously accepted as the ultimate source of the collection of stories nowadays known as *The Thousand and One Nights*.[13] This collection, moreover, serves as an additional argument for the high esteem story-telling enjoyed in pre-Islamic Iran. The collection's well-known frame-story is already outlined by both Ebn al-Nadim and al-Mas'udi with reference to King Shahriyār and the story-teller Shahrazād, two characters who undoubtedly bear Persian names. The frame-story in which Shahrazād tells stories to Shahriyār for a thousand nights apparently did not change much in the course of time. Yet the stories originally contained within that frame might well have been quite different from what they came to be after the work's translation into Arabic. Recent scholarship has drawn attention to a short mention of the *Hazār afsān* in an Arabic book on secretaries compiled by a certain Abdallāh b. Abd al-Aziz, where the collection's translation into Arabic is attributed to Abdallāh b. al-Moqaffa'.[14] This author, who was apparently a Manichaean convert to Islam originally bearing the name of Ruzbeh, is credited with an Arabic rendering of the *Khwadāy-nāmag* which, though lost, served as the principal source from which Muslim historians drew their knowledge of pre-Islamic Iran. He is most famed for his Arabic translation of another monument of transnational narrative tradition, the collection of fables known as *Kalila wa Demna*, whose lost Middle Persian version was an augmented rendering of the Sanskrit *Panchatantra* that is attributed to the physician Borzūy during the reign of Sasanian emperor Khosraw Anushirvān (531–79).[15] While the Iranian origin of the book *Hazār afsān* is beyond doubt, the extent to which the contents of its presently known version, *The Thousand and One Nights*, are representative of the Iranian original is a matter of dispute. *The Thousand and One Nights,* as we know them today, mainly comprise three genres: tales of wonder and magic, short entertaining anecdotes of a pseudo-historical or edifying character and a few long epics.[16] The original work, in comparison, might have focused on fables and other didactic tales, as is suggested by the attribution of the book's translation to Abdallāh b. al-Moqaffaʿ, the translator of *Kalila wa Demna*. Or, then again, the original Persian version of the *Nights* might also have consisted of tales about the heroes of ancient Iran. According to the testimony of the quoted Persian poets of the tenth and early eleventh century, Ebn al-Moqaffaʿ was also well versed in the history of ancient Iran. A definitive solution to this question will have to await the discovery of additional information. Meanwhile, the great narrative collections prevalent in early Islamic Iran – *Kalila wa Demna*, *Hazār afsān* and also the *Sendbādnāmeh*, a mirror for princes that in later world literature became known as *The Book of the Seven Sages* – leave no doubt as to the continuity of the pivotal values of pre-Islamic Iran: model behaviour was exemplified by the heroes of ancient Iranian tradition and model moral precepts were propagated by the protagonists of fables and other didactic narratives as well as wisdom literature. Incidentally, the 'Persian versions of animal tales' have been discussed by the French scholar Henri Massé in his contribution to the 1951 collected volume on 'The Spirit of Iran'[17] and the position of Arabic wisdom literature *vis-à-vis* the Persian sources has recently been discussed in Mohsen Zakeri's rich study, *Persian Wisdom in Arabic Garb*.[18] At any rate, the continuity of ancient Iranian values might also, to a certain extent, account for the fact that the Arabic version of *The Thousand and One Nights,* with its apparently newly integrated tales of magic and its lack of appreciation for the history and values of ancient Iran, did not meet with great approval in later Iranian tradition, where the tales were only translated much later on account of their enthusiastic reception in the West.

To return to my main topic, we might have a quick glance at the only tale of *The Thousand and One Nights* in which a Persian *pari* makes a major appearance, namely the tale of *Ahmad and Pari Bānu*. In structural terms, this tale is a combination of two originally separate stories.[19] The first story is about three brothers, one of whom is the eponymous hero Ahmad, competing for a princess bride. While the brothers manage to cure the ailing princess with the combined help of the magical objects each of them has acquired during their quests, none of them manages to win her hand. The subsequent task of shooting an arrow leads into the tale's second part, in which Prince Ahmad meets the beautiful Pari Bānu, the daughter of the king of the *jinn*, who, being in love with him, has lured him to her abode. They marry and for some time enjoy a pleasant life in her land. The main action of the second part, however, deals with a set of difficult tasks the hero is asked to perform for the malicious king and that he manages to perform with the help of his fairy wife. The tasks set by the king eventually lead to his destruction, with Ahmad becoming his successor.

Both the character of the *pari*/fairy and the term 'Bānu' as a respectful term of address for a woman might be taken as pointing to the tale's Iranian origin. It is, however, important to note that the tale owes its introduction into the European corpus of the *Nights* to the Syrian Maronite story-teller Hannā Diyāb, whose oral performance Antoine Galland, the French translator of the *Nights*, later reworked by elaborating the rudimentary notes he had taken during the performance. Considering the tale's Arabic origin, its fairy character is probably less indicative of an Iranian background, showing rather that the early eighteenth-century Syrian Christian story-teller perceived Iran as the realm of wonder, magic and all kinds of fantastic creatures and events. This perception is also apparent in other stories of the *Nights* that derive from different sources, most prominently the tale of As'ad and Amjad in which a group of magicians makes its appearance.[20]

Leaving detailed philological speculations about the ultimate origin or 'Iranianness' of specific tales or collections aside, we should tackle the main theme of this chapter, namely the question to what extent the character of the *pari* and other exemplary supernatural beings are connected to pre-Islamic concepts that survived in the Islamic period. Not being a specialist in pre-Islamic Iran myself, I admit to having relied heavily on published studies on this topic.

The *pari*, as imagined as the Qajar prince's object of desire, is a vague echo of a supernatural being already known from Zoroastrian scripture.[21] In the *Avesta*, the *pairikā* is an evil being that in formulaic phrases is often associated with sorcerers and demons. It has, however, been pointed out that this association belongs to the youngest layers of Zoroastrian scripture, with the further implication that the association developed after the older Avestan texts were composed. In a detailed study focusing on the historical development of the concept of *pari*, Bahman Sarkārāti has suggested that the *pairikā*s were a class of pre-Zoroastrian goddesses who were concerned with sexuality and were closely connected with sexual festivals and ritual orgies.[22] While the sexual connotation lingers on in the character's subsequent development, later texts also elaborate the *pari*'s magical powers. In the Middle Persian *Selections of Zatspram*, for instance, the hero Srit fights with a *pari* in the shape of a dog. Every time he cuts the dog in half, the *pari* multiplies until the hero is finally overcome and killed by the multiplicity of dogs. Incidentally, this episode is mirrored in Goethe's ballad of the sorcerer's apprentice (*Der Zauberlehrling*) who unsuccessfully attempts to destroy the magic broom he has created without knowing how to control its action fully. In classical Persian literature of the early Islamic period, such as the poetry of 'Onsori, Farrokhi, Asadi and Nāser-e Khosraw, the *pari* is imagined as extremely beautiful, invisible and capable of flight. According to the evaluation of Mahmoud Omidsalar, 'it is often a metaphor of spirituality, and stands in opposition to man's baser instincts'.[23] While *paris* make their appearance in the mythological part of the *Shāhnāmeh*, fighting in the army of Gayumars and Hushang against the Evil Spirit and his hosts, in the heroic part of the epic the word is used almost exclusively in the sense of 'beautiful', particularly in the compound *pari-chehre*, literally meaning 'with a face like a *pari*', or '*pari*-faced'. Both the secondary epics *Farāmarznāmeh* and *Sāmnāmeh* mention a union between a male human and a female *pari*. The erotic attraction of the female *pari* as well as her magical powers are further elaborated in the Persian prose romantic epics such as *Samak-e ayyār*, *Eskandarnāmeh* and *Romuz-e Hamza*, as well as in the *tumār*s used by professional story-tellers. Here, the *pari* to some extent merges with the concept of the swan–maiden, in particular when she disappears in the form of a dove or when the hero summons his *pari* helper by burning a bit of the *pari*'s feather that he has kept for this purpose.[24] And, finally, in contemporary Persian folk-tales the *pari* has matured into the acme of both physical and moral perfection, two qualities that ensure her human husband is ultimately inferior to her. As an inevitable outcome of this disparity she is often obliged to leave him since he is incapable of understanding and accepting her rules. The folk-tale of the jeweller Salim, *Salim-e javāheri* – an eighteenth-century romance that is, in terms of content, vaguely related to the travels of Sindbād the sea-faring merchant[25] – expresses the *pari*–wife's perfection by allotting the different roles of a man's relation to women to females of three different characters: the human wife bears him offspring, the animal wife (a monkey) is the ideal partner for the joyful execution of sex unburdened by responsibility, and the *pari*–wife is simply superhuman understanding and tolerance. Even so, it is interesting to note that the text of this romance explicitly has the *pari*–wife leave her husband every month for ten consecutive days to visit her father – leaving it open to interpretation whether this absence coincides with her menstruation or her most fertile days.

Popular narratives, as is well known, need conflict to develop a dynamic plot. While the union with a *pari* serves well as a male hero's ultimate goal, the hero must first overcome obstacles, perform difficult tasks and, most important, subdue evil forces or, in other words, vanquish the ultimate Bad. In folk-tales, this ultimate Bad finds its expression in two concepts, both of which, similar to that of the *pari*, are also linked to ancient Iranian tradition: the *div*, or demon, and the *ezhdehā*, or dragon.

The short definition of the *ezhdehā* which introduces a highly detailed exposition in the relevant entry of the *Encyclopaedia Iranica* describes them as: 'various kinds of snake-like, mostly gigantic monsters living in the air, on earth, or in the sea... sometimes connected with natural phenomena, especially rain and eclipses.'[26] Myths about dragons and heroes slaying them are said to have been 'common among the Indo-European peoples and the Near-Eastern peoples with whom the Iranians came into contact from the first half of the first millennium B.C.'[27] While there are several dragon-like characters in the *Avesta*, the most immediate precursor of the *ezhdehā*, as encountered in Persian literature of the Islamic period, is Azhi Dahaka, a character belonging 'to the realm of mythologized history or historicized mythology'.[28] It is, however, not altogether clear 'whether he was originally considered as a human in dragon-shape or a dragon in man-shape'. This dichotomy later gave rise to two separate entities. The evil human character Zahhāk, similar to the Avestan Azhi Dahaka, is imagined as a three-headed creature that, in addition to its human head, has two snake heads on his shoulders. While this character by later tradition was incorporated into mythology and mythical history, the second embodiment of the Avestan concept plays the major role in the popular narrative literature of the Islamic period. This is the animal *ezhdehā* or dragon making its appearance in a large number of Persian legends, including those of dragon-slaying heroes Fereidun, Garshāsp, Rostam, Farāmarz, Borzu, Esfandiyār, Alexander, Bahrām Gur and many others.[29] Fighting and slaying a dragon is a hero's most valiant task. In fact, a warrior has to slay at least one dragon to be constituted as a true hero. In the later religious epics of the Islamic era this feature is epitomized by the episode of Ali, the Shi'i equivalent of the national Iranian hero Rostam, who rips a dragon apart when still an infant in the cradle.[30] Slaying a dragon is, moreover, not only a demonstration of prowess. In Iranian mythology, the dragon is a symbol of drought, often preventing the people's access to water. In the Iranian versions of a folk-tale that is widespread in Indo-Iranian tradition, a dragon occupies a country's well or spring and thus its indispensable source of life.[31] In addition, it also threatens human reproduction by demanding the sacrifice of a virgin (and, ultimately, the princess) in exchange for allowing the people to fetch water. Quite obviously, the people's choice is for the bad or the worse, and so the dragon-slaying hero's interference is their only chance of survival. As the standard reward for his valiant deed, the hero is promised marriage with the princess. In passing, it might be mentioned that the future union of princess and hero constitutes a good choice, not only from the latter's perspective. Even if the ancient story-tellers probably did not think of the union in these modern terms, by uniting the ruler's daughter with the hero who had secured their survival, the people could profit from the hero's genetic potential for the procreation of the country's future rulers. Out of the characters discussed in the present survey, the *ezhdehā* is the one elaborated in most detail in pre-Islamic sources and also in both the elite and popular literatures of the Islamic period.

While the *ezhdehā* was perceived as an evil character from the very beginning, the *div*, as the second impersonation of the quintessential Bad in Persian literature of the Islamic period, apparently relates to a class of gods from the Indo-Iranian period.[32] It is extremely difficult to determine the various stages of this development, but undoubtedly at some stage the Avestan *daiva*s were demonized. In the Gathas, the *daiva*s still 'constituted a distinct category of quite genuine gods, who had, however, been rejected' due to the fact that they were 'incapable of proper divine discernment'. Though the existing evidence is said to be 'full of gaps and ambiguities', it has been suggested that *daiva*s should be regarded as beings who, similar to humans, have been endowed with the freedom of choice but have not put their freedom to proper use. Their religion is false, and humanity's main weapon to defend itself against them is the proper observance of ritual and liturgy. In later Zoroastrian ritual and theology, the concept of the *dēv* is central and in Zoroastrian religious books they serve as the stereotypical personifications of every imaginable evil. This image is mirrored throughout their appearance as *div* in the Persian literature of the Islamic period.[33] *Div*s are often imagined as hideous creatures, sometimes black and furry, with long teeth, black lips and claws on their hands. Some *div*s have several heads, while others have monstrous ears or gigantic teeth. The land of Māzandarān mentioned in the *Shāhnāmeh* even depicts a land of *div*s whose organization resembles that of the human world. Here, 'they have a king, with all the trappings of kingship, including armies, demon generals, cities, fortresses, farms, herds, etc.' While the *div* has thus become the ultimate representative of evil forces hostile to humanity, attributes derived from its ancient Iranian roots have also mingled with, and to certain extent incorporated, additional features originally pertaining to demons of Arabic tradition, such as the *ghul*, the *jinn* or the *ifrit*.

Within the numerous details characterizing the *div* in the Persian epics as well as later popular literature, several peculiar traits are of particular interest. One curious characteristic is the *div*'s tendency to do the opposite of what it is asked to do. This is the reason why Rostam, when carried through the air by the *div* Akvān, asks to be thrown down to the earth: he is certain that Akvān will then throw him into the sea.[34] Another peculiarity is that when fighting a *div*, the hero must strike the *div* only once, since a second stroke will restore the *div*'s powers.[35] Consequently, when the *div* asks to be struck a second time, the informed hero will normally respond: 'My mother only bore me once, and so I will not strike again...', thus delivering the *div* to final annihilation. As a third peculiar point, we might mention that a *div* can also, even if it does so rarely, enter into sexual union with a human being. Mostly, though not exclusively, imagined as a male creature, the *div* could thus sire offspring with a human woman. A fairly recent instance of such a union is encountered in the narrative of *Khosraw-e divzād*, in folklorist terms a version of the popular tale of the faithless sister.[36] In this tale, a royal brother and his sister are driven away from their home. Unnoticed by her brother, the young woman falls in love with a *div*, becomes pregnant and gives birth to a son. Due to the qualities inherited from his demon father, the son possesses supernatural strength, whereas in terms of ethics he is firmly committed to human (though not necessarily his mother's) standards. Consequently, when his uncle has been mortally wounded by his mother's *div*–lover, he saves his uncle from imminent death or even resuscitates him by procuring the water of life before going on to slay his demon father.

The final point to be addressed in the present survey is the impersonation of Good. As might well be imagined, this feature is stereotypically impersonated by the hero. But whereas the forces of evil are pure and unambiguous in their determination to destroy humanity, the hero of Iranian legend and epic does not manifest positive characteristics alone. As a telling example, we might remember Rostam's fight with his son Sohrāb. When Rostam has been overcome by Sohrāb and the latter has already drawn a dagger to sever the hero's head, Rostam resorts to trickery to save his life.[37] He tells Sohrāb that, according to the laws of his land, a hero may not strike a fatal blow the first time he vanquishes his enemy, but only when he has overcome him twice. Sohrāb trusts Rostam's words and lets him go. Having been alerted to the folly of his action by a third party, he soon returns to fight Rostam again. This time, however, Rostam seizes him by the shoulders and forces him to the ground. Knowing the young man will not lie there for long, Rostam plunges his dagger into the young man's chest – only to find out soon afterwards that he has unwittingly killed his own son. Incidentally, Rostam's trick mirrors the above-mentioned rule that a hero should never attempt to strike a *div* twice lest he restores his enemy's power.

In order to avoid tragedies like Rostam's, the hero character in Persian epics of the Islamic period is often split up into two distinct characters, leaving an unambiguous positive role to the main hero. In particular, the Persian romantic epics relegate the more dubious activities of a warrior to a separate character, the *ayyār*.[38] The *ayyār*, who is best perceived of as the hero's *alter ego*, is absolutely loyal to the hero. Yet, while the hero challenges his foes directly, to further the hero's ultimate success the *ayyār* is permitted to lie and spy, to drug and abduct the enemy and to perform all kinds of ethically questionable activities that would spoil the image of the pure hero. Interestingly, both the valiant hero and the tricky *ayyār* share a common pre-Islamic origin in being related to the prototypical ideal of *javānmardi* (Arabic *futuwwa*) as exemplified by members of the Sasanian cavalry who were bound together by a code of honour.[39] Thus the hero character of much of the Persian literature of the Islamic period also relates directly to a pre-Islamic concept. Abstracting the role of the hero even further, one is tempted to interpret most of the action in Persian epics, legends and folk-tales as exemplifying and elaborating the quintessential basics of a pre-Islamic world-view that sees human existence as being governed by the constant battle between the forces of Good and Bad. At this point, however, the analogy becomes so generally applicable that it appears hardly profitable to develop it any further.

In conclusion, I would like to mention two theoretical assumptions underlying this chapter, even though I have not voiced them explicitly. First, it is a commonly acknowledged paradox that detailed knowledge of events, characters and concepts multiplies in inverted proportion to their historical proximity. In other words, numerous historical events and other features of history are with time relegated to oblivion or all but disappear. Conversely, those that persist in tradition are often embellished and adorned with numerous additional traits so as to develop an attractive and convincing image of how posterity imagines them to have been. This process is particularly evident in the phenomenon of '*Kristallisationsgestalt*', a term denoting certain characters from historical or pseudo-historical tradition that have the capacity of attracting and adding to their own repertoire all kinds of traits and narratives that might or might not originally have been attached to other characters.[40] As a folklorist I am rather less concerned with the question of historical truth, particularly since the concepts of truth or reality are not as unambiguous as we would hope them to be. Studying the survival of ancient concepts, my focus is rather on meaning. Seen from this perspective, the features I have discussed demonstrate their meaningful position in Iranian tradition not only by their longevity but also by their characteristics as articulated in the Persian literature of the Islamic period. In addition, it is significant that the features discussed unquestionably relate to pre-Islamic tradition and that their present shape is an imaginative and often fanciful transformation of ancient models. We should, however, be extremely diligent not to hypothesize pure and uncontaminated origins, nor to presume direct and unbroken chains of tradition. From their inception, or at least from the earliest sources we can fathom today, the underlying concepts were subjected to a variety of influences arising from the differing ethnic and religious backgrounds with which they came into contact. Consequently, and not only from the point of view of popular literature, my 'Idea of Iran' is not that of a pure nation whose pivotal values might or might not have been contaminated by later developments. Rather, I see it essentially as a hybrid entity that over the thousands of years of its existence has successfully managed to incorporate a plethora of elements of varying origins. Seen against this theoretical backdrop, the enduring power of the 'Idea of Iran' would thus not arise from a nostalgic adherence to values of times that have irretrievably gone by. Rather its powerful potential relates to its constant ability to preserve a limited array of core values while adapting them to the exigencies of constantly changing circumstances.

Notes:

1. Arthur, Comte de Gobineau, *Trois ans en Asie (de 1855 à 1858)*. vols 1–2 (Paris: Bernard Grasset, 1922), vol. 2, 54–66.
2. Arthur de Gobineau, *Essai sur l'inégalité des races humaines* (Paris: Belfond, 1967); Arthur de Gobineau, *The Inequality of Human Races* (New York: Fertig, 1915 [1999]); see Janine Buenzod, *La Formation de la pensée de Gobineau et l'essai sur l'inégalité des races humaines* (Paris: Nizet, 1967); Günther Deschner, 'Gobineau und Deutschland. Der Einfluß von J. A. de Gobineaus "Essai sur l'inéqualité des races humaines" auf die deutsche Geistesgeschichte 1853–1917', unpublished PhD dissertation Erlangen-Nürnberg, 1967; Jean Boissel, *Gobineau. Biographie, mythes et réalité* (Paris: Berg, 1993).
3. de Gobineau, *Trois ans en Asie*, 66: '*l'esprit de la nation est porté au merveilleux*'.
4. Abbas Amanat, *Pivot of the Universe: Nasir al-Din Shah and the Iranian Monarchy, 1831–1896* (Berkeley: University of California Press, 1997), 49–50, 66; see Ulrich Marzolph, 'The Persian "Nights": Links between the "Arabian Nights" and Iranian Culture' in *The 'Arabian Nights' in Transnational Perspective*, ed. by Ulrich Marzolph (Detroit: Wayne State University Press, 2007), 221–43 (231).
5. Marzolph, 'The Persian "Nights"', 231–2.
6. Ulrich Marzolph, *Narrative Illustration in Persian Lithographed Books* (Leiden: Brill, 2001), particularly 26–7.
7. Bahman Sarkārāti, 'Pari. Tahqiqi dar hāshiya-ye ostura-shenāsi-ye tatbiqi', *Nashriya-ye Dāneshkada-ye adabiyāt va 'olum-e ensāni-ye Tabriz*, 23 (1350 / 1971), 1–32; Mehrān Afshāri, 'Pari' in *Dāneshnāma-ye jahān-e eslām*, vol. 5. Tehran 1379 / 2000, 593–7; Mahmoud Omidsalar, 'Peri (Pari)' in *Enzyklopädie des Märchens*, vol. 10 (Berlin: Walter de Gruyter, 2002), cols 743–6.
8. Arthur Christensen, *Essai sur la démonologie iranienne* (Copenhagen: Einar Munksgaard, 1941).
9. *The* Fihrist *of al-Nadîm: a Tenth-century Survey of Muslim Culture*, vols. 1–2, trans. and ed. by Bayard Dodge (New York: Columbia University Press, 1970), vol. 2, 714.
10. The wording of the following passage relies to some extent on the last published discussion of this anecdote in Mohsen Zakeri, *Persian Wisdom in Arabic Garb. 'Alî b. 'Ubayda al-Rayhānī (D. 219/834) and his* 'Jawāhir al-kilam wa-farā'id al-hikam', vols 1–2 (Leiden: Brill, 2007), vol. 1, 129–30; see also Charles Pellat, 'al-Nadr b. al-Hārith' in *EI²* 7 (1993), 872–3; Mahmoud and Teresa Omidsalar, 'Narrating Epics in Iran' in *Traditional Storytelling Today: An International Sourcebook*, ed. by Margaret Read Macdonald (Chicago and London: Fitzroy Dearborn Publishers Inc., 1999), 326–40, (329).
11. Omidsalar, 'Narrating Epics in Iran', 329; Zakeri, *Persian Wisdom in Arabic Garb*, vol. 1, 129.
12. Ibid., 329.
13. Marzolph, 'The Persian "Nights"', 222–5; Ulrich Marzolph and Richard van Leeuwen, *The Arabian Nights Encyclopedia*, vols 1–2 (Santa Barbara: ABC-Clio, 2004), vol. 2, 588–9; Aboubakr Chraïbi, *Les Mille et une nuits. Histoire du texte et classification des contes* (Paris: L'Harmattan, 2008), 24–45.
14. Dominique Sourdel, 'Le "Livre des secrétaires"' de 'Abdallāh al-Baghdādī', *Bulletin d'études orientales* 12 (1947–8), 115–53; Zakeri, *Persian Wisdom in Arabic Gard*, vol. 1, 128; Chraïbi, *Les Mille et une nuits*, 24–6.

15. François de Blois, *Burzôy's Voyage to India and the Origin of the Book of Kalīlah wa Dimnah* (London: Royal Asiatic Society, 1990); see also Heinz and Sophia Grotzfeld and Ulrich Marzolph, 'Kalīla und Dimna' in *Enzyklopädie des Märchens*, vol. 7 (Berlin: Walter de Gruyter, 1993), cols 888–95.

16. Chraïbi, *Les Mille et une nuits*.

17. Henri Massé, 'Les versions persanes des contes d'animaux' in *L'Âme de l'Iran* by Georges Contenau et al. (Paris: Albin Michel, 1951), 129–49.

18. Zakeri, *Persian Wisdom in Arabic Garb*.

19. Marzolph and van Leeuwen, *The Arabian Nights Encyclopedia*, 80–82.

20. Ibid., vol. 1, 343; see Jean-Louis Laveille, *Le Thème du voyage dans Les Mille et une Nuits: Du Maghreb à la Chine* (Paris: L'Harmattan, 1998), 189; Marzolph, 'The Persian "Nights"', 225–7.

21. The following passage draws from Mahmoud Omidsalar's unpublished original English version of the encyclopaedic entry 'Parî' whose edited German version is published in Omidsalar, 'Peri (Pari)'. I would like to thank my colleague for kindly granting permission to quote his work. Passages in quotation marks are his wording.

22. Sarkārāti, 'Pari'.

23. Omidsalar, 'Peri (Pari)'.

24. Jörg Bäcker, 'Schwanjungfrau' in *Enzyklopädie des Märchens*, vol. 13 (Berlin: Walter de Gruyter, 2007), cols 311–8; see also Christine Goldberg, 'Pars pro toto' in *Enzyklopädie des Märchens*, vol. 10 (2002), cols 590–95.

25. Ulrich Marzolph, 'Social Values in the Persian Popular Romance "Salīm-i Javāhirī"' *Edebiyat*, New Series 51 (1994), 77–98, also in Ulrich Marzolph, *Ex Oriente Fabula. Exploring the Narrative Culture of the Islamic Near and Middle East*, vol. 2 (Dortmund: Verlag für Orientkunde, 2006), 29–56; Mohammad Ja'fari (Qanavāti), *Do revāyat az 'Salim-e Javāheri'* (Tehran: Māzyār 1387 / 2008).

26. 'Aždahā', *EncIr* 3 (1989), 191.

27. P.O. Skjærvø, 'Aždahā. 1. In Old and Middle Iranian' in *EncIr* 3 (1989), 191–9, quotations at 191, 194; see also Ali Hasuri, 'Ezhdehā' in *Dāneshnāme-ye Irān*, vol. 2 (Tehran 1386/2007), 777–86.

28. Skjærvø, 'Aždahā. 1. In Old and Middle Iranian'.

29. J. Khaleghi-Motlagh, 'Aždahā. 2: In Persian Literature' in *EncIr* 3 (1989), 199–202; M. Omidsalar, 'Aždahā. 3: In Iranian Folktales' in *EncIr* 3 (1989), 203–4.

30. Marzolph, *Narrative Illustration*, 77, fig. 13.4; for Ali as the equivalent of Rostam see Sorour Soroudi, 'Islamization of the Iranian National Hero Rustam as Reflected in Persian Folktales', *Jerusalem Studies in Arabic and Islam* 2 (1980), 365–83.

31. Ulrich Marzolph, *Typologie des persischen Volksmärchens* (Beirut: Orient-institut der Deutschen Morgenländischen Gesellschaft, 1984), 62–4, tale type *302 B; see also Lutz Röhrich, 'Drache, Drachenkampf, Drachentöter' in *Enzyklopädie des Märchens*, vol. 3. (Berlin: Walter de Gruyter, 1981), cols 787–820, particularly cols 792–3.

32. Clarisse Herrenschmidt and Jean Kellens, '*Daiva' in *EncIr* 6 (1993), 599–602, quotations at 599.

33. Mahmoud Omidsalar, 'Dīv' in *EncIr* 7 (1996), 428–31, quotation on 428–9; see also Msia Čačava, 'Dev' in *Enzyklopädie des Märchens*, vol. 3 (1981), cols 569–73.

34. Abolqasem Ferdowsi, *Shāhnāma. The Persian Book of Kings*, trans. by Dick Davis (New York: Viking, 2006), 301–2.

35. Fritz Meier, 'Orientalische belege für das motiv, nur einmal zuschlagen' in *Mélanges d'Islamologie. Volume dédié à la mémoire d'Armand Abel*, vol. 1, ed. by Pierre Salmon (Leiden: Brill 1974), 207–23.

36. *Wenn der Esel singt, tanzt das Kamel. Persische Märchen und Schwänke*, narrated by Maschdi Galin Chanom, collected by L.P. Elwell-Sutton, trans. and ed. by Ulrich Marzolph (Munich: Diederichs, 1994), 112–27; *Qessahā-ye Mashdi Galin Khānom. 110 qessa-ye 'āmiyāna-ye irāni. Gerd-āvarda-ye L.P. Elwell-Sutton,* ed. by Ulrich Marzolph, Azar Amirhosseini-Nithammer, Ahmad Vakiliyān (Tehran: Markaz, 5th edn 1386/2007), no. 80; see also Christine Shojaei Kawan, 'Schwester: Die treulose S. (AaTh/ATU 315)' in *Enzyklopädie des Märchens*, vol. 12 (Berlin: Walter de Gruyter, 2002), cols 434–439 (col. 435).
37. Ferdowsi, *Shāhnāma. The Persian Book of Kings*, 208.
38. William L. Hanaway, ''Ayyār. 2: 'Ayyār in Persian Sources' in *EncIr* 2 (1987), 161–3; Marina Gaillard, *Le Livre de Samak-e 'ayyār. Idéologie et structure du roman persan médiéval* (Paris: Centre National de la Recherche Scientifique, 1987), 27–42.
39. Mohsen Zakeri, *Sāsānid Soldiers in Early Muslim Society. The Origins of 'Ayyārān and Futuwwa* (Wiesbaden: Harrassowitz, 1995).
40. Ines Köhler-Zülch, 'Kristallisationsgestalten' in *Enzyklopädie des Märchens*, vol. 8 (Berlin: Walter de Gruyter, 1996), cols 460–66.

3

Arts of Iran in Late Antiquity

Oleg Grabar
(Institute for Advanced Study, Princeton University)

The title I have chosen for my chapter reflects the main conclusion I will propose: that the arts of whatever we can call Iran during the period extending roughly from the late sixth century to the tenth can best be defined or explained through the characteristics of what is becoming known as Late Antiquity all over Eurasia, rather than as the expression of an existing or recently (that is to say in our own time) formulated Iranian purpose and identity. But I will also try to show that unevenness and lacunae in our knowledge and the consequent methodological deficiencies in scholarly thinking may be partly responsible for the difficulties we face in dealing with these centuries in the Iranian world, as opposed, for instance, to the Mediterranean or to China, where political and social structures are reasonably well connected to beliefs and to languages so as to allow matching art and history in a reasonable way, or else to the post-Mongol period in Islamic history, when linguistic and ethnic divisions are more closely connected to territories.

My thoughts on these questions lie somewhere between an incomplete scholarly statement and the rambling of a long-standing, but not always coherent, meditation. It will try to provide the arguments which have led to my conclusion, but the justification for the research which has led to this chapter lies in several, at first glance unrelated, sets of visual or written documents, and also in queries which have plagued me for most of my long professional life and which came to a head in the past decade or so, when several new discoveries, especially in China, Central Asia and Afghanistan, complicated matters enormously but perhaps also lead to new interpretations and new labels for the history of the Eurasian continent.

Within this continent, a central area, roughly between lower Mesopotamia in the west, the Gobi desert in the north and the Hindu Kush in the east, can be identified as Iranian or Iranocentric during the first ten centuries of the common era, because it was for the most part dominated or even ruled by Iranian regimes of many different sorts and because Iranian languages predominated over other existing ones. And then, at a completely different level of thought and knowledge, exactly one hundred years ago, an extraordinary book, Smirnov's *Oriental Silver*, gathered excellent photographs of some 325 silver objects, nearly all of which fall within the first millennium, and called them 'oriental', in accordance with a meaning of the word 'oriental' which is no longer acceptable.[1] Smirnov's book implied what was confirmed by later discoveries, that many different spatial and chronological origins can be assigned to these 'oriental' objects in silver, always within the same general boundaries. Two subsidiary questions emerge from Smirnov's book. One is a methodological one, whether a category consisting of objects in a single material constitutes a valid category for historical, as opposed to aesthetic or technological, arguments. I will not deal with this question in theoretical terms, but it emerges constantly for this period of history, partly because of Smirnov's book, which provided a skewed emphasis on silver within our documentation. The second question is whether all these objects, or most of them, are in fact 'Iranian'? Or should we learn to define a whole range of sub-groups which might end up by making the term 'Iranian' meaningless or extremely limited, perhaps applicable only to Sasanian royal objects, as I recall a distinguished archaeologist and historian of art telling me at an exhibition some forty years ago: that only Sasanian silver plates count as works of Iranian art and that only the ones in the Hermitage count altogether?

What is fascinating is that exactly the same sorts of observations and queries surround the term 'Islamic'. The Islamic faith and a political structure attached to it spread from the seventh century onwards and rapidly took over most of what was known as the Iranian world and thus included the latter in a much vaster entity extending from China to the Atlantic. But is it justified to label 'Islamic' all the arts which flourished within its political and religious sphere? We are all aware of the dangers of broad labels like 'Gothic' or 'French' in defining the arts, for we never quite know when such labels are just conveniences for sorting things out and when they are acceptable or objectionable expressions of possession or formal judgements. But the point remains that groups of related objects deserve a patronymic, even if such patronymics reflect the prejudices of the time when they were first established.

Such questions may be thought to be unnecessary because there is no clear answer to them, but not to deal with them implies the acceptance of two propositions which can be and have been misused. One assumes a fundamental unity across time and space of all works of art made by or for Muslims – and we all know the constrictions this position has put on exhibitions, interpretations and contemporary creativity as well as judgements. The second maintains the existence across the centuries of an Iranian artistic expression which, in spite of formal differences, perpetuated a uniquely Iranian set of subjects and approaches to forms. The second proposition is not really compatible with the first one or else a different set of cognitive and descriptive categories would have to be developed. The arts, possibly, operate according to a different pattern from whatever is defined by a specific space or a specific time, as happens with words like 'Iranian' and 'Islamic'. That the former adjective belongs to an area, whose borders are always difficult to define but whose core lies between the Tigris and the Hindu Kush, is obvious enough. The latter refers to a time beginning with the moment of conversion from whatever was an area's set of beliefs to Islam. Here again there are murky edges, especially at the beginning, but, on the whole – with the notorious exception of Spain and less clearly the region to the south of Russia and Ukraine – areas that became Muslim have tended to remain Muslim. But art and material culture, while made in a specific area and at a specific time, can and – according to some contemporary thought – must be defined and judged independently of their time and space and thus become useless for history, even if wonderful for the pleasure of the senses.[2]

These abstract queries and remarks are troublesome and perhaps a sign of *fin de carrière* scholarship, but they are important for me in focussing on the problem I will address, which during these centuries concerns both Iran and Islam: did a new Islamic formal and iconographic umbrella transform or cover whatever artistic expression existed in the eighth to the eleventh centuries? Or did an Iranian tradition maintain itself in spite of a radical change in religion and social as well as linguistic structure? If the latter, was it a fairly unified tradition or a hotchpotch of styles and subjects? Or, perhaps, is neither label appropriate to whatever happened during these fascinating times?

In order to try to answer these questions, we must first either identify the terms in our possession, the visual dialects from which we will be able to define a language, or decide that there was no unifying system at all. For a period roughly extending from 600 CE to 1000 CE and comprising the world between Iraq and the Gobi desert, I have identified five or six (I still have not made my mind up, as you will see shortly) groups of sources to study, some of which are fuzzier to define than others. Most of them have not been investigated in sufficient depth to allow for more than tentative conclusions and no one scholar is likely to develop the linguistic, historical and archaeological competencies needed to deal with them all. What follows therefore is an invitation to a research whose results will only emerge over time.

Of my five (or six) groups of sources two are better known than the others, having occupied at least three generations of scholars. I shall begin with these.

Sasanians

The arts associated with the Sasanian dynasty (225–640 CE) are relatively well known as is their alleged impact on the art of both the Christian Mediterranean and China, at least with respect to textile designs found all over Asia and Europe. But, in reality, we are dealing with a very limited and restricted body of monuments, especially when compared with the wealth of the arts around the

Mediterranean or in the Buddhist world further east. With the exception of usually undated fire temples, and possibly textiles, most of its surviving examples are unique, or almost unique, and it is difficult to know whether the Taq-e Kesra of Ctesiphon, the palatial compound at Qasr-e Shirin, the fascinating sculptures of Taq-e Bustan, the stucco panels from southern or northern Iran, the standard hunting scenes on silver plates, the elegant ewers with scantily clad women (among several other subjects), the crystal and gold plate at the Bibliothèque Nationale and several representations of royalty or of what seem to be cosmic themes – such as in the recently published hunter with a bull found in western Siberia – are all idiosyncratic items fulfilling specific and unique purposes or uniquely preserved samples of otherwise typical series. The date of most of these items is not known and, whether correctly or out of academic despair, a large percentage is set in the seventh century, even the eighth, that is to say after the end of the Sasanian dynasty. The issue has in the past drawn the amused and slightly unfair ire of Jean Sauvaget who made fun of the term 'post-Sasanian' to identify an art, arguing that 'post-Sasanian' meant 'early Islamic'.[3]

To bicker about exact appellations might be childish, but what is not childish is our persistent difficulty in identifying the – or a – patronage for the objects or for buildings with such consistently clear features. Too many works of Sasanian art are unique and historians of art are, or should be, aware of the dangers involved in identifying a style or a patron through unique works. A look at a map with Sasanian sites known in 1980 and prepared by a well-known expert in the field shows how restricted they are in terms of both area and number.[4] This is partly the result of limited archaeological investigations, but if we compare this map to what was known in Syria, Tunisia or Italy as early as a century ago it is evident that we are not simply dealing with an absence of archaeological and other research but with a far lesser density of occupation and creativity than existed in the Mediterranean or in Central Asia. As I will suggest below, there is another way to define the Sasanian legacy, but as far as physical or visual remains are concerned, it is a limited one.

In addition to the core of Sasanian objects, we can identify – as a separate set or not – a para-Sasanian mix of other artefacts, mostly silver but also ceramic and glass remains as well as stuccoes. This group of objects manifests techniques characteristic of allegedly official Sasanian art but for purposes other than the proclamation of royal power and wealth. Thus there are Jewish and Christian motifs on objects made in the Sasanian manner; these objects were often carried to (or made in) Central Asia, whence they found their way to territories in what is now Russia. To my knowledge, there are not enough of these to propose the existence of clearly defined Christian or Jewish strands within the arts of Iran in the eighth and ninth centuries, but they certainly formed a significant and restricted set within the societies of the time.[5]

Another group within this para-Sasanian category consists of dozens of works, mostly in silver, that copy, imitate or paraphrase Sasanian royal works.[6] They are probably all later than the dynasty itself and we can only speculate on who sponsored these works and why. For example, the fairly recent discovery of a typically 'Sasanian' relief in Afghanistan shows a king hunting a rhinoceros, an animal unknown in the Sasanian world.[7] We encounter here a fairly classical problem of art historical research which is to understand the motivations of people one does not know, through one's own contemporary reaction to images one does not quite understand. What is needed here is a series of thorough analyses of individual pieces comparable to the ones which led Marshak to explain the Anikova plate as the taking of Jericho and a strange, much later, small ewer of the Golden Horde as the burning bush seen by Moses.[8] Are these works of Jewish art using Sasanian or later techniques or of Iranian art with a Jewish patronage or purpose?

Dealing with these matters requires a different type of discussion from the one that prevails today, but it is a time-consuming one and involves groups of scholars and students working in a laboratory atmosphere which can easily be imagined on the internet, not the showy presentation of travelling exhibitions. Some time we will get there, but in the meantime I propose the notion of para-Sasanian objects (mostly in silver thanks to Smirnov, but possibly also with stuccoes) waiting in limbo for a place in the formal Linnaean tables of learning.

Sogdians

My second clear set of sources consists of what we are beginning to call, accurately, Sogdian art. We know something about its urban architecture and temples, even palaces and wealthy houses, but Sogdian art is mostly known through its wall paintings thanks to the excavations carried out in Panjikent, Varahsha, Balalykh Tepe, Afrasiyab and other Central Asian sites.[9] There are also silver objects connected with Sogd, mostly boat-shaped containers with variants, and possibly plates as well. We also know quite a bit about Sogdian expansion eastwards along the Silk Route and the culture's encounter with Buddhist art from China and Tibet. Thanks primarily to the work of Boris Marshak, we know about the wealth of Sogdian religious and, especially, secular subjects and their connection to artistic trends in western Asia and even the Mediterranean basin as well as to the east in India (especially in sculpture) and China.[10] Sogdian forms and subjects have, moreover, frequently been found in Buddhist sites in Central Asia.

The real problem, however, from the point of view of my theme is whether we should consider Sogdian painting as the remaining expression of what could have been 'Sasanian' painting, as many thought when Panjikent was first studied in the 1950s, or whether it illustrates and reflects an original north-eastern Iranian milieu significantly different from the western one and, for a variety of reasons of its own, particularly brilliant just as Islam appeared on the horizon. Its taste in topics to be illustrated is less consistently royal than what is known of western Iranian art and perhaps it illustrates the needs and interests of the merchant aristocracy of the area rather than those of a fancy imperial court, such as we assume to be the patron of high Sasanian art. We must also decide whether the early Islamic mural paintings found in Nishapur, Lashkari Bazar or now Afrasiyab should be considered as continuations of a Sogdian Iranian tradition or the creation of new forms for art, as seems to be the case for architecture. The matter is particularly important when we consider the important place of epic narratives in Sogdian painting, which perhaps, as I thought some forty years ago, could be seen as models for the illustration of *Shahnama* manuscripts in the fourteenth century.[11] I am far less certain now than I was then of a formal relationship, but, as I shall discuss shortly, another kind of thematic relationship may well have existed.

Manicheans

The basic Manichean story is well known. A religious system which owes a great deal to Zoroastrian beliefs and practices appears in third-century Mesopotamia and then travels westwards as a doctrine and eastwards also as a doctrine, but one which becomes a state doctrine under Uighur rulers in Central Asia from the eighth to the eleventh century, when it disappears as an distinct form of belief and merges with the dominant doctrines of Christianity, Islam and Buddhism. During its several centuries of more or less independent presence, the Manichean streak was mostly found in the Iranian world and, what is more important, its doctrines and ideologies were formally expressed visually, essentially in painting, and specifically in illustrated books. The surviving examples come primarily from Central Asia and date to the eighth and later centuries. According to the most recent investigation of these paintings known to me, that by Zsuzsanna Gulacsi, most are identified as belonging to a 'west Asian' group associated with Sasanian Iran or Abbasid Iraq.[12] The fact that no clear distinction is made between these two centres, separated by more than two centuries and with totally different religious systems, illustrates the uncertainty of our historical understanding of this period in the arts. An original drawing style, probably brought from China, appears in ninth-century Turfan and is often seen on textiles, but the bulk of Manichean painting constitutes the earliest-known book illustration in Iranian lands and persists until as late as the eleventh century, a point of considerable importance when we compare it to what is known about book-making by communities other than the Manicheans.

Northern and Southern Iran

I will be brief on these key provinces, because the evidence is slim, except on a literary level, to which I will come back shortly. Several excavations have taken place there, but to my knowledge no one has tried to summarize their results. There is the celebrated site of Sarvestan, long thought to be a palace and now accepted as a tenth-century Zoroastrian sanctuary.[13] There is the fascinating sequence of Buyid inscriptions at Persepolis which imply a certain sacralization of the old Achaemenid site by this tenth and eleventh-century Muslim dynasty apparently without their possessing any clear knowledge of what the site had signified for its original builders; hence its attribution to Jamshid, a mythical king.[14] But who individually or what social group made these identifications and why? We may be on slightly safer grounds when we turn to the eleventh-century tomb towers of northern and north-eastern Iran, two of which, at Radkan and Lajim, have a Pahlavi inscription from the eleventh century.[15] Is it a leftover or a revival? And in a general way the early Islamic appearance of mausoleums, domed or towers, in north-eastern Iran is probably connected with pre-Islamic practices, Zoroastrian or other, Sogdian or other.

Literary Sources

All the examples I have given so far can be illustrated with specific examples and arranged into visually definable clusters or sets – through subject-matter, technique of execution, or manner of execution – even if we cannot always provide an exact time and space definition it can be assumed that there was one. But, in order to understand the arts of the time, we must also turn to a different source, the written record, which contains enormous quantities of information, but information which is very biased because it is influenced by, but removed from, visual knowledge and therefore difficult to use properly. I will give two examples.

The first one is the story of *Vis u Ramin* written between 1050 and 1055 by Fakhr al-Din Gorgani. It is based on a Parthian original and has recently been made available through a wonderful translation by Dick Davis.[16] In contrast with the *Shahnama*, with which it is almost contemporary, it is a long and fascinating love story; its Freudian implications are quite surprising, as are its descriptions of love-making. But what struck me mostly as I read it recently is that the description of royal feasts, which are quite numerous, could be illustrated with sixteenth-century miniatures of the *Shahnama* or of the *Khamsa* of Nezami. Here are two examples:

> The king sat in his court surrounded by his nobles like the full moon in the sky among its stars... His nobles were like lions ranged in rows, the women of the court like graceful does; the lions gazed with longing and the deer bravely returned their stares and showed no fear. Goblets went around, all filled with brimming wine... Musicians drank and sang, and told their tales... everywhere the spring's new blossoms made the earth as lovely as a rich brocade... (2)

Vis sat, a vision of magnificence, of loveliness, and shifting tints and scents, upon her throne, within an audience hall with golden pictures painted on each wall; three doors led to a garden, and three more to private rooms reached by a corridor... she cleared the room of strangers and prince Ramin appears from the rooftop. (124–5)

Here we may recall the importance of roof pavilions in the design of sixteenth-century palaces in miniatures.

It is relatively easy to reconstruct in sketches the palaces that provide the setting for these scenes, but this leaves open the question whether they are based on real palaces, like the Ghaznavid ones in Afghanistan and the Samanid ones in Transoxiana, or whether they are fantasies from older times. And why are they so strikingly reminiscent of sixteenth-century representations, when we have no illustrations of the text and no contemporary images even remotely comparable to the text's description?

A similarly tantalizing visual parallel can be derived from Daqiqi's poetry, once again of palaces and of gardens which may have been literary inventions, but their precision suggests that such gardens did exist in fact.[17] In other words, there seems to have existed within a literary tradition developed primarily in Khorasan a visually definable vision of royal paradises. Were they fictions or reflections of reality? If the latter, are they creations of already Islamic dynasties or memories of earlier glories? Is it a north-eastern Iranian fantasy that was Arabicized into the mythology surrounding Khawarnaq in Iraq, which then entered Iranian legends?

And these literary descriptions should be connected with the last of my examples of sources for the arts during these complex centuries. These deal with concrete stories which were to become standard features of the *Shahnama* and of later poetry and prose.

The first example is that of the Throne of Khosrow, mentioned in the *Shahnama,* in Bal'ami and in Tha'alabi, but not in Tabari. It was one of the twelve (the number itself makes the list suspicious as a reflection of reality) marvels belonging to Khosrow that included musicians, singers, Shirin, Ctesiphon, and the horse Shabdiz (like Rostam's Rakhsh). The throne was in the shape of a dome, made of ivory and teak with gold and silver plaques with seats of ebony on steps and a baldachin (canopy) of gold and lapis with signs of the zodiac represented there, together with the seven climes and kings of the world in all sorts of poses: eating, battling, and hunting. It also featured a mechanism indicating night and day. Ferdowsi relates that it was inspired by a throne of old. Herzfeld interpreted it as a huge clock, but this interpretation has not generally been accepted. The Byzantine chronicler Kedrenos claims that it was part of Khosrow's palace taken and then destroyed by the Byzantines.[18] The question is not what it was, nor whether it was an actual object or the representation of an object. It is why is all of this associated with Khosrow Parviz, the last major ruler of the Sasanian dynasty (591–628), but one whose

life of conquests was also a string of failures and defeats and who ended up
assassinated by one of his sons somewhere in Khorasan? The wealth and
acquisitiveness of Khosrow is not unusual for either the image or reality of
kingship, even if it is exaggerated. The 'throne', however, is a unique
monument. We shall never know whether it existed in reality or not, but why
was something so symbolically spectacular attributed to a ruler who failed in
his politics as well as in his private life, when Khosrow I, 'the one with an
immortal soul', would have been a perfect candidate for such a monument? A
possible answer was suggested to me by my teacher E. Baldwin Smith some
fifty-five years ago, after I had given a seminar report on Sasanian palaces. He
pointed out that the sources which mention the throne are all of the tenth and
eleventh centuries, essentially Muslim sources, and, he argued, Muslim sources
had an appropriate hero, Solomon, whose mythical palace and encounter with
Bilqis was already suggested by the Qur'anic scripture and the commentaries
surrounding the story.[19] For my argument today, the throne of Khosrow would
have been the Iranization of Solomon at a time when a new Iranian purpose or
ideal sought to replace or to naturalize myths brought by Muslim Arabs, the
ones who profited from the chaos brought by Khosrow's failures. The throne's
extraordinary brilliance served to provide a moral justification for Khosrow's
defeat, something later picked up by Nezami among others. These failures
themselves became the stories of Persian epic and lyric literature, mixing
medieval Islamic moralism with the epic history of the Iranian kings.

For the purposes of this chapter, the importance of the argument does not lie
in the specifics of the Khosrow–Solomon relationship, but in the suggestion
that it occurred in the tenth or eleventh centuries, the very time when Bahram
Gur and Azada appear in images and the first steps are taken in the literary
transformation of the Sasanian king Bahram Gur, the pre-Islamic Iranian ruler
with the closest Arab connections. This is also the time when Persepolis
becomes Takht-e Jamshid and when a Takht-e Solaymān appears in both
Azerbaijan and Central Asia.

The further examination of these sources requires much more work in
written sources than I have been able to accomplish so far. My point is simply
that these were centuries during which choices were made in whatever Iranian
legend or patrimony existed and these choices created a new vocabulary of
images and gave new names to the ruins of the past. In a few cases, thanks, for
instance, to the inscriptions of Persepolis, we know that the sponsors of these
changes were the new Iranian dynasties of early Islamic Iran.[20] But so were the
new Turkish dynasties farther east.[21] I am less clear whether a similar process
can be identified within Samanid culture, whose visual vocabulary, known
mostly through ceramics, seems to be different. Why? Why is it also that, in the
rich repertoire of later images on Islamic pottery, we have several images of
Bahram Gur and Azada, a few Rostams, and no other subject that can be clearly
identified with any of the characters and stories of the *Shahnama*? Is it that we

have not learned to recognize these subjects or that some special meaning was attached to Bahram Gur?

What then are the conclusions I can propose from these rambling remarks and examples? First, I would like to argue that from the sixth through to the eleventh century there were several artistic trends within the Iranian world corresponding to the variety of very different communities in Iran: Pahlavi-speaking and writing Sasanians, Sogdians in Central Asia (who in this period were Bactrian speakers), Jews, Christians, Manichaeans, Buddhists and many types of Zoroastrians. A very rich and very heterogeneous set of forms and subjects could be construed as Iranian, rather than there being a clear main stream with dependencies. The type is best identified as Late Antique because it does not centre on formal features that created styles, but on cultural habits that admitted and even welcomed co-existing differences. What changes all of this is the success of Islamization, just as the equally complex and relatively slow cultural Christianization of the west led to what we call the Middle Ages. Within this new Islamic synthesis of the eleventh and later centuries, Iranian traditions played a significant role, but it is only with the architecture of the late eleventh and later centuries and the ceramics of the twelfth that an identifiable Iranian streak appears in western Asia under the umbrella of Islamic art.

And, secondly, as we are only now slowly beginning to understand the extraordinary complexity of these earlier centuries, we must also realize that they will only be understood through a large-scale collective effort, since no one person can control the immense written and visual documentation which is gradually coming to light or which is already known but without having been seriously noticed. The new techniques to communicate knowledge that have been developed over the past ten years should help the next generation of scholars to make it all available in a clear, intelligent and creative fashion.

Notes:

1. Iakov I. Smirnov, *Vostochnoe Serebro* (St Petersburg, 1909).
2. The issues of terminology and of the many meanings of the word 'Islamic' underlie many recent publications. See Sheila Blair and Jonathan Bloom, 'The Mirage of Islamic Art', *The Art Bulletin* 85 (2003) and Sibel Bozdoğan, and Gülrü Necipoğlu 'Entangled Discourses', *Muqarnas* 24 (2007), 1–6. On the Iranian issue, see, as the latest example, Abolala Soudavar, *The Aura of Kings: Legitimacy and Divine Sanction in Iranian Kingship* (Costa Mesa: Mazda Publications, 2003).
3. The latest catalogue of Sasanian art is François Demange, Musée Cernusci, *Les Perses Sassanides: fastes d'un empire oublié, 224–642* (Paris: Findakly, 2006). For architecture, the latest summary is in *The Arts of Persia*, ed. by Ronald W. Ferrier (New Haven: Yale University Press, 1989). For silver, see Prudence O. Harper and Pieter Meyers, *Silver Vessels of the Sasanian Period* (New York: Metropolitan Museum in association with Princeton University, 1981). The unusual plate from Siberia is found in A.V. Baulo, 'A Sasanian Silver Plate from the Synya River', *Archaeology, Ethnology and Anthropology of Eurasia* 1(9) (2002), 142–8. Sauvaget's caustic remarks are in Jean Sauvaget, 'Observations sur les monuments omeyyades II', *Journal Asiatique, janvier-mars* (1940), 222, 1–59.
4. For instance, the map in Roman Ghirshman, *Iran, Parthes et Sassanides* (Paris: Gallimard, 1962), fig. 453.
5. Typical examples in Boris Marshak, and V.P. Darkevich, 'O tak nazyvaemom siriiskom bliude', *Sovetskaia Arheologiia* (1974), which includes the Anikov plate whose subject is now accepted to be the taking of Jericho.
6. Examples are in Harper, *Silver Vessels*, pls. 18, 19, 26, 32 and 34.
7. Frantz Grenet, 'Découverte d'un relief sassanide dans le nord de l'Afghanistan', *Comptes-rendus des séances de l'Académie des Inscriptions et Belles-Lettres*, (2005), 149 (1), 115–34.
8. Boris Marshak, 'Persian Silver and Gold' in *The Treasures of Khan Kubrat* (St Petersburg: The Hermitage Museum, 1997), 50–71, (68–9).
9. Easiest access is through Frantz Grenet and Boris Marshak, 'L'art soghdien' in *Les Arts d'Asie Centrale*, ed. by Pierre Chuvin (Paris: Citadelles & Mazenod, 1998), 114–80.
10. The easiest introduction is through Boris Marshak, *Legends, Tales, and Fables in the Art of Soghdiana* (New York: Persica Press, 2002).
11. Oleg Grabar, 'Notes on the Iconography of the Demotte Shahname', in *Paintings in Islamic Lands* ed. by Ralph Pinder-Wilson (Oxford: Cassirer, 1969), reprinted in Oleg Grabar, *Constructing the Study of Islamic Art*, vol. II (Hampshire: Ashgate Publishing Ltd, 2006).
12. Zsuzsanna Gulasci, *Medieval Manichean Book Art* (Leiden: Brill, 2005).
13. Lionel Bier, *Sarvistan. Study in Early Iranian Architecture* (University Park: Pennsylvania State University Press, 1986).
14. Souren Melikian-Chirvani, 'Royaume de Salomon', *Le Monde Iranien et l'Islam*, vol. I (1971).
15. Ernest Diez, *Persien: Islamische Baukunst in Churāsān* (Hagen I.W.: Folkwang-Verlag, 1923); Ernest Diez, *Churasanische Baudenkmäler* (Berlin: D. Reimer, 1918); Sheila Blair, *The Monumental Inscriptions of Early Islamic Iran and Transoxiana* (Leiden: Brill, 1992), 85–92.
16. Fakhruddin Gorgani, *Vis & Ramin*, trans. by Dick Davis (Washington: Mage, 2008).

17. Gilbert Lazard et al, *Anthologie de la Poésie Persane, XIe – Xème siècles* (Paris, 1964).
18. The texts have been assembled by E. Herzfeld, 'Thron'; summary of the arguments in A. Christiansen, *L'Iran sous les Sassanides* (Copenhagen, 1944), 464–8.
19. Valérie Gonzalez, *La Piège de Salomon: la pensée de l'art dans le Coran* (Paris 2002).
20. Blair, *Inscriptions*, 32, 34, 36, 60 and 118.
21. Alessio Bombaci, *The Kufic Inscription in Persian Verses in the Court of the Royal Palace of Mas'ud III at Ghazni* (Rome Instituto Italiano per il Medio ed Estremo Oriente, 1966).

4

Sindbādnāma: A Zurvanite Cosmogonic Legend?

Mohsen Zakeri
(Georg-August University, Göttingen)

B y cosmogony (*āfarinesh*) is understood an account of how the cosmos first came into being. The word cosmogony is, however, generally applied to mythic–religious accounts of the world's origin current among the peoples of antiquity. Ancient cosmogonic myths provided speculations to account for the existence and harmony of the cosmos. Aristotle declared: 'The myths and stories were devised to make the religious systems intelligible and attractive to the people, who otherwise would not give them any regard or veneration.' Thus the stories of Jamshid, the brain-devouring snakes of Zahhāk, the ordeal of Siyāvash and the adventures of Rostam and Isfandiyār, are but tales and fables that convey a deep religious meaning.

Whereas popular creation myths and epic tales of the kind we find in Ferdowsi's *Shāhnāma* are perceptibly etiological and offer narrative accounts of first causes, there are other kinds of entertaining tales in Persian literature which seem to have been nourished from the same fount with the same explicative purpose, though such an intention is less apparent. One such example is the famous collection of amusing tales commonly known in world literature as *Sindbādnāma*, or 'The Prince, the Concubine and the Seven Viziers', a classic work allegedly about women's cleverness and infidelity, which is celebrated in Europe as 'The Seven Wise Sages'. This folkloristic compilation, which at some point was attached to the *Thousand and One Nights*, has received vast attention for its entertaining contents, but has not yet been approached from the perspective of cosmogony.

While studying the main story that frames the contents of the *Sindbādnāma*, it suddenly occurred to me that its narrative moves along the pattern we know from the Zurvanite myth of creation. The link between the two sounded far-fetched and strange at first, but it was curious enough for me to undertake a comparison. What follows is a product of that curiosity. A simplified version of the Zurvanite myth is presented here and then it is compared with the framing story of the Persian *Sindbādnāma*, which I shall refer to as *SN*.[1] My brief comments are motivated by a dual goal: removing some misconceptions with regard to the Zurvanite cosmogonic scheme and showing how it continued to live on in classical Persian literature – epic or otherwise – disguised in almost completely unrecognizable garb. Zurvanite influence on Persian literature is perennial.

Zurvanism is a sect which believed Time (Zurvan) to stand at the top of the divine hierarchy, to be the source of all things and to be the father of Ahura Mazda (Ohrmazd) and Angra Mainyu (Ahriman). Zurvanism elevated Zurvan, the god or genius of Infinite Time, to a supreme position over and above the twin spirits of good and evil. Here Ahura Mazda was held to be not God eternal but a subordinate creator-god, one of the twin sons of Zurvan. Zurvanism is regarded either as the continuation of an Iranian religion parallel to Mazdaism, a Mazdean heresy, or simply a theological trend peripheral to orthodoxy.[2] There is reason to believe that Zurvanism was already in existence in the sixth century BCE. For Zaehner, the pied piper of Zurvanism studies, 'The mysteries of Mithra are Zurvanite in so far as they place Kronos–Zurvan at the head of the Pantheon.'[3] Christensen saw Zurvanism as the predominant form of Sasanian Zoroastrianism.[4] Mary Boyce called it the monist heresy of Zurvanism, which evolved probably in the late fifth century BCE The Sasanian dynasty was Zurvanite, though it declared its devotion to Ohrmazd in diverse ways.[5]

As a heterodox branch of Zoroastrianism, Zurvanite dogma offered a multifaceted theology, very confused, with at times a naively contradictory concept of life, in addition to an elaborate myth of creation, which has been a subject of great interest to many historians of religion in modern times. It is a relief that we only need to focus on the question of Zurvanite cosmogony, for this is the best-known part of the sect's conceptions and is reported rather frequently in Iranian (*Bundahishn*, *Selections of Zādspram*, *Dēnkard*, *Mēnōg ī Khrad*, etc.) and foreign sources (Greek, Armenian, Syriac and Islamic), all, of course, with divergences in details, misunderstandings and misrepresentations. I generally follow the account of the *Bundahishn* (BD).[6]

Periodization

The Zurvanite world-view is based on two pillars: first the belief in two eternal and contradictory principles of good and evil, which are in constant struggle against one another in an arena that is the entire universe, and secondly the belief in the time limit of this universal battle, which signifies the duration of the world. To understand this concept better, one needs to imagine a condition and time when there was no wind or rain, no warmth or coldness, no creatures or creation, no heaven or hell, no movement, nothing, and go to that remote conceivable moment which the Neoplatonians call hypostasis (the fundamental reality that supports all else). This moment is magnificently formulated in New Persian parlance with *yakī būd yakī nabūd, ghayr az khodā hīch kas nabūd,*

'There was one, there was no one' (with the extension 'except God, there was nobody'), used to transpose listeners immediately to a time when time, space and place as we understand them now had no meaning yet. This brief and, on the surface, trivial expression is without doubt one of the most profound sentences the Persian language has ever produced. It is usually rendered into English as 'Once upon a time,' which is harmless for ordinary communication, but definitely hides the ingenuity of the original. This is Zurvan, the Infinite Time. The concise and enigmatic statement above is then reflected in the formulaic phrase *be-nām-e khodāvand-e jān o kherad* (without rhyme: *kherad o jān*; Arabic *'aql wa nafs*), which is again the Neoplatonic notion of the One (Transcendental Good, *khodāvand*), the Nous (Divine Consciousness, *kherad*) and the Psyche (The Universal-Soul, *jān*), with its correspondence in Zurvan, Ohrmazd and Ahriman.

Zurvan, who is transcendent and has no particular attributes, had always lived in his primeval state, until at some point he felt that the lack of existence was rather unsatisfying. It would perhaps be better, he thought, to have a son to rule over everything. To fulfill his wish, Zurvan began offering sacrifices for a thousand years, but with no success. Then for a moment he doubted whether it was a good idea to offer sacrifices for a son. At that rare instant of hesitation, an emanation took place and two sons were conceived in him, one all light and goodness, the reward for his sacrifice, and the other all darkness and evil, the result of his doubt. He had spoken out to make his first born ruler over the entire world. Due to his prescience, Ohrmazd, had known this and now informed his brother of it. Ahriman, rebellious as he was, cut his father's side, came out first and presented himself to Zurvan. Thus Zurvan, in accordance with his pledge, unwillingly gave him sovereignty over the world.

Ohrmazd lived in his domain of endless light busy with creating the *mēnōg*, or immaterial state of the world. For 3,000 years, all creatures remained in a spiritual state, that is, they were unthinking, unmoving and intangible (the sun, moon and stars all existing in a state of motionlessness). During all this time Ahriman was roaming around in his own realm of endless darkness, separated from Ohrmazd's realm of light by a *tuhīgīh* (void). Towards the end of this period, during one of his wanderings, Ahriman happened upon the boundary of light unawares, cut through it and presented himself to Ohrmazd. Ahura, aware that he could not stop Ahriman from harming his creations offered him peace, an offer that Ahriman arrogantly rejected. Hence Ahura proposed a period of combat limited to 9,000 years, the 'time of long dominion' (*zamān i drang khwadāy*) incised from the 'unlimited time' (*zamān i akenārag*), which is Zurvan. Being nescient of the end result, Ahriman agreed. This agreement is called the *paymānag* 'covenant' ('measure'). At this juncture, by invoking the Ahunvar (Ahuna Vairya) prayer, Ohrmazd put him in a state of prostration and sent him back to hell, whence he had come. Ahriman remained in a state of stupefaction for 3,000 years, at the end of which period he was awakened from his stupor by Jeh, his daughter and wife, the mother of all prostitutes, and attacked the realm of Ohrmazd that had meanwhile taken the *gētīg* form.

The attack of Ahriman took place 6,000 years after his and Ohrmazd's birth (3,000 *mēnōg*, 3,000 *gētīg*). Ahuraic emanations stood in a *mēnōg* state for 3,000 years, that is, they had not yet been subjected to *gētīg* or corporeal form: they existed as formless spirits. Their physical period lasted 9,000 years, out of which they were free from Ahrimanic pollution for 3,000 years. In other words, the first 6,000 years went by eventless and rather peacefully. *Dīd ēn kū tā madan ī petyārag 6,000 sāl zamān widard ēstad, 3,000 sāl mēnōgīhā, 3,000 sāl gētīghā, andar abēzagīh.*[7]

Ohrmazd knew that his *mēnōg* creation, without form, motion and life, was useless in the fight against Ahriman, therefore he planned and executed the material creation in order to tie up and detain the king of darkness. The *gētīg* creation was to be a snare for Ahriman and his demonic creatures, for this was the only way to give material form to them and make them visible to men of good thought, good words and good acts, so they could fight back against them. *Zātspram* (3.23) and Shk. (4.63-79) clearly state that the world was created by Ohrmazd as a trap for Ahriman. 'By his very struggles in the trap and snare the beast's power is brought to nothing.'[8]

Upon reaching the sphere of light for the second time, Ahriman made a hole in the outer crust of the earth, polluted the waters, made the plants wither, killed the bull and Gayōmart, tainted the fire with smoke, darkened the world and became the sole ruler over it; meanwhile Ohrmazd only managed to save the seeds or prototypes (*karp*) of his creation, each kept hidden on one of the planets. The *Avesta* refers to this desperate moment as the great winter (*zemestān*), during which the prototypes of man and animals were kept in *var-e Jamshid* (this is a version of the great deluge). At the end of this icy period of 3,000 years, during which Ahriman was the sole ruler in the universe, Zoroaster rose and equipped humanity for the great fight to end the Ahrimanic rule. Thus the last period was inaugurated, the period of admixture (*gumēzishn*) of the forces of good and evil, which in turn was to take 3,000 years. Ahriman was now kept in check (in the epic version of this phase he was put in chains and kept in a hole at Damāvand) till the end of the appointed time, when the *rastākhiz*, 'resurrection' happens and *frashkart* [*frashegird;* Av. *Frashō.kərəti*], or renovation, takes place, light and darkness are separated and a new cycle of life begins.

An important point in the above account, often overlooked or misunderstood, is the period of Ahriman's sole rule, in its epic presentation, that of Zahhāk, who is Ahriman's mythic personification (and in other cycles, epic characters of *anairya* such as Afrāsiyāb). The Zoroastrian clergy, not able to justify it, have resorted to ignoring it. Plutarch (*c.* 46–120 CE), citing Theopompus, a source from the fourth century BCE, wrote: 'Ohrmazd and Ahriman reigned alternately for 3,000 years, then they fought each other for

3,000 years, one destroying the domain of the other, at the end of which Ohrmazd comes out victorious.'[9] Plutarch's report is partially obscure, but this is certainly one of the best we have. It is the Mazdean doctrine that has difficulty with Ahriman's absolute rule of 3,000 years, not the Zurvanists.

It is after Ahriman's initial excursion into the realm of light at the end of the neutral state of 3,000 years period of *mēnōg* that Ahura determined a limited period of 9,000 years in order to put an end to the evil intentions of Ahriman successfully. Hence he offers this to Ahriman, who unaware of the inevitable result, accepts the deal. Ahura knows that of these 9,000 years, 3,000 are his, 3,000 are his adversary's, and 3,000 are in a mixed state, that is, the period in which we are now living (BD. 1.28). Although the three distinct eras are clearly expressed, the period of Ahriman's supremacy is regularly left out of discussions. Thus Kreyenbroek gives the three stages after the pact between Ohrmazd and Ahriman as creation, mixture and separation.[10] The period of creation is identical to Ohrmazd's unhindered act of emanation, but the next step, the rule of Ahriman, is left out of the concept and replaced with that of the mixture, which is, in fact, the third and last period. This misplacement has then led to an imaginary period of 'separation' or *wizārishn*, which actually has no duration and merely signifies the end of time and the renovation of the cycle in a new form. In this scheme, all that has ever happened and all that will ever happen is included and is foreseen.

The Seven Ameshaspands

'Zurvanite teaching was profoundly influenced by astronomy and astrology; a preoccupation with the zodiac may have inspired the belief in a 12,000-year period of limited time.'[11] The period of material creation (*gētīg bundahishn*) starts with the treaty (*paymānag*) between the two antagonists. Earth is the battlefield in which the struggle between good and evil must work itself out. After creating the world, which the ancient Iranians thought of as seven creations – *dahishnān* – Ohrmazd put each section under the guardianship of one of the Ameshāspands (Aməsha Spəntas), 'the beneficent, or bounteous immortals', which are different manifestations of the deity himself. According to the Persian *Rivāyat of Hormazdiyār*, Zurvan had seven faces and seven names,[12] all of which belong to the process of personification of abstractions:

1. Sky (made of crystal) encircling the world like a shell, personified as Shahrēvar (Khshathra Vairya), translated as 'sovereignty' or 'ideal dominion'. His charge is that of metals, which included, in Old Iranian physics, crystal, taken as the substance of the sky. Thence, Shahrēvar is the guardian and lord of the sky, as well as of weapons made from stone.

2. Water that filled the bottom half of the world egg, personified as Hordād (Haurvatāt, Av. Haurva, OI. haruva + dād, a suffix for an abstract feminine name), variously translated as 'wholeness', 'health', 'healing',

'salvation', 'well-being' or 'spiritual perfection'; the personification of perfection and completion.

3. The earth that floated on the water to Spandārmad, (Spenta Ārmaiti), 'holy devotion', 'the goddess of the earth'.
4. Plants (the unique plant of all plants), personified as Amurdād, (Amərətāt) 'the eternal', 'undying', 'immortality'.
5. Animals (the cattle), personified as Vahman/Bahman (Vohu Manah), 'good thought', 'good mind', 'holy spirit'.
6. Man (the just), Gayōmart, personified as Ohrmazd.
7. Fire, which permeated all other creations, personified as Ardvahisht (Asha.vahishta) 'perfect existence', 'best righteousness'.[13]

This sevenfold division of the deity finds its epic transposition in the myth or legend of Sindbād.

Sindbādnāma

The *Sindbādnāma* offers a collection of stories within a framework which is in place from the beginning of the story to the end, comparable in some ways to the *Thousand and One Nights*, which also offers a large number of diverse stories within a general framework. Ever since the time of Mas'udi (d. 345 / 956) and Ebn al-Nadim (d. 380 / 990), scholars working in the field of Near Eastern literatures have been divided with respect to the origins of *Kalīla wa Demna* (*KD*) and *SN*. In contrast to *KD*, which has Indian antecedents, no such Indian derivation has been found for *SN*. In an exhaustive survey, B. E. Perry tried to put an end to disputes surrounding the background of this outstanding work of literature by vigorously establishing its Near Eastern, or better, Persian origins.[14]

Sindbādnāma belongs to the group of Middle Persian books which were translated into Arabic very early in the second / eighth century. Abān al-Lāhiqī (d. *c.* 200 / 815) versified *SN* and *KD*.[15] Only a few samples of his Arabic verses can be found in the scattered literature.

Despite its various Arabic translations, the original Middle Persian text continued having a life of its own until Abu al-Favāres Fanāruzi rendered it into Persian (Darī) in 339 / 950, a version which is also lost. Zahiri Samarqandi, the author of the available New Persian *SN* (written in 556 / 1160), considered the Darī version of the *SN* to be plain and devoid of artistic excellence. Hence he decided to make it beautiful and attractive by transforming it into an ornamented rhymed prose. Following the current literary style of his time, he heavily interposed his Persian source with material taken from the Qur'an, *hadith* and Arabic and Persian poems, proverbs and proverbial phrases, thus truly changing the character of the original and extending its size considerably. It is this text that my comments are based on. It consists of a long and highly ornate introduction by Zahiri, a frame-story that runs throughout and a total of thirty-four short stories told by major participants.

The main theme in most of the tales assembled within the central frame seems to have been tied initially to the cleverness and disloyalty of women, though the present collection has stories which contradict that theme. The third-century historian Ya'qūbī (d. 284 / 897) knew *SN* as *Makr al-nisā'* ('The Craft and Malice of Women').[16] In Zahiri's Persian version seventeen out of the thirty-four stories have nothing to do with women; only eight deal with women's craftiness, while four emphasize their piety and trustworthiness. It is likely that interpolations have in the course of time replaced many of the earlier tales.

We do not know how much of the introduction of the present *SN* was part of the Pahlavi text and to what extent Zahiri, a Muslim author, has modified it. It is noteworthy that he starts with an exposition of the Neoplatonic notion of hypostasis, though he is by no means unique in doing so.

Mythic speculations about the universe, and later philosophical, primarily Neoplatonic, notions of hypostasis and emanation or the successive stages in the process of creation (universal intellect [or reason], the universal soul [or world-soul] mentioned above, the spheres and stars, the four basic elements, nature, plants, animals and, finally, the first man), have provided a conceptual framework within which Iranian artists of all denominations have, consciously or unconsciously, taught and entertained their public for centuries, among them Zahiri Samarqandi. He writes: God (*parvardgār*) created the sky (*āsmān*) without means from nothing, brought forth the plan of time (*zamān*), produced earth, water, air, *hayulā* (i.e. primal matter) and fire; the seven heavenly fathers (*haft pedar-e 'olvi*; i.e. the planets) and the twelve stations (i.e. the signs of the zodiac); the four lower mothers (*chahār mādar-e sofli*, i.e., the four basic elements); caused the mixture of steam and smoke responsible for all meteorological products, as well as the *javāher* of the mines; and from the *chahār ustuqus,* or four basic elements, came the three offspring (*se mawlud*), that is, minerals, plants, animals; and topped all this with reason (*'aql*) to enable man to differentiate between right and wrong and live a good life (*SN*, 2–3).

Since Zahiri's presentation is not all that consistent in the form we have it, let us examine another sketch of this scheme. The Iranian Ismā'ili theoretician Abū Ya'qub al-Sejestāni (died soon after 361 / 971) studied with the grand master Mohammad al-Nasafi (d. 332 / 943) and followed his teachings. He calls the lords who govern the motion of the spheres 'fathers' (*abā'*). Once the four 'natures' (Arabic *tabā'i, mufradāt*; Persian *ākhshijān*, that is, the contrary powers of hot, cold, wet and dry) are activated by the soul, they climb to produce the four elemental bodies (*'anāser*)[17] called 'mothers' (*ummahāt, mādarān, chahār mādar*), that is, earth, water, air and fire. As Paul Walker succinctly explains, fathers and mothers are metaphors for the interaction between the revolutions of the spheres (those of the seven planets and the orb of the twelve signs of the zodiac, which is the eighth *falak*, or sphere beyond and above the other seven), and the effects of their combined movements on the mixing of the elements. What is thus conceived are the 'offspring' (Arabic *mawālid*), that is, the mineral, vegetable and animal kingdoms (the best of which is man).[18]

Having prepared the philosophical setting, Zahiri then moves on to articulate the intrinsic ties between sovereignty and prophecy. He quotes the famous Arabic saying *al-dīn wa'l-mulk taw'amān* 'religion and kingship are twins', which he attributes to the Prophet Mohammad (*SN*, 4). In fact, it is the first Sasanian king Ardashir who in his *kārnāmak* addressed his son Shāpur: 'O my son, know that religion and kingship are two brothers, and neither can dispense with the other. Religion is the foundation of kingship, and kingship protects religion. For whatever lacks a foundation must perish, and whatever lacks a protector disappears.'[19] We may recall that when Zurvan gives sovereignty over the world to his unwanted son, he hands him a diadem as the sign of royalty. He gives his son Ohrmazd a bundle of *barsom* (Av. *barəsman*) (twigs of the *haoma* plant), as a sign of spiritual leadership in the world. Zaehner is certainly correct in making the distinction between these two symbols. It is in the Zurvanite doctrine that the twin sons of Zurvan represent spirituality and sovereignty in the world. Thus it is no surprise that Zahiri immediately takes recourse to Goshtāsp to complete the saying by adding: 'Religion is strengthened by kingship, and kingship endures with religion.'[20]

The framework narrative that sets the scene for the other stories to be told runs as follows.[21] Late in life and after long praying and doing of good deeds, the one-hundred-and-something-year-old king of kings Kurdis (for which OP. Kūrush, i.e. Cyrus, has been suggested) finally receives the child he has longed for all his life. At the age of twelve the prince is given to master trainers and expert teachers. Ten years of hard work go by, but he learns nothing. The king's seven wise viziers choose Sindbād, the most learned among them, to educate the prince. He is to instruct him for six months and then present him to the court at a set date. Just as the date arrives, the prince's star of destiny indicates that he has to keep silence for seven days; otherwise he would be in grave danger. The prince enters the court and the teacher, fearing punishment, goes into hiding. One of the king's favourite concubines, who is in love with the prince, tries to win him over but to no avail. Rebuffed and fearing retribution, the stepmother accuses him of attempting to violate her. The prince, doomed to silence, is condemned to death. His life is saved by the seven wise men, who take turns with the king's favourite wife to tell him stories so they can secure a stay of execution by entertaining the king through seven days with tales showing the wickedness of woman, the queen (concubine) meanwhile recounting stories to offset those of the sages (Perry, 97–8). The motif of rescue-by-narrating-stories is established. On the eighth day the prince, who has remained silent up to that time, speaks in his own defence, and the queen is found guilty.

Sindbādnāma has been compared with the Greek story of the *Life of Secundus*, the Silent Philosopher (for example by Paulus Cassel).[22] Perry emphasizes the unmistakable influence of the *Life of Secundus* upon the frame-story of the book of *Sindbād*.[23] The similarity is at times astonishing, though the motivation and operating factors are fundamentally different. The philosopher's motive for silence is to check the sensational proposition that no woman is chaste, whereas that of the prince is to protect himself from the unrestricted desire of a woman. The philosopher's silence is a matter of choice, dictated by the death of his mother; that of the prince unavoidable, imposed by an inauspicious conjunction of stars. His silence is purely mechanical and arbitrary, for it depends only upon a horoscope taken at the last moment. The prince starts talking as soon as the externally imposed period of silence is over; the philosopher pledges to stay silent for the rest of his life.

Shifting the emphasis to a literary–historical approach allows us to question whether the Greek *Life of Secundus* (from *c.* 200 CE) has not been under the spell of the Iranian tale. After all, the *Book of Shimās* (Shīmās), perhaps the *Vorlage* of *SN*, is said to have been written under the Parthians (and the *SN* itself is occasionally attributed to them).[24] Shimās stands alone for all the seven wise men and alternates his tales with those of the concubine. Both books are recasts of one another; the frame-story is the same and the wisdom of the sages is also secular in both.

In the Greek *Syntipas* (a translation of the Syriac rendition of *SN*), after the dust is settled and the truth is revealed, the king asks twenty questions of his son. The contents of this session are identical to the questions put to the silent philosopher Secundus by the Emperor Hadrian. Zahiri has only four of these. However, Perry argues convincingly that the Pahlavi original should have also contained this question-and-answer session with all its examples.[25] Hadrian asks Secundus to write out answers to twenty questions for him, which he does. The prince does the same, but answers verbally. As will be seen, the motivation for the question and answer at the end of *SN* is yet another clue to Sindbād's ties with Zurvan.

Characters in the Drama

Zurvan, Ohrmazd, Ahriman, Ameshāspands, Frēdōn

The King, Prince, Queen, Sindbād and the Wise Sages, Feridun

With the exception of the king with the corrupt name Kūsh, Kurdis or Kūrush, and the prince's teacher Sindbād, who gives his name to the collection, none of the characters, neither the prince nor any of the other viziers has a name. The prince's mother is never mentioned and for all practical purposes she is non-existent; this is in line with the hermaphrodite Zurvan who gives birth to the two twin spirits, being both their father and mother. Here the king plays the role of the father and the husband. Very few personal names appear in the text, but the ones that do appear provide the necessary clues to disclose the initial purpose of the tale.

The King

The King is old and of undetermined age. Just like Zurvan, he has lived his life in luxury and peace, fulfilling all his wishes except having a son. One day the king thought to himself and said: 'I have come to this time of life and I have no son to carry on my name and to be king after me.'[26] He prays and sacrifices for a long time until he receives what he wants (*SN*, 41). All this is almost identical to what is reported of Zurvan.[27] He is transcendent and has no apparent function other than watching how events unfold in his presence.

Zurvan spent a 1,000 years sacrificing (in the Zurvanite myth the issue of sacrifice is significant) for a progeny, then doubted (or pondered) whether his sacrifice had been worthwhile. As a result two sons were born: one a product of his sacrifice, the other a product of his doubt. The king was rewarded with a son, who 'grew up like a cedar', but no sooner had he come of age, than he attracted the lust of a concubine.

'Sacrifice accompanies the actualization of Ohrmazd; Ohrmazd himself performs sacrifice to form his creation, and at the end of time sacrifice is held in order finally to annihilate the power of evil and to inaugurate the "Final Body".' 'Through sacrifice multiplicity is produced from unity, and by sacrifice is the essential unity restored.'[28]

Zurvan's desire to have a son, who would create heaven and earth and rule over it, is the king's wish to have a wise prince to rule over his imperium of peace and prosperity. This very desire begins the process of self-actualization of the deity; its absence would have kept the imperfection of the deity latent. The thousand-year sacrifice that accompanies the desire is a necessary accompaniment of the creative act.

Perry surmises that the childlessness episode in the *SN* is a borrowing from the frame-story of the *Book of Wise Achigar*.[29] If true, this can only reinforce the antiquity of the motif in Persian literature. Another borrowing from this source could then be the question-and-answer part at the end of *SN*.

The king is assisted by seven learned viziers, whereas Zurvan has seven faces, each in charge of part of his affairs. His kingship is the most auspicious (*sa'd akbar*) of all reigns in the realm of Saturn (*eqlim-e zohal*) (in fact Saturn is inauspicious; the asterism here is imprecise); the rulers of the farthest reaches of the earth follow his example, and the invisible administrator behind the movement of the day and night is in contact with him (*SN*, 32–3); and one wishes that the king lives to the end of time (*SN*, 37).

The Prince

As the prince is born the astrologers at the court predict that he will live a long life, like Jamshid and Feridun. He will encounter great danger for a while, but

will emerge victorious to rule over the world with justice (*SN*, 43). He grows up
an eventless but unusually long period of twelve [three x four] years before
being sent to school; Ohrmazd experiences 3,000 [three x a thousand] years of
undisturbed *mēnōg* period. In later sources the 3,000 year periods of the
cosmogony appear often in fractions of it: 3, 100, 1,000, and so on. The
Manichaeans even spoke of the three successive ages as the Three Days.[30]

The prince attends school for ten years and receives education from the best
teachers and philosophers, but he does not learn anything. His ten-year period
of apparent ineptitude in learning corresponds with Ohrmazd's *gētīg* age during
which the forces of goodness have prepared themselves but have nothing yet to
say.

Similar to the Zurvanite cosmogony in Pahlavi sources, the era of
Ahriman's domination over Ohrmazd's creation and the latter's saving only the
seeds and archetypes of his creatures has not been articulated properly. Its
parallel in the tale must have been when the prince is in great danger and on the
verge of being executed; but in his case this has been relegated to the next
phase. As in the cosmogony, the boundaries between the periods are blurred
here.

In the final stage, the prince is well prepared to demonstrate his learning and
wisdom, but having been born at an inauspicious constellation, he has to keep
silence for seven days; his acquired wisdom helps him to pass through this
perilous situation. As in the Zurvanite myth and the Ameshaspands, here the
seven viziers come to his assistance and help him to put his antagonist in check.

The prince's ordeal resembles that of Siyāvash of the Persian epic cycle,
and that is certainly not accidental. The two tales are part and parcel of the
same tradition of expounding the intricacies of the ancient religious world-
view.

Sindbād

Sindbād is a fictive and conventional name. That Sindbād is a meaningless
personal title for a sage has been recognized for over a century and despite the
fact that it has found a rival in Sindbād the Sailor; it is still used conventionally
as an easily recognizable title. Elsewhere I have reviewed the discussions about
this fanciful name and established that Sindbād سندباد is a nonsensical corruption
of the Middle Persian Spandyād.[31] Av. Spentō.dāta > *spanta'dāda [-dāta >
- dād > -yād] (Yt. 13.103, etc.) meaning 'created or given by the holy or
beneficent spirit' becomes Spandi-dāt [spndd't'], Spanddād/Spandyād in
Pahlavi and thence the New Persian and Arabic Isfandyār (Sifandyār) or
Isfandyād (Sifandyād), which in Arabic letters would also give سينداد، سبنتدات,
سبنداد (*sipand* سپند = saint, righteous, divine). The Middle Persian form may be
read Spandadāt سپينددات or Spandyād سپينديا (d and y have the same sign in
cursive Pahlavi script) reflected in Arabic as Isfandyādh اسفنديا,[32] and
Isfandyār اسفنديار.[33] We also have Spandidātān, 'patron of the spandi-dāt'.[34]

Spandmat or Spandarmat [spndrmt'] is one of the seven Ameshaspands, 'holy immortals' and corresponds with the goddess of the earth, as well as the twelfth month of the year in the Persian calendar: Avestan Spənta.ārmaiti- 'bounteous devotion'; *spenta-* < *suanta-*; hence NW *spanta-*, SW *santā* سنتا, both represented in Armenian lws: *spandaramet*; *sandaramet* <*santā aramati 'abyss, hell.' The Armenians still have the old name Spandarat, Spandiyat.[35] Another example is *Spentā* 'bounteous, holy', which is a characteristic term in Zoroaster's revelation and signifies those who use their powers to further the good creation.

In the Gāthās, Angra Mainyu [Aŋra Mainiiu, 'evil spirit'] plays the role of an adversary to Spenta Mainyu [Spəntāg Mēnōg, 'bounteous spirit'] in the cosmic drama. In later Pahlavi literature when Ohrmazd takes the place of Spenta Mainyu, Ahriman becomes his direct contender. Spenta Mainyu, who is only the first and highest aspect of Ohrmazd, becomes his attribute and is then identical to him. As such he himself has been placed in opposition to Ahriman, and so gives rise to the apparent dualistic nature of Zoroaster's message. On the one hand, Sindbād is Spenta Mainyu, the head of the Aməsha Spəntas, on the other, a kind of alter-ego of the prince. The association of Sindbād with the prince reflects the identification of the Spenta Mainyu with Ohrmazd.

Sindbād is one of the wise sages who, due to his superior knowledge and wisdom, is entrusted with the duty of teaching the prince, for: 'Any bird trained by him will be able to compete with simurgh in flying, and build its nest next to the pheasant' (*SN*, 46). The metaphorical comparison of Sindbād's pedagogical abilities as equivalent to training birds to attain the rank of the simorgh is not merely accidental hyperbole; it echoes the protective relationship between the bird and the hero. Hanns-Peter Schmidt has dedicated a study to the simorgh (senmurv), drawing on all the available literary and iconographical sources about this mythical bird. He depicts the symbolic significance of its constituent parts: head of a dog, tail of a pheasant, etc., presenting a critical synthesis of the innumerable works published on the subject. Schmidt concludes that the most common significance of senmurv is its relation with *khwārna* (Av *Khvarənah*), while the very rich symbolism of this animal has made of it a manifestation of Veretragna 'victory,' combined with the tree of life and, through an astral plan, with Tishtar (Sirius). The tail of the pheasant makes of senmurv a herald of the rainy season, and a psychopomp, having the head of a dog indicates his role as the protector of justice.[36]

The Seven Wise Sages

After the prince's failure in learning, the king discusses his case with his seven viziers, who are all sages (*hakims*) selected from among 7,000 philosophers. They consult on the matter but each one is reluctant to accept responsibility, until Sindbād, who is one of them and knows that the unfavourable time for the prince is over, accepts the task of teaching him (*SN*, 46). Later on in the text this point is forgotten, and seven sages are listed in addition to Sindbād. This is another sign of the difficulty facing the authors of whether or not to include Ohrmazd among the Amesha Spentas, causing the number to fluctuate between six or seven. As in the Zurvanite myth, with the exclusion of Ohrmazd/Sindbād, there should have remained six, and not seven, wise men to intercede in favour of the prince. It is also noteworthy that it is Sindbād who knows in advance that the adverse period in the prince's horoscope has passed.

The viziers are nameless, but it is said expressly that 'the seven viziers to the king were like the seven planets in the sky', who were by 'good fortune' at his service and ordered the affairs of the kingdom with their penetrating intelligence (*SN*, 78). Their attributes come to the fore only sporadically: one is the 'Moon' (*māh*) of sagacity and the Mercury (*tir*) of contemplation (*SN*, 84); the second is unequalled in science, philosophy and art (*SN*, 117); the sharp intellect of the third has taken the light of the fourth planet (i.e. the Sun) away from it (*SN*, 146); the fourth is of great splendour and widespread celebrity (*SN*, 171); the fifth is the highest star in the assembly of the kingdom (*SN*, 204); the sixth is in charge of the four elemental bodies (*arkān*, i.e. earth, water, air and fire), and his influence on the affairs of the realm is as that of the king of the stars (i.e. the Sun) in the sky (*SN*, 225); and the seventh embodies the resolution of Saturn (*zohal*), the luck of Jupiter (*moshtari*) and possesses *farr-e homāy* (*Khvarr* 'fortune, glory' created by Ohrmazd) (*SN*, 256). The seven planets are all present, one way or another, keeping danger away from the prince.

The Concubine

After the truth is revealed and the queen is exposed, the king asks his son what punishment she should receive, and whether or not she should be killed. The prince says:

> women cannot be killed. I think that the most appropriate punishment for her is to cut off her hair, blacken her face, put her on a black donkey, [facing backward], and parade her all around town. Let two heralds accompany her, one preceding, the other following behind, proclaiming loudly to the people that this is the punishment for whoever acts treacherously against his master and his king.

So they brought retribution upon her and punished her treachery in this way. (*SN*, 330; Perry, *Origin*, 74–5). Her life is spared and peace is established.

This episode has its parallel in the fate of the mythic Ahriman and that of his epic counterpart Bewarasp (Bēvar-Asp, Aži-dahāka, Arabic/Persian Zahhāk). One recalls that Ahriman takes the form of a snake, lizard, fly or man, though Pahlavi texts speak of Aži-dahāka as being only one of Ahriman's creatures.

Ahriman, the darkness, cannot be eliminated while the brightness of light is defined by it. This concept has created endless debates. Manicheans argued that the darkness will be imprisoned in the belly of light. Those opposing Mani responded that *rōšan ī bun rōšn* (the realm of light) is at first on one side (the lower side) adjacent with darkness, the direction from which it is attacked, but if Ahriman falls out at the end and is engulfed by the boundless light, it can harm the light from all directions. The authors of the *Dēnkard* are clearly against the Manicheans on this point and criticize them for it (*DK*, 3.114). This all goes back to the fact that supporters of Mani have conceived of darkness as boundless, just as the light is boundless.

Ahriman cannot die (*BD*, I. 6–7). The principles of Spenta Mainyu and Angra Mainyu, the good and the bad spirits, are eternal (*Y*, 30.4). Since 'All creatures are created by Ohrmazd, he will return them to himself', (*DK*, 6.279) at least in the Zurvanite heresy, one could expect that his son Ahriman would also return to him. Ahriman, who is not infinite and has no material existence of his own, is the finite time which at expiration will dissolve into infinite time.

In the majority of our sources, Ahriman is only reduced to powerlessness though some – definitely secondary – sources mistakenly or for theological reasons speak of his annihilation. The *Bundahishn* and *Māh Fravardīn*, 38, recount that he is led back through the same hole through which he had first entered the world. In *Mēnōg ī Khrad* (8.11–15), Ahriman survives in a state of incapacity even after the final renovation; in Yashts (*Yt.* 19.96), Ahriman will be vanquished and reduced to impotence in the final struggle; yet according to the *Dēnkard* (Bombay, XII, 13, no. 297) he is eliminated.

In this cosmic drama the entire historical concept of man's existence is comparable to an ordeal: sinners will be purified of all faults by a final punishment and will experience a renaissance. The final renovation of the world will consist of a return to its initial perfection (*mēnōg*) (*Zādspram*, 34.25).

Frētōn/Feridun

The king praises Sindbād for having taught his beloved son so successfully and then asks his son how it was possible for him to learn such a vast amount of knowledge in such a short period of time. The prince tells him about the ten maxims of wisdom that embody the essence of all knowledge and ancient science as written on the walls of Frētōn's palace. Amongst all recensions of the book, only three have this section. The Greek *Syntipas* has all ten maxims. The Persian *SN* has eight, as does its poetic version. From the ten maxims of *Syntipas*, four have their parallels in the Persian, so Perry concludes that at least these four should have existed in the Pahlavi original. The other adages are of doubtful provenance and may have been introduced in part by Andreopulus or Musā the Persian, who prepared an early Arabic version of *SN*.[37] Perry observes that the original number of maxims should have been ten and shows that such forms of decalogue had been popular in the Near East as well as in the west.

Of greater significance for our proposal, however, is that the content of the prince's teaching material comes from Frētōn who plays a key role in the ancient Persian cosmogony.

In the *Shāhnāma*, Feridun strikes Zahhak (Aži.dahāka) down with his ox-headed mace, but does not kill him; on the advice of an angel he imprisons him in a cave underneath Mount Damāvand, binding him with a lion's pelt fixed onto the walls of the cave, where he will remain until the time of *frashkart* [*frašogird*] 'restoration'. In the *Dēnkard* (*DKM*, 811.13–20) we read about the reasons why Frētōn does not kill Zahhāk and puts him in chains instead: in order to kill Zahhāk, Frētōn hit him on the head, shoulders and all over his body with his club; but Ohrmazd told Frētōn not to cut him in half, for by doing so the world would be filled with harmful insects and *khrafstar*s, (repugnant or harmful creatures), disease, stink, etc., in other words, all Ahrimanic creatures which can still cause havoc. By winning over Aži.dahāka and putting him in chains, Frētōn restores the balance of forces in accordance with the accepted rules of the *paymānag*; his appearance in the tale inaugurates the period of *gumēzishn*. However, the battles fought until this time will be replicated at the end of time. Notably the demiurgic exploits of Frētōn reappear at the time of resurrection and, according to Bahman Yasht (*Yt.* 9.13 f.), they require Frētōn to be resurrected to preside over the process of restoration of a preliminary order.

In the *Avesta* Frētōn (Therita; θraētaona) is the first doctor. Ahura helps him to keep death and sickness away from people by putting at his disposal 10,000 medical plants, all grown around the eternal tree of *gaokərəna*, or the white *haoma* tree in Paradise. Frētōn's father Āthviya (O.I. Āptya; etc.) is the second person after Jamshid's father to press the *haoma* tree to prepare the ritual drink, as a reward for which Frētōn is born to him with *farr-e īzadī*, which had left Jamshid. The successive ages of Jamshid, Aži.dahāka and Frētōn represent the three periods of 3,000 years. The story of the prince in *SN* is a typical one: he is to become king like Jamshid and Frētōn and restore the glory of the kingdom (*SN*, 42). In other words, *farr-e kiyānī* (*khvarənah*), the glory or royal fortune which had left them will now reach him.

Let us encapsulate: The king who has all that his heart desires but a son (= Zurvan), the prince (= the Good, Ohrmazd / Spenta Mainyu), who has to keep silence for a while due to his horoscope (= the period of Ahriman's dominance), the queen (= Ahriman), the seven viziers (= Ameša Spentas), Sindbād (the Saviour/ Spenta Mainyu), and the final victory of good over evil at the auspicious moment.

The above comparison suggests that the book *Sindbādnāma* has been originally composed in a Zurvanite milieu. This opens a new vista not only for interpreting and placing the *SN* in the history of fiction, but also for the *Shāhnāma* and other similar epics in Persian.

Notes:

1. Mohammad al-Zahiri al-Samarqandi, *Sindbādh-nāme* [Sindbādnāma], ed. by Ahmed Ateş (Istanbul : Chāpkhāna-e Wezārat-e Farhang, 1949). This was poorly versified in 776 / 1374 by a poet who called himself 'Azod Yazdi; see Mohammad Ja'far Mahjub, 'Sindbādnāma-ye manzūm' in *Pazhūheshhā-ye Irāni* (= Nāmvāra-ye, Dr Mahmud Afshār). XI (Tehran 1378 AH), 561–622. Here Mahjub introduces 'Azod's work in detail and later attaches this as an introduction to his edition of it, published in Tehran in 1381. W.H. Clouston's *The Book of Sindibād. Or, The story of the king, his son, the damsel, and the seven vazirs*; from the Persian and Arabic, with introduction, notes and appendix, (Glasgow: privately printed, 1884), is in the main a translation of 'Azod's work.
2. G. Gnoli, 'Iranian Cosmogony and Dualism', *EncIr*, vol. VII (1996), 576–82.
3. R.C. Zaehner, *Zurvan. A Zoroastrian Dilemma* (Oxford: Clarendon Press, 1955), 19.
4. A.Christensen, *L'Iran sous les Sassanides*, 2nd edn (Copenhagen: Eniar Munksgaard, 1944), 141–78.
5. Mary Boyce, 'Ahura Mazdā', *EncIr*, I, 687a.
6. See C. Cereti and D.N. MacKenzie, 'Except by Battle. Zoroastrian Cosmogony in the first chapter of the Greater *Bundahišn'* in *Religious Themes and Texts of pre-Islamic Iran and Central Asia. Studies in honour of Professor Gherardo Gnoli on the occasion of his 65th birthday on 6th December 2002*, ed. by C.G. Cereti, M. Maggi and E. Provasi (Wiesbaden: Reichert Verlag, 2003), 31–59.
7. *Bundahishn*, Ervand Tahmuras Dinshaji Anklesaria, The Bundahishn, being a Facsimile of the TD Manuscript no. 2, (Bombay: 1908), 58.
8. J. Duchesne-Guillemin, 'Ahriman', *EncIr*, I, 672b.
9. J. Duchesne-Guillemin, *La religion de l'Iran ancien* (Paris: Presses Universitaires de France, 1962), 319.
10. 'On Spenta Mainyu's role in Zoroastrian cosmogony', *Asia Institute*, 7 (1993), 97–103 [published in Oct. 1994]; = Iranian Studies in Honor of A.D.H. Bivar; here 97.
11. Philip G. Kreyenbroek, 'Cosmogony and Cosmology: I. In Zoroastrianism / Mazdaism', *EncIr*, VI, 304b.
12. Zaehner, 408–9.
13. Consult Mary Boyce, 'Aməša Spənta', *EncIr*, I, 933-6.
14. B.E. Perry, *The Origin of the Book of Sindbad* (Berlin: Walter De Gruyter & Co., 1960).
15. Ebn al-Nadim, *Ketāb al-Fehrest*, ed. by R. Tajaddod (Tehran 1971; reprint published by Enteshārāt Asātir, 1381 / 2003), 132, 186.
16. He says: The king Kūsh, a contemporary of Sindbād the Wise, compiled a book which he called *Makr al-nisā'* (*Ta'rīkh*, [Leiden: Brill 1883], I, 105).
17. In other sources these are also called *murakkabāt*, *arkān*, *mabādi*, *basāyit*, *ustuqusāt*; Greek: *stoicheion*, pl. *stoicheia*; Latin elementum; Persian *astawmandān* or *gōhrān*; in the *Dēnkard chahār zāhagān/zādagān*; or *chahār rastagān*; NP. *anāser-e chahārgāna*, etc. = *The Complete Text of the Pahlavi Dinkard*, published by The Society for the Promotion of Researches into the Zoroastrian Religion under the supervision of DM Madan (Bombay, 1911), III, 121, 123-6.
18. Paul Walker, *Abū Ya'qūb al-Sijistānī: Intellectual Missionary* (London and New York: IB Tauris in association with the Institute of Ismaili Studies, 1996), 103.
19. Al-Mas'ūdī, *Murūj al-dhahab*, ed. by Charles Pellat (Beirut: Université Libanaise, 1965), I, 289; Zaehner, 36 n. 3.

20. *SN*, 5; see, *'Ahd Ardashīr*, ed. by I. 'Abbās (Beirut: Dār Sādir, 1967), 53; *Dēnkard* 58: *ērīh khwadāyīh mehēnīdārīhā' az dēn; 'ohrmazd bandagīh' <ud> 'māzdēsnīh dēn' az khwadāyīh*; for a slightly different transliteration and translation of the whole passage see M. Molé, 'Culte, mythe et cosmologie dans l'Iran ancien', *Annales du Musée Guimet* (Paris: Bibliothèque d'études, 1963), 51–2.

21. The frame-story of *Sindbādnāma* is present in *Gesta Romanorum* ['Deeds of the Romans'], ed. and trans. by Charles Swan 1824, re-edited by Wynnard Hooper 1877; reprint (NY: George Bell and Sons, 1950). This is a collection of tales from the thirteenth or fourteenth century.

22. Paulus Cassel, *Mischle Sindbad, Secundus-Syntipas* (Berlin: Richard Schaeffer, 1891).

23. Greek, Syriac, Armenian, Arabic, and Ethiopian versions of the *Life* exist (see Perry, 84–5).

24. M. Hermann Zotenberg, 'L'histoire de Gal'ad et Šīmās', *Journal Asiatique* 8 (1886), 97–123.

25. Perry, 80–82.

26. Perry, 66 (from the Arabic version).

27. Zaehner, 60–61, 421–3.

28. Zaehner, 271–2.

29. Perry, 89.

30. 'al-Ayyām al-thalātha' was the title of a chapter of Mani's book *Sifr al-asrār*; see Ebn al-Nadim, 399.

31. M. Zakeri, *Persian Wisdom in Arabic Garb*, 2 vols (Leiden: Brill, 2007) I, 100–15.

32. Abu Hanifa al-Dinawari, *al-Akhbār al-tiwāl* (Cairo: Wizārat al-Thiqāfa wa'l-Irshād Qawmi, 1960) 25, 26, 79; al-Tha'ālibi al-Marghani, *Ghurar al-mulūk*, ed. by H. Zotenberg (Paris: Imprimerie nationale, 1900), 256.

33. al-Tabari, *Ta'rīkh al-rusūl*, ed. by M. Hārūn (Cairo: Dār al-Ma'ārif, 1967) I, 562; al-Tha'ālibi al-Marghani, 256 n. 3; cited by E. Yarshater, 'Esfandīār', *EncIr*, VIII, 584.

34. The name of the magus Sphandadates is the Median *Spandadāta, see Lloyd Llewellyn-Jones and James Robson, *Ctesias' History of Persia, Tales of the Orient* (London and New York: Routledge, 2010), 178, 179, 228.

35. See J. Marquart, 'Beiträge zur Geschichte und Sage von Eran', *ZDMG*, 49 (1895), 639; M. Brosset, *Histoire de la Georgie* (St Petersburg: Académie des Sciences de Saint-Pétersbourg, 1849), 484.

36. Hanns Peter Schmidt, 'The Sênmurv. Of Birds and Dogs and Bats', *Persica* 9 (1980), 1-85; + 11 plates.

37. Perry, 77–8.

5

Early Persian Historians and the Heritage of Pre-Islamic Iran

A.C.S. Peacock
(University of St Andrews)

The rise of ethnically Iranian dynasties and the emergence of literature in New Persian – the Persian written in the Arabic script which came to replace Pahlavi (Middle Persian) – in the third century after the Muslim conquest of Iran have often been linked. Starting in the ninth century, the Persian Taherids dominated much of western Iran while the Saffarids of Sistan held sway in the east. The political dominance of Iranians in the eastern Islamic world – Iran, Iraq and Central Asia – was consolidated in the tenth century by the Buyid and Samanid dynasties. The Buyids from the Caspian region of Daylam seized Baghdad in 944 CE and gained control over most of what is now western Iran and Iraq, while the Samanids, whose capital was the Transoxianan city of Bukhara, ruled over Muslim Central Asia and eastern Iran. Meanwhile, the emergence of literature in New Persian is traditionally dated to the reign of the Saffarid Ya'qub b. Layth (861–79), who was of humble origins and is said (probably apocryphally) to have been unable to understand the Arabic panegyrics dedicated to him, forcing his court poet, Mohammad b. Vasif, to resort to Persian.[1] The birth of New Persian was certainly a good deal less sudden than this suggests, and fragments of poetry indicate the survival of some forms of Persian in the provinces as a literary language throughout the early Islamic period.[2] Yet it received little elite patronage until the tenth century when the Samanids started to promote both New Persian poetry and prose, including the first historical work written in the language. This was a translation and adaptation of the Arabic chronicler Abu Ja'far al-Tabari's great *Ta'rikh al-rosul wa'l-moluk* (History of Prophets and Kings) composed by the Samanid vizier Abu Ali Bal'ami at the command of the amir Mansur b. Nuh in 962. As the development of New Persian literature seems to be associated with its patronage by these ethnically Iranian dynasties, it has often been assumed that the latter must have been motivated by patriotic considerations.[3] Scholars who have doubted the extent to which rulers promoted Persian literature out of some sense of Iranian national feeling have suggested its rise was connected to

a supposed devotion to ancient Iranian traditions on the part of the *dehqān* class
of gentry in the Iranian east, distant from the more thoroughly Arabized and
Islamized centres of the west.[4]

The best-known example of this revival of interest in pre-Islamic Iran is
Ferdowsi's *Shāhnāma*, completed in 1010, which presents a versified panorama
of Iranian history from creation down to the Arab conquests. Ferdowsi's work
is reputed to have met with a cool reception from the Ghaznavid ruler Mahmud
to whom it was dedicated, but some rulers did show an active concern for
Iranian antiquities. The Buyid ruler Azod al-Dawla (936–83), for instance,
visited the ruins of Persepolis in the company of a Zoroastrian priest who read
the Pahlavi inscriptions there to him. So impressed was Azod al-Dawla that he
added his own inscriptions recording his visit next to the ancient ones.[5]
Alongside the relatively humble title of *amir* or *amir al-omarā'*, commander or
commander-in-chief, which the caliphs granted to the military men who
wielded actual power, dynasties started to arrogate to themselves titles and
styles reminiscent of the Sasanian past such as the ancient Iranian title of
shāhanshāh.[6] There also developed a fashion among the new Iranian rulers,
later to be adopted by their Turkish successors, for forging themselves
genealogies claiming descent from more illustrious predecessors, especially
Sasanian rulers.[7]

Yet the connection between the rise of ethnically Iranian dynasties and
Persian literature is less clear cut than at first appears. Some, like the Taherids,
showed little interest in promoting Persian letters or even, it is alleged by later
sources, an active aversion to them.[8] In western Iran and Iraq where the Buyids
held sway, there was no linguistic or literary Persian renaissance: Arabic
remained the language of literature and bureaucracy, while Zoroastrians
continued to use Pahlavi. Meanwhile, far from everything written in New
Persian can easily be connected with any kind of 'national feeling'. Most of the
Persian works sponsored by the Samanids were firmly religious, expressions of
the piety-minded Sunni environment of tenth-century Transoxiana, and were
translations from Arabic originals: the anti-heretical tract *al-Sawād al-a'zam*
and the Persian versions of Tabari's history and his Qur'anic commentary, the
Jāme' al-bayān.[9] Even where antiquarian interests can be observed, these were
by no means necessarily linked to the use of Persian as a literary language. As
we shall see, Esfahāni's *Ta'rikh seni moluk al-arz*, the historical work which is
by far the most hostile to the Arabs and the most strident in stressing the central
place of Iran in history and geography, was written not in Persian but in Arabic.

In this chapter I wish to explore the various ways in which ancient Iranian
history was interpreted and used during the Iranian Intermezzo, as this period
has been named, through examining some of the major historical works
produced in the period. The 'early Persian historians' of the title is not
restricted to those who wrote in Persian, but includes many who wrote in
Arabic although they themselves were of Iranian descent. Some were active in

Baghdad, but many more lived in the heartland of Iran itself. I shall take the story down to the early twelfth century, for, apart from the example of Bal'ami, the first flourishing of historical writing in Persian took place not under the ethnically Iranian dynasties of the tenth century, but under their Turkish successors. However, as we shall see, that did not mean that the latter were devoid of interest in the heritage of pre-Islamic Iran: far from it.

Iranian History in Arabic, Eighth to Tenth Centuries

Although Arabic historiography originated in *hadith* and *akhbār* – reports about the Prophet, his companions and their deeds – from the eighth century a certain interest in ancient Iranian history was evident. The bureaucrat and littérateur Ebn al-Moqaffa' (d. 757), who served both the Umayyads and the Abbasids, produced an Arabic translation of the *Khwadāy-nāmag*, the Pahlavi book of kings.[10]Although Ebn al-Moqaffa''s version has not survived, it became a major source for subsequent historians, especially when in the ninth century Arabic historiography started to diverge from its pious origins and evince a greater interest in pre-Islamic history.[11] The Abbasid court fostered a cultural environment that sought to engage with the Iranian heritage. By making Iraq the centre of their empire, the Abbasids were emulating their Sasanian predecessors, and near their newly-founded capital of Baghdad the ruins of the Sasanian city of Ctesiphon could be observed. The poet Bohtori was inspired by Ctesiphon to write a *qasida* lamenting the Sasanian dynasty, but which also linked the latter to the Abbasids as part of 'a project to assimilate their heritage'.[12] The Abbasid court lay claim to many of the imperial traditions of their predecessors, as well as the learning for which Iran was famed.[13] Pahlavi texts were translated into Arabic, ranging from scholarly works to wisdom literature to selections from the *Avesta* to more popular affairs like the fables of *Kalila wa Demna*.[14] In place of recording traditions about the early (and more recent) traumas of the Islamic community and its victories, historians became more ambitious and related Islamic history to the broader history of what they knew of the civilized world – or, more precisely, one could say they sought to situate the history of the world in Islamic history. The outstanding example of such a history is Tabari's annals, on which Bal'ami's Persian version was loosely based. In Tabari and Bal'ami, tales of ancient Iranian kings are interwoven with stories of the Israelite prophets, who are depicted as the forerunners of Mohammad, the last Prophet. Other authors, however, went much further in their efforts to connect Iran and Islam.

The ninth-century Arabic history by Dinawari entitled the *al-Akhbār al-tewāl* is perhaps the clearest early example of this attempted integration of Iranian and Islamic history.[15] Whereas Tabari and Bal'ami start their works with long discussions on the duration of the world – a very popular topic in tenth-century historiography – Dinawari launches his history by trying to establish the centrality of Irānshahr, the land of Iran, the centre of the world according to ancient Iranian thought. Arabs and Persians are given a common origin in their descent from Shem, whom, Dinawari says, 'the Persians call Iran; he settled in Iraq and made it his private domain so it was called Irānshahr'.[16] Later on, another descendant of Noah, Afraskhad, is described as 'ancestor of the Arabs and the kings of Iran'.[17] Nor does Dinawari stop at annexing the Arabs to Iran. Alexander the Great is both made into a proto-Muslim, performing the *hajj*,[18] and a legitimate Iranian monarch through Persian descent on his mother's side (although Dinawari does recognize that Greeks did not accept this).[19] Indeed, Dinawari even manages to invent what he claims is a Persian etymology for Alexander's name.[20] Such is the prominence that Dinawari gives to his Iran-centred outlook that the amount of space he devotes to the Prophet Mohammad seems almost embarrassingly short, as several scholars have noted.[21] None the less, Dinawari's commitment to Islam cannot be doubted and he was himself the author of a commentary on the Qur'an. Significantly, Dinawari made no effort to bring his history up to his own days, but ended it with the rebellion of Bābak, suppressed in 837, several decades before the work was probably composed.[22] Bābak's rebellion is often considered an early expression of Iranian national feeling, but the general who suppressed it, Afshin, was also suspect in his adherence to Islam. With Afshin's execution and exposure as a non-Muslim, Dinawari concludes his work. It seems that despite his anxiety to uphold the centrality of Iran, Dinawari was keen to stress that this should not be used as an excuse for deviating from Islam.

The next generation produced another Arabic-language historian who was exactly the kind of individual Dinawari seems to have been worried about, Hamza al-Esfahāni (d. after 961). As far as we can judge from his use of the appropriate honorifics after the names of the Prophet Mohammad, Hamza was a Muslim, or at least was not prepared to confess openly to Zoroastrianism. Most likely, however, he adhered to the old faith to some degree, as is suggested by his interest in Zoroastrian traditions, whose perspective he largely adopts. Hamza's aim was to explain the rise and fall of states and the transfer of power between them:

> I have prefaced to these histories an introduction so that [the reader] can be informed of the vicissitudes of history, and may thereby understand the iniquities that befell them and the resemblances between them. I mention the places where great nations have settled, and the place of small nations among them, so that it may be seen how one has power over the other, and how some are eliminated when their time is up by the advent of states of other people, so that these events became a cause for the iniquity of history.[23]

The centrality of Iran is stressed right from the start. Hamza writes in terms that would not have been out of place in Sasanian times or even earlier, reflecting the Avestan idea of Iran at the centre of the world surrounded by six other climes on its peripheries.[24]

> Know that the inhabited parts of the earth are divided between seven nations: the Chinese, the Indians, the Blacks [al-Sudān], the Berbers, the Greeks [al-Rum], the Turks and the Aryans. The Aryans [al-Aryān] – who are the Persians [al-Fors] – occupy the middle of the realms [of earth], surrounded by the [other] six nations. For the south of the earth is in the possession of the Chinese, and its north in that of the Turks... These six nations are all situated on the edges of the populous areas of the earth, around the realm of the Aryans which is in the middle of them.'[25]

Even with regard to chronology, Hamza stresses the superiority of the Iranian solar dating system – at one point offering a detailed hijri–solar calendar conversion table – and insists that even the Arabic word for history, ta'rīkh, is of Persian origin.[26] Indeed, the range of sources Hamza refers to is itself strong testimony to the continuing interest in pre-Islamic Iran. He refers to eight different 'manuscripts' (nosakh) on Iranian history he consulted: among them was Ebn al-Moqaffa''s version of the Khwadāy-nāmag and another a work from the caliphal library in Baghdad,[27] but he further mentions another three works by local authors from Isfahan on pre-Islamic kings.[28] Hamza also had access specifically to histories of the Sasanian dynasty, such as one edited by a mōbed, a Zoroastrian priest, from Fārs named Bahrām b. Marwānshāh. Another was illustrated, and Hamza describes its depictions of individual Sasanian rulers.[29] Although he does not explicitly state so, it is tempting to suppose these works were written in Pahlavi. Yet there were major discrepancies between these sources, especially over chronology. Although Hamza – or Hamza's sources – place the blame for disagreements in the accounts of Iranian kings squarely on their Arabic translators,[30] it is evident there was much variation in the Persian tradition too. The desire to clean up these inconsistencies and establish an authoritative version of Iranian history prompted scholars like the mōbed Bahrām to seek out numerous different manuscripts on which to base their editions. Bahrām, we are told, collected no fewer than twenty manuscripts for his history of Iran from Gayumars (the first man according to Iranian tradition, widely equated with Adam) to the Arab conquest.[31]

Thus, even in the mid-tenth century, there was a substantial volume of Iranian historical literature beyond Ebn al-Moqaffa''s version of the Khwadāy-nāmag on which Hamza could draw.[32] Despite the centrality of Iran to his work, Hamza was also motivated by more narrowly local concerns, repeatedly drawing out historical associations with his home town of Isfahan and its surroundings, and stressing especially the foundation of nearby fire temples by ancient rulers.[33] As was to become popular among New Persian authors, Hamza divided Iranian rulers into the conventional four dynasties of Pishdadid, Kayanid, Ashkhanid and Sasanian, but his treatment of some figures is strikingly different from that of his contemporaries. Nowhere is this more noticeable than with his account of Alexander the Great, whom Dinawari had attempted to appropriate as a legitimate Iranian monarch, and whose career as an Islamic saint is stressed by Hamza's contemporary Bal'ami.[34] For Hamza, though, Alexander is a bloodthirsty monster, a destroyer of civilization who ruined Iran's cities, killed its priests and burned its books.[35] This is much more in accordance with the traditional Iranian depiction rather than the tales of Alexander's Iranian kinship, ultimately derived from the *Alexander Romance*, which Dinawari appropriated.[36]

Hamza does allot some space to Lakhmid, Ghassanid, Jewish and Islamic history and concludes with a brief account of the Buyids bringing the work up to the date of its composition in the year 350 AH / 961 CE.[37] It might be tempting to dismiss Hamza's work as something of a curiosity, an expression of the last gasps of Zoroastrian culture in western Iran, very probably written for the Buyid dynasty who controlled Hamza's hometown of Isfahan and who, as mentioned above, on occasion evinced an interest in Iranian antiquities which they employed *mōbed*s to interpret to them. Yet a striking passage in Hamza's account of the chronology of the world suggests that in fact it may have been composed with an eye to contemporary political concerns, which was perhaps why it was written in Arabic rather than the Pahlavi that remained current in Zoroastrian circles. Just before his section on Islamic history – or as he puts it perhaps rather disparagingly 'the history of the kings of the Qoraysh',[38] Mohammad's tribe – Hamza cites traditions concerning astrological portents of the rise of Islam and the Prophet on the authority of Abu Ma'shar and others.[39] He goes so far as to suggest that the acceptance of the Prophet's message was merely due to the fortunate alignment of the stars, claiming that if Mercury had been in a slightly different position at the time, the Qoraysh would have continued to resist Islam and the new religion would never have caught on.[40] The agency for the transfer of rule from the Persians to the Arabs is likewise attributed to planetary alignments.

> The conjunction of the stars necessitated the transfer of rule [*enteqāl al-dawla*] from the Persians to the Arabs. The sun was in Scorpio and Mars was in Cancer, which indicated that [Arab] kingship will wax from the birth [of the Prophet] for no more than 220 years. The [Arab] nation shall dominate for three hundred and sixty years after the birth [of the Prophet]. Three hundred years after [the Prophet's] death the decline in the rule of the Arab nation will begin from the direction of the west.[41]

The idea that a force from the west would inflict a crushing defeat on the Arabs is found in several Pahlavi and New Persian Zoroastrian apocalyptic texts.[42] Yet while Zoroastrians envisage a saviour at the end of time, Hamza makes no such eschatological references. It is not the end of the world he predicts, but of Arab rule. As Hamza tells he was writing in year 350 of the hijra, this passage suggests that the end of Arab, Islamic rule brought about by the Prophet was nigh. Although apocalyptic prophecies were common in Zoroastrian circles, it is unusual to find such ideas so openly expressed in Arabic and for the timescale for their realization to be so imminent. Hamza expected the collapse of the caliphate in his own lifetime, presumably paving the way for a rebirth of Iranian rule under the Buyids and perhaps, by implication, the fall of Islam itself, which, after all, in Hamza's view is nothing more than an astrological accident. It is hard to tell quite how far such predictions permeated Muslim consciousness, but it is noteworthy both that Hamza is frequently cited by later Persian historians and that historical works composed in the tenth and eleventh centuries show an acute interest in the related themes of the duration of the world and chronology. Bal'ami, for instance, Hamza's exact contemporary, devoted much attention to these problems. While some scholars have associated this interest with the need of pious Sunni circles to refute Isma'ili ideas that the end of time was imminent,[43] it may just as well have been a response to equally dangerous currents of thought like those represented by Hamza, writing just two years before Bal'ami.

The Birth of Persian Historiography

The first extant work of New Persian historiography – and in all probability the first such work to have been composed – is Bal'ami's great Persian version of Tabari. The Samanid dynasty that commissioned the work claimed descent from the Sasanian general Bahrām Chubin, as Bal'ami advertizes in his preface.[44] This fact, the choice of language for the text and the numerous discrepancies between the translation and the original, have suggested to many scholars that Bal'ami and his masters were motivated by a desire to promote a specifically Persian perspective on history. Although analysis is hindered by the vicissitudes of the work's textual history – meaning it is difficult to reconstruct exactly what the original text of Bal'ami said – the surviving manuscripts do not in the main bear this out. Indeed, compared to the Arabic original of Tabari – also, it should be remembered, ethnically Iranian, a native of the Caspian who spoke a dialect of Persian as his native language – Bal'ami actually reduces the amount of space given to tales of the pre-Islamic past, has nothing significant to say about the rise of the Persianate dynasties of the ninth and tenth century and concentrates on early Islamic history.[45] Iranian rulers of course have a place in Bal'ami's work – just as they had in Tabari's – but it is not the principal one. Prophecy and kingship are Bal'ami's themes, not the centrality of Iran, which is hardly surprising given it was compiled in a territory that had not been part of the Sasanian empire, and whose rulers showed only a passing interest in the pre-Islamic past. Even the Samanids' putative ancestor, Bahrām Chubin, was not a Sasanian monarch such as the Buyids and the Ghaznavids claimed for their forefathers, but a rebel against the Sasanian crown, a usurper of dubious legitimacy.[46]

Thus the first Persian-language history is entirely free – as far as we can judge from the extant manuscripts – of Hamza's Iranian patriotism. Far from espousing the latter's hopes for the end of Islamic hegemony, Bal'ami's work is an expression of Sunni orthodoxy and piety-mindedness. As an example of historiography inspired by national sentiment, Bal'ami's work is disappointing. Only the fact of it having been written in Persian is at all suggestive in this respect. Most probably Persian was chosen largely because, as the preface to the work indicates, Arabic was not that widely understood on the eastern frontiers of Islam in Central Asia where it was composed.[47] Indeed, in contrast to the Pahlavi and Arabic-using western Iran and Iraq where Hamza was active, antiquarian Iranian traditions cut little ice in the Persophone eastern Islamic lands, at least during the tenth century. From what we know of the predecessors to the *Shāhnāma* that were composed in the east, they do not seem to have been written at the behest of the court. True, individuals may have preoccupied themselves with tales of the pre-Islamic past, like Abu Mansur, who compiled a lost prose *Shāhnāma*. Both Abu Mansur and Ferdowsi were natives of Tus in Khorasan, rather far from the Transoxianan centre of the Persian Renaissance and the court patronage which provided the impetus for the growth of literary Persian, and there is little reason to think their interests reflected the tastes of Bukharan *sophistiqués*.[48] Of course, references to the mythical Iranian past might also on occasion furnish court poets like Rudaki and Daqiqi with apt similes, but its relevance to contemporary dynasties was limited.[49] Indeed, it has been suggested that Ferdowsi's work, with its failure to integrate Iranian and Islamic history, ending at the Arab conquest, was very much the exception rather than the rule, and the *Shāhnāma*'s sheer oddity in this respect may have been a factor behind its cold reception.[50] Court audiences in the east were simply not ready to take their Iranian history in unadulterated form.

Like their Samanid predecessors, the Turkish Ghaznavid dynasty sponsored literature in both Arabic and Persian. The earliest extant Ghaznavid historical work bears the title *Ghorar akhbār moluk al-fors wa siarehem* ('Highlights of the History and Biographies of the Persian Kings'), written in Arabic by the well-known littérateur Abu Mansur Abd al-Malek b. Mohammad al-Tha'ālebi shortly before 1021, when the work's dedicatee died.[51] This was Abu 'l-Mozaffar Nasr, brother of the Ghaznavid sultan Mahmud (997–1030), and governor of Sistan which perhaps explains why Tha'ālebi dwells at length on Sistan-related episodes of Iranian mythology, such as stories of Rostam. The *Ghorar* was originally a history in four volumes continuing down to the days of Mahmud of Ghazna himself. Only the first two volumes have been preserved, however, and the second, which covers the life of the Prophet Mohammad and early Islamic history, is as yet unpublished.[52] The published volume deals with the kings of Iran, but is very different in tone from Hamza's work, which is none the less cited from time to time as a source,[53] or Ferdowsi's.[54] The victory of Islam is seen unequivocally in a positive light, and despite Ghaznavid claims to descent from the last Sasanian monarch Yazdgerd III, Tha'ālebi makes no reference (at least in the extant parts of the work) to his patron's putative ancestor, who is here presented as a hopeless extravagant lacking any military prowess.[55] Tha'ālebi himself underlines the strongly Islamic flavour of his work when introducing the far-fetched story of the youth of Zāl, father of the Iranian hero Rostam, who is said to have been brought up in the nest of the mythical *anqā'* bird:

> I do not take responsibility for [the veracity of] this story. Were it not for its fame in every time and place and on every tongue, and were it not one of those tales by which kings are pleased and entertained, I would not have written it down... everything except the miracles of prophets are just pleasant tales.[56]

At the same time, Tha'ālebi tries to Islamicize ancient Iranian history. References to the single monotheist God abound and there are few hints of any of the fire temples in which Hamza was so interested. Indeed, in gratitude for the birth of his son Rostam, Zāl is depicted as giving alms (*sadaqa*) to the poor to thank God (*shokran lellāh*), a distinctly Muslim act.[57] Gayumars, the Iranian first man, is connected with Adam and made a prophet – the first of the line of prophet kings (*moluk al-anbiyā'*) with whom Tha'ālebi equates a number of legendary Iranian rulers, as well as Jewish ones like Solomon.[58] Tha'ālebi's purpose is not antiquarian or patriotic, but exemplary. In some respects, the *Ghorar* seems to have been intended as a mirror for princes designed to give ethical advice to Tha'ālebi's patron Abu 'l-Mozaffar Nasr as to how to behave with, for instance, pointed stories about the necessity of lowering taxes in times of famine[59] – a field in which the Ghaznavids had a terrible reputation. Tales of the Iranian past thus aim at imparting ethical values: Tha'ālebi approvingly notes the great Sasanian ruler Anushirvān the Just, who spent much of his time reading books of history which provided a model for his conduct.[60] Yet even if Iranian history did not hold the central place for Tha'ālebi that it did for Dinawari or Hamza, old Iranian concepts remain influential, above all the idea that *farr* – divine favour – (here rendered as *al-sa'āda al-elāhiya*) is essential for Iranian kings to remain legitimate.[61] Even the pre-Islamic concept of Irānshahr – Tha'ālebi repeatedly uses the ancient word – as the centre of the world survives in the *Ghorar*.[62] Despite his claim to prefer stories of prophetic miracles, the fact that the first volume of Tha'ālebi's work is devoted to tales of ancient Iran, albeit in Islamized garb, suggests that, like Dinawari, he too was trying to feel his way towards some kind of Iranian–Islamic synthesis. It is a great loss that we are unable to see how this theme was developed with regard to more recent history, and what place Mahmud of Ghazna would have had in it: in all likelihood he was envisaged as the inheritor of this Islamized Irānshahr.

The eleventh century saw the composition of two Persian-language histories under Ghaznavid tutelage, the first to survive since Bal'ami's work nearly a century earlier. On present evidence there is little to suggest there was much in between; in other words the first attempt at Persian-language historical writing – if that is the correct way to describe Bal'ami's piety-minded agenda – was something of a damp squib. These mid-eleventh-century works, the *Zayn al-akhbār* ('Adornment of Historical Reports') by Gardizi and the history of the Ghaznavids by the former bureaucrat Bayhaqi owe nothing to Bal'ami. The two works – neither of which has survived complete – are very different. Bayhaqi's choice of Persian for his vivid chronicle of court life in the 1030s probably lies in his bureaucratic background, for Persian was increasingly used as the language of administration from the tenth century onwards. As a chronicler of his contemporaries, Bayhaqi rarely refers to the pre-Islamic Iranian past, except as a source of stock moral exemplars in figures like Anushirvān.[63]

Gardizi's chronicle is much broader in scope than Bayhaqi's – if shorter – and written in a plain, unembellished Persian in contrast to the latter's sophisticated prose. Gardizi's aim was to glorify the deeds of Mahmud of Ghazna, he tells us,[64] but he also includes substantial sections on the pre-Islamic Iranian past as well as the history of Khorasan after the Muslim conquests. If Tha'ālebi's work suggests that by the eleventh century Iranian history had lost some of the political potency it had for Hamza al-Esfahāni and indeed Ferdowsi, Gardizi reminds us that the heritage of Irānshahr could still act as a focus for loyalties. The *Zayn al-akhbār* was written for the Ghaznavid sultan Abd al-Rashid around the years 1051–2,[65] when the Ghaznavid state had lost its major territories that were traditionally part of Irānshahr, Khorasan and Sistan. Gardizi's work seems to aim to assert the Ghaznavid place as the true heirs to Iranian kingship, at least in the lost territories of Khorasan.[66] History is explicitly used to explain the present. Gardizi stresses the permanence of Muslim rule: with the killing of Yazdgerd III 'the Muslims seized Irānshahr and they hold it to this day and will do so until the end of time, God willing.'[67] The Turanian chief Afrāsiyāb's wars with Iran are explicitly mentioned as the origin of the present hostility between the Turkish and Iranian worlds[68] – perhaps an allusion to tense relations with the Qarakhanids who themselves claimed descent from Afrāsiyāb. Likewise, customs current in Khorasan in Gardizi's day are explained through their introduction by famous caliphs: the amount of the *kharāj* of Marv, for instance, is said to have been set by Mo'āwiya, while many of the descendants of Hārun al-Rashid's governor of Chaghāniān are said still to live there.[69] Thus Gardizi's version of history – rather like Tha'ālebi's – situates the Ghaznavid dynasty in Iranian and Islamic history, even if the two are not merged quite as explicitly as they are in the *Ghorar*. If Gardizi's interest in the past is tied up with contemporary events, his reference points remain more ancient concepts: he defines Iran, for example, as including not just Khorasan and Sistan, but also Iraq, part of Syria, Mecca and

Medina, and Yemen.[70] This clearly reflects the concept of Irānshahr as stretching from the Nile to the Oxus we find in Sasanian works, and indeed some other eastern Islamic ones,[71] but also serves to assert implicitly the unity of Iranian and Islamic history.

The historiographical model pioneered in Ghaznavid times shaped future Persian historical writing. Whereas authors like Dinawari and Bal'ami had conspicuously avoided bringing their works down to their own days, the Turkish Ghaznavids' desire for legitimacy may have given the impetus for historical works that sought to show an unbroken continuity of Iranian history down to its present Turkish rulers. A later example is the anonymous *Mojmal al-tawārikh wa'l-qesas* ('Compendium of Stories and Histories'), composed around 1126, which brings Iranian and Islamic history down to Saljuq times. Again, the ancient idea of Iran as the centre of the world makes its appearance from the very beginning.[72] Alongside this, historical writing focused on a particular geographical area developed. In some ways, Hamza al-Esfahāni, with his anxiety to relate ancient Iranian history to his home town of Isfahan, can be seen as the pioneer of this type of localized historiography, in contrast to Bal'ami's work which contains few indications of its Transoxianan background. Later historians too often show a strong regional interest, such as Gardizi's emphasis on Khorasan, and that of the author of the *Mojmal* on the primacy of the Jebāl region of which he must have been a native.[73] The anonymous *History of Sistan* (*Tārikh-e Sistān*), a first draft of which was probably composed around 1050,[74] is the earliest example of a history devoted to a particular region in Persian, but was followed at the beginning of the twelfth century by a Persian history of Fārs, the *Fārsnāma*, which also sought to highlight that province's links with ancient Iranian rulers.[75] For instance, Estakhr is said to have been built by Gayumars, the first man, who adopted it as his residence (*dār al-molk*),[76] while much emphasis is put on the role of nearby Mount Nafasht in the revelation of the *Zend* (commentary on the *Avesta*), which here seems to be accorded the status of scripture.[77] Even at this late date (before 1116), a region's Zoroastrian connections could evidently be a source of pride to a (presumably) Muslim author, indicating the extent to which ancient Iran remained a key theme for historians. On the whole, then, early Persian historiography was shaped by this concern to integrate Iranian and Islamic history, often tinged by local pride. It was not until the end of the Saljuq period, the late twelfth century, that Persian started to be used for purely dynastic histories or those of individual rulers, even though this had become an increasingly popular genre in Arabic from the tenth century onwards. Bayhaqi's experiment in court-centred Persian historiography was not one that had found any imitators.[78]

The nature of the sources on which these late Ghaznavid and Saljuq histories claimed to be based is particularly striking. About the same time as Persian historiography revived in the second half of the eleventh century, a series of epic poems based loosely around the heroes of the *Shāhnāma* became popular: first the *Garshāspnāma*, later, in the twelfth century, the *Bahmannāma*, the *Farāmarznāma* and others.[79] Alongside works like Hamza al-Esfahāni's and Tabari's, these poems – which were entirely romances void of any true historical content[80] – start to be cited as sources in works like the *Tārikh-e Sistān* and the *Mojmal al-tawārikh*.[81] This stands in sharp contrast to Hamza's painstaking efforts, and those of his sources like Bahrām b. Marwānshāh, to gather multiple manuscripts and to sort out problems of chronology. However much their end product was deliberately political, in the sense of addressing contemporary concerns about the rise and fall of states rather than being purely antiquarian, Hamza's method still resembled that of the scholar. This is suggestive of the shift in treatment of ancient Iran between the tenth and twelfth centuries. For Hamza, Iranian history was intensely potent and in establishing its chronology and understanding the messages of the stars, the forthcoming end of Islam could be seen. By the eleventh century, and certainly by the twelfth, ancient Iranian history was shorn of this immediate political relevance and reduced to romantic stories that could edify the Turkish rulers of the day and provide convenient fictions to legitimize these newcomers both to Iran and Islam. Yet although all the historians discussed (with the exception of Hamza) sought a synthesis between Iranian and Islamic history, they rarely referred to contemporary rulers as king, *shāhanshāh* or ruler specifically of Iran. Thus, while the continuity of the idea of Iran, the centre of the world, is stressed and while these histories are clearly intended to underline contemporary rulers' places in Iranian history, there is little attempt to suggest they might be anything but indirect heirs to parts of the Sasanian empire, regardless of whatever forged genealogies they might have. Even ancient titles like *shāhanshāh*, which we know from other sources were certainly used by dynasties like the Buyids, on rare occasion the Samanids, and even the Saljuqs, tend not to be applied to contemporary rulers by these historians.[82] It was not until the Mongol period that Iran was revived more fully as a political term.[83] None the less, the idea of Iran, of Irānshahr, did not die out during this epoch of political division, but was kept alive by these historians for whom, along with Islam, it consistently provided a central focus for their works, whatever other concerns they were addressing. This perhaps was the most enduring legacy of the historical traditions on ancient Iran.

Notes:

1. *Tārikh-e Sistān*, ed. by M.T. Bahār (Tehran, 1381 AH), 214–16.
2. G. Lazard, 'The Rise of the New Persian Language' in *The Cambridge History of Iran*, IV: *The Period from the Arab Invasion to the Saljuqs,* ed. by R.N. Frye (Cambridge: University Press, 1975), 605.
3. Behrooz Mahmoodi-Bakhtiari, 'Planning the Persian Language in the Samanid Period', *Iran and the Caucasus* 7/1-2 (2003), 251–60.
4. Lazard, 608–9.
5. John J. Donohue, 'Three Buwayhid Inscriptions', *Arabica* 20/1 (1973), 74–80, esp. 77–8.
6. Luke Treadwell, '*Shāhanshāh* and *al-Malik al-Mu'ayyad*: the Legitimation of Power in Samanid and Buyid Iran' in *Culture and Memory in Medieval Islam: Essays in Honour of Wilferd Madelung,* ed. by Farhad Daftary and J.W. Meri, (London: I.B.Tauris, 2003), 318–37.
7. C.E. Bosworth, 'The Heritage of Rulership in Early Islamic Iran and the Search for Dynastic Connections with the Past', *Iran* 11 (1973), 51–62.
8. C.E. Bosworth, 'The Tahirids and Persian Literature', *Iran* 7 (1969), 103–6.
9. See the discussion in A.C.S. Peacock, *Mediaeval Islamic Historiography and Political Legitimacy: Bal'amī's* Tārīkhnāma (London: Routledge, 2007), 35–48.
10. J. Derek Latham, 'Ebn al-Moqaffa', Abu Mohammad 'Abdollāh Rōzbeh' *EncIr* online. On the text see A. Shahpur Shahbazi, 'On the *Xwadāy-nāmag*', *Varia Iranica: Papers in Honor of Professor Ehsan Yarshater* (Leiden 1990: Acta Iranica 30), 208–29.
11. This was not necessarily restricted to Iran. Ya'qubi, for instance, makes very little of Iranian history, which is just one among many stories of pre- and non-Islamic peoples he discusses in his *Ta'rikh*. However, at the risk of a generalization, it is probably true that for most historians who attempted to write universal or general histories which cover pre-Islamic history, Iran was one of their major themes, along with Israelite prophets and, to a lesser extent, ancient Yemen.
12. Samer M Ali, 'Reinterpreting al-Buhturī's Īwān Kisrā Ode: Tears of Affection for the Cycles of History', *Journal of Arabic Literature* 37/1 (2006), 46–67.
13. Dimitri Gutas, *Greek Thought, Arabic Culture: The Graeco-Arabic Translation Movement in Baghdad and Early 'Abbāsid Society (2nd–4th / 8th–10th centuries)* (London: Croom Helm, 1998), 28–60.
14. On one such ninth-century translator from Pahlavi to Arabic see Mohsen Zakeri, *Persian Wisdom in Arabic Garb: 'Alī b. 'Ubayda al-Rayhānī and his* Jawāhir al-kilam wa-farā'id al-hikam (Leiden: Brill, 2006).
15. A recent study of this work is Hayrettin Yücesoy, 'Ancient Imperial Heritage and Islamic Universalist Historiography: al-Dīnawarī's Secular Perspective', *Journal of Global History* 2 (2007), 135–55.
16. Al-Dinawari, *Ketāb al-akhbār al-tewāl*, ed. by Vladimir Guirgass (Leiden, 1888), 4.
17. Ibid., 11.
18. Ibid., 36; see the discussion in Yücesoy 142–4.
19. Al-Dinawari, 31–2.
20. From *āl sandar*, meaning, according to Dinawari (Ibid., 32), 'how strong is the smell of the sandarac', the herb that was used to cure the bad smell of Alexander's mother.
21. Yücesoy, 145–6.
22. Dinawari died *c.* 895, so the work in all likelihood dates to the second half of the ninth century.

23. Hamza b. al-Hasan al-Esfahāni, *Ta'rikh seni moluk al-arz wa'l-anbiyā'* (Beirut, n.d.), 6.
24. See the discussion in Touraj Daryaee (ed. and tr.), *Šahrestānīhā ī Ērānšahr: A Middle Persian Text on Late Antique Geography, Epic, and History*, ed. and trans. by Touraj Daryaee (Costa Mesa: Mazda Publishers, 2002), 4–7. For a parallel example of the survival of ancient Iranian geographical concepts in a mid-tenth century Persian source, see Vladimir Minorsky, 'The Older Preface to the Shāh-nāma' in V. Minorsky, *Iranica: Twenty Articles* (Tehran: University of Tehran, 1964), 268–9.
25. Hamza al-Esfahāni, 6.
26. Ibid., 7–8, 127.
27. Ibid., 10: *Ketāb moluk al-Fors al-mostakhraj men khezānat al-Ma'mun*: on this phrase, see Gutas, 54–5.
28. Ibid., 10: *Ketāb seyar moluk al-Fors* transmitted by Zaduya b. Shahuya al-Esbahāni, *Ketāb seyar moluk al-Fors* transmitted or compiled by Mohammad b. Bahrām b. Mazyār al-Esbahāni and the *Ketāb moluk Bani Sāsān* transmitted or compiled by Heshām b. Qāsem al-Esbahāni.
29. Ibid., 37, 39, 39 (descriptions of pictures of Ardashir b. Bābak, Shābur b. Ardashir and Hormoz b. Shabur).
30. Ibid., 16.
31. Ibid., 22.
32. See ibid., 50, where Hamza mentions reading in the *Khwadāy-nāmag* information not mentioned by Ebn al-Moqaffa'.
33. For example, ibid., 30: Kayqobād enlarges Esfahān; ibid., 30-31: Kaykhosrow fights a dragon at Mount Kushd near Esfahan, which he kills, and sets up a fire [temple] there; ibid., 31: Kay Garshasf accepts Zoroaster's religion and builds a fire temple at Anārabād near Esfahān; ibid., 32: Kay Ardashir builds fire temples and other buildings around Esfahān, building a beautiful new city in the Esfahān region by Homāy Chahrāzād.
34. See Peacock, *Mediaeval Islamic Historiography*, 114–18.
35. Hamza al-Esfahāni, 33–4.
36. Ehsan Yarshater, 'Iranian National History' in *The Cambridge History of Iran* III/i: *The Seleucid, Parthian and Sasanian Periods*, ed. by Ehsan Yarshater (Cambridge: Cambridge University Press, 1983), 377.
37. Hamza al-Esfahāni, 183.
38. Ibid., 125.
39. Ibid., 123–4.
40. Ibid., 124: *wa law kāna yadollo woqu' 'otared le-esteqāma wa woqufoho lel-roju' la-tamma emtenā 'ohom wa dāma eltewā 'ohom fa-lam yaqboluho.*
41. Ibid., 124.
42. Touraj Daryaee, 'Apocalypse Now: Zoroastrian Reflections on the Early Islamic Centuries,' *Medieval Encounters* 4/3 (1998), 195–9.
43. See the discussion with references in Peacock, *Mediaeval Islamic Historiography*, 79–81, 153–5.
44. *Tārikhnāma-ye Tabari gardānida-ye mansub be Bal'ami*, ed. by Mohammad Rowshan (Tehran, 1999), vol. I, 2.
45. See Peacock, *Mediaeval Islamic Historiography*, 97–8, 106–8, 114–30.
46. For Bal'ami's treatment of Bahrām Chubin, see ibid., 118–23. Although Bahrām was not of Sasanian descent, his ancestry is said to have gone back to the Arsacid (Parthian) dynasty which he claimed to be reviving (see A. S. Shahbazi, 'Bahrām vi.

Bahrām Čubin', *EncIr,* vol. 3, 519–22). It is interesting to note in this respect that
the Samanid Mansur b. Nuh had a commemorative medallion struck in 258 AH /
968–9 CE which draws on pre-Islamic models, but these are eastern Iranian, not
Sasanian. Treadwell, 328.

47. *Tārikhnāma-ye Tabari,* vol. I, 2: 'I translated it into Dari Persian that the intellects
of the populace and the authorities might share in reading it... and it might be easy
for anyone who examines it'. Arabic of course was current in the east, where there
was substantial literary production of Arabic poetry, philosophy and theology.
However, this represented the culture of the elite, whereas the Tabari translations
were probably aimed at a rather wider audience (see Peacock, *Mediaeval Islamic
Historiography,* 35–38, 41–2, 171).

48. Daqiqi and Asadi (author of the *Garshāspnāma*) were also natives of Tus who
produced epics. True, Daqiqi received Samanid patronage, but it is far from clear
this was for his epic poetry rather than other genres. As for the slightly later Asadi,
he had to go to Nakhchevan, an utterly remote frontier region, to find an obscure
local potentate, otherwise unknown to history, to whom he could dedicate the
Garshāspnāma.

49. Peacock, *Mediaeval Islamic Historiography,* 38–40, 48.

50. See Dabiri, 25–6.

51. The authorship of the work has been a matter of some dispute, with doubts
expressed as to whether the Abu Mansur al-Thaʻālebi who composed the *Ghorar*
can be identical with the famous Nishapuri littérateur, Abu Mansur Abd al-Malek b.
Mohammad al-Thaʻālebi. See C.E. Bosworth, 'al-Thaʻālibī, Abu Mansūr,' *EI²,*
vol. X, 425. However, a passage in the unpublished second volume of the *Ghorar*
indicates that the author was indeed the famous Nishapuri *adib.* In MS Süleymaniye
Library, Istanbul, Damad Ibrahim 916, f. 250b, the author inserts an aside at the
mention of the Arab name al-Hasan b. al-Hasan b. al-Hasan: 'these names reminded
me of Ma'mun b. Ma'mun b. Khwārazmshāh, who called his son – who is in Sistan
– Ma'mun, so he is Ma'mun b. Ma'mun b. Ma'mun' *(fa-dhakarto bi-hadhehe al-
asmā' Ma'mun b. Ma'mun b. Khwārazmshāh fa-sammā ebnaho alladhi howa be-
Sejestān Ma'munan fa-howa Ma'mun b. Ma'mun b. Ma'mun*). Abu Mansur Abd al-
Malek b. Mohammad al-Thaʻālebi had served the Khwarazmshah Ma'mun b.
Ma'mun and dedicated several works to him before continuing his career with the
Ghaznavids who overthrew the Ma'munid dynasty of Khwarazmshahs, taking all
remaining descendants into captivity in the Ghaznavid lands. The acquaintance with
Ma'mun b. Ma'mun and his little-known son's fate – currently, apparently, in
Sistan, presumably a hostage at the court of the provincial governor, Abu 'l-
Mozaffar Nasr b. Sebüktegin, the *Ghorar*'s dedicatee – strongly suggests this
connection with the famous al-Thaʻālebi of Nishapur. On him see E.K. Rowson, 'al-
Thaʻālibī, Abu Mansūr Abd al-Malik b. Muhammad', *EI²,* (2011), vol. X, 426–8; on
the end of the Ma'munids, see Muhammad Nazim, *The Life and Times of Sultan
Mahmūd of Ghazna* (Cambridge: Cambridge University Press, 1931), 59–60; W.
Barthold, *Turkestan Down to the Mongol Invasion* (London: Luzac, 1958), 278–9.
For further evidence for the identity of the author of the *Ghorar* see the important
article by Mahmud Omidsalar, 'Thaʻālebi-ye Nishapuri yā Thaʻālebi-ye Marghāni',
Nāma-ye Bahārestān 8–9, ser. nos. 13–14 (2007–8), 131–43.

52. The first volume was published with a parallel French translation as Aboû Mansoûr
'Abd al-Malik ibn Mohammad ibn Ismâ'îl al-Thaʻâlibî, *Histoire des rois des Perses,*
ed. and trans. by Hermann Zotenberg (Paris: Lemercier, 1900); the second,

unpublished volume is in MS Damad Ibrahim 916 referred to above, along with the first volume.

53. Ibid., xix–xx.
54. Tha'ālebī does refer from time to time to a work called the *Shāhnāma*, but Zotenberg did not believe it was Ferdowsi's. See ibid., xxiii–xxli.
55. Ibid., 737ff.
56. Ibid., 69–70.
57. Ibid., 104.
58. Ibid., 1, 3.
59. See, for example, the homily under the reign of Manuchehr about the mutual obligations of rulers and subjects: in the event of a disaster, the ruler is obliged to reduce the *kharāj* (land-tax) proportionally. Ibid., 66–7.
60. Ibid., 606.
61. See for example, ibid., 109, 129: King Nuzar and his sons, the successors to Manuchehr, fail as rulers or are rejected because of their lack of *sa'āda elāhiya* (i.e. *farr*).
62. Ibid., 41.
63. On Bayhaqi's history, see Julie Scott Meisami, *Persian Historiography to the End of the Twelfth Century* (Edinburgh: Edinburgh University Press, 1999), 79–108.
64. Gardizi, *Zayn al-akhbār*, ed. Rahim Rezāzāda Mālek (Tehran, 1384 AH), 252.
65. For the date of composition, see the editor's introduction in ibid., 24–8.
66. See Meisami, 68–9.
67. Gardizi, 105.
68. Ibid., 75: *miyān-e Irān u Turān ta'assob u fetna oftād tā bedin ghāyat hanuz andar ān-and.*
69. Ibid., 165, 195; for further discussion of Gardizi's references to contemporary events, see ibid., introduction, 52–5; Meisami, 78–9.
70. Gardizi, 368.
71. See Daryaee, *Shahrestānīhā ī Ērānshahr*, 6–7, 19.
72. *Mojmal al-tawārikh wa'l-qesas,* ed. by M.T. Bahār (Tehran, 1381 AHS), 4: *sharh-e akhbār-e moluk-e 'Ajam keh miyāna-ye jahān ast va az atrāf marja'... miyān-e zamīn Irān-ast*; also ibid., 478.
73. Meisami, 189, 192, 204–206.
74. Ibid., 131–2, 133–4.
75. *The Fársnáma of Ibnu 'l-Balkhí*, ed. by G. Le Strange and R.A. Nicholson (London: Luzac and Co, 1921), 8ff.
76. Ibid., 26.
77. Ibid., 49–51.
78. The first extant Persian dynastic history is the *Saljuqnāma* of Zahir al-Din Nishāpuri (*c.*1176); there may, however, have been earlier works which are now lost. The eleventh-century *Maleknāma*, a history of the early Saljuqs, had its origins in Turkish oral tradition, and also existed in a written Arabic version; when the Persian text which survives in revised form in Mirkhwānd's *Rawzat al-safā* was composed is unclear. In addition, the early twelfth-century Saljuq vizier Anushirvān b. Khāled composed his memoirs in Persian, which survive in a much-altered Arabic form in 'Emād al-Din al-Esfahāni's chronicle of the Saljuqs. However, uncertainty about the language of the *Maleknāma* and about the contents of Anushirvān's work means it is not possible at the moment to state unequivocally that they were works of Persian historiography. On the *Maleknāma*, see A.C.S. Peacock, *Early Seljūq History: A New Interpretation* (London: Continuum, 2010) 8–9, 27–33; on Anushirvān and his

work see David Durand-Guédy, 'Mémoires d'exilés: lecture de la chronique des Saljuqides de 'Imād al-Dīn Isfahānī', *Studia Iranica* 35 (2006), 181–202.

79. For an overview, see François de Blois, 'Epics', *EncIr*.

80. It has been argued that Ferdowsi's *Shāhnāma* is a valuable historical source in its own right for the Sasanian period; see Parvaneh Pourshariati, *Decline and Fall of the Sasanian Empire: The Sasanian-Parthian Confederacy and the Arab Conquest of Iran* (London: I.B.Tauris, 2008), 14–15.

81. *Tārikh-e Sistān*, 49, citing the *Garshāspnāma*; *Mojmal al-tawārikh*, 2–3, citing the *Shāhnāma* of Ferdowsi, the *Garshāspnāma*, the *Farāmarznāma*, the *Bahmannāma* and the *Kushnāma* among others.

82. See Treadwell, and Peacock, *Early Seljūq History*, 91, for the Saljuq use.

83. Bert Fragner, 'The Concept of Regionalism in Historical Research on Central Asia and Iran: a Macro Historical Explanation' in *Studies on Central Asian History in Honor of Yuri Bregel*, ed. by Devin DeWeese (Bloomington: Indiana University Press, 2001), 341–54.

6

Advice Literature in Tenth and Early Eleventh-Century Iran and Early Persian Prose Writing

Louise Marlow
(Wellesley College)

The production of works offering counsel for kings flourished in the courtly cultures of many pre-modern societies.[1] The rich advisory literatures composed for Muslim rulers in the centuries following the establishment of the caliphate were paralleled by extensive traditions in Byzantium, the Latin west and elsewhere. In the context of western Asia, however, it is the Persian language and Iran that are associated most closely with the composition and appreciation of this kind of literature. Of the pre-modern advisory works that have survived in the Islamicate languages, the most admired examples, among medieval and modern readers alike, are almost certainly the celebrated Persian compositions of the later eleventh century: the *Qābusnāma* or *Andarznāma* (475 AH / 1082–3 CE) of the Ziyarid ruler 'Onsor al-Ma'āli Kaykā'us b. Eskandar (r. from 441 / 1049), the *Siyar al-moluk*, also known as the *Siyāsatnāma*, of the vizier Nezām al-Molk (410–85 / 1019–92) and the *Nasihat al-moluk* attributed to Abu Hāmed Ghazāli (450–505 / 1058–1111).

Although often grouped together, these pre-eminent Persian books of advice differ significantly in their structure, organization and contents, and each reflects the unique experience and insight of its remarkable author. The three compositions also stand apart from the larger tradition of advisory literature: while sometimes revised in subsequent centuries in the form of translation–adaptations, they were rarely imitated directly.[2] They were, however, composed within twenty years of one another and they were all shaped to some degree by the historical experience and distinctive culture of the eastern Iranian world. Nezām-al-Molk and Ghazāli both hailed from Tus and spent their formative years in Khorasan; for several Hanbalis of Baghdad, Nezām al-Molk long remained 'the man from Tus',[3] and Ghazāli composed his *Nasihat al-moluk* after his departure from the Nezāmiya in Baghdad and his return to his native Khorasan in 493 / 1100.[4] Kaykā'us, whose territories lay in Gorgān and

Tabaristān, was related on his mother's side to the Ghaznavid ruling family and had spent eight years in Ghazna as the companion (*nadim*) of Sultan Mawdud b. Mas'ud (r. 432–41 / 1041–50), an experience likely to account for his inclusion of several anecdotes relating to individuals who lived in the eastern regions and a number of quotations from Khorasanian poets.[5]

The *Qābusnāma*, *Siyar al-moluk* and *Nasihat al-moluk* are in many respects exceptional texts and, as examples of lucid, often graceful prose, they occupy a particular place in the history of Persian literature. Their distinctiveness should not, however, obscure the earlier history of advisory writing in Iran; the eleventh-century texts did not emerge *ex nihilo*, and their appearance did not mark the end of a literary hiatus following the composition of the last Sasanian works of *andarz*. In an effort to elucidate this history, this chapter explores the advice literature produced in eastern Iran in the tenth and early eleventh centuries. This earlier literary activity, much of it conducted in Arabic but with the integration of copious materials associated with Iran as well as more distant regions, established a repertoire and context for the celebrated eleventh-century Persian works.

It is proposed in what follows that the advisory literature produced in the eastern parts of Iran in the tenth and early eleventh centuries is likely to have possessed distinctive characteristics shaped by its regional context. Three locally specific aspects of this literary corpus will be emphasized: its relationship to the contemporaneous local historiographical tradition, its function as a purveyor of diverse cultural materials to a large west Asian and even European audience, and its particular importance as a receptor, preserver and transmitter of wisdom literatures and other cultural materials of Indic or South Asian provenance or association. Because of the probable relevance of Abu Zayd Balkhi (d. 322 / 934) to all three of these concerns, his likely role in the shaping of a locally distinctive advisory literature will be considered in some detail.

It must be acknowledged that of the abundant advisory literature recorded as having been produced in the period and region under study, little has survived. Much of the following discussion necessarily draws on a relatively small sample of extant texts and depends heavily on circumstantial and contextual factors. It should also be noted that perhaps the best-known early Khorasanian advisory work, the moral exhortation (*wasiya*) of Taher b. Hosayn (r. 159–207 / 775–822) to his son Abdallāh on the occasion of the latter's appointment to the province of Diyar Rabi'a in 206 / 821, yields few obvious indications of its author's local environment; more evident are Taher's close connections with the political culture of Baghdad.[6] The favourable reception of Taher's missive throughout western Asia and North Africa may, however, have stimulated the continuing composition and appreciation of works of counsel in Khorasan,[7] where Taher's grandson Obaydallāh b. Abdallāh (d. 300 / 913) would also compose an (apparently lost) *Ketāb resālatihi fi'l-siyāsa al-molukiya*.[8]

In contrast to Taher's ninth-century work, the advisory literature that has survived from the eastern regions in the tenth and early eleventh centuries reflects its distinctive regional milieu. Two pertinent books, both in Arabic, are available in their entirety: the *Nasihat al-moluk* attributed to the eminent Sunni jurist and caliphal envoy Māwardi (364–450 / 974–1058), and the *Ādāb al-moluk* of the celebrated poet and philologist Abu Mansur Abd al-Malek Mohammad Thaʿālebi (350–429/961–1038). The *Nasihat al-moluk*, though often attributed to Māwardi, is more likely to have been, at least in its earliest form, the work of an as yet unidentified author who lived in eastern Iran, possibly Balkh, in the first half of the tenth century.[9] Balkh is one of the very few locations mentioned in the text,[10] which displays several characteristics that render that exceptionally cosmopolitan city a likely environment for its composition. Thaʿālebi, whose authorship of the *Ādāb al-moluk* is not in question, spent his entire life in the eastern regions, where he composed his work of counsel between 403 / 1012 and 407 / 1017 for the Khwarazmshāh Abu 'l-Abbās Maʾmun II (r. 399–407 / 1009–17), brother-in-law of the Ghaznavid sultan Mahmud (r. 388–421 / 998–1030), who later deposed him. These two works constitute recognizable literary antecedents to the *Siyar al-moluk* of Nezām al-Molk and the *Nasihat al-moluk* of Ghazāli.[11]

Biographical, bibliographical and historiographical sources record the titles of several additional (mostly Arabic) compositions, but so far scholars' knowledge of these works is limited to, at most, occasional quotations that appear in later writings. The advisory literature of tenth-century eastern Iran is known to have included at least one Persian text: Thaʿālebi reports having read and heard a composition on the manners of kings (*ādāb al-moluk*), in Persian, by the amir Abu 'l-Hasan Mohammad b. Ebrāhim b. Simjur (d. 378 / 988).[12] A member of the Simjurid line of Turkish commanders and governors, Abu 'l-Hasan, during the reign of the Samanid amir Nuh II b. Mansur (r. 365–87 / 976–97), was confirmed as *sepahsālār* of Khorasan and awarded the title of Naser al-Dawla.[13] According to Samʿāni (d. 562 / 1166–7), he was an excellent ruler and an intelligent man (*kāna min fudalā' al-umarā' waʿuqalā' al-rijāl*), whose favourable reputation had reached Mecca.[14] Thaʿālebi was struck by the similarity of a passage in the amir's work to examples known to him from books on the Arabic language.[15] It is quite likely that the Arabic and Persian advisory discourses of the Samanid realms evolved, if at different rates and for different audiences, alongside one another and that they both drew on the broad repertoire of wisdom literature, much of it with broadly Iranian associations, that was in circulation in oral and written forms in the eastern regions. Notably, the earliest extant work of advice in a language other than Arabic was a product of Central Asia: *Kutadgu bilig* (462 / 1069–70), the didactic poem of Yusof Khāss Hājeb, written not in Persian but in Qarakhanid Turkish, was composed in Kashghar and dedicated to the Qarakhanid prince Tavghach Boghrā Khān (Hasan b. Solaymān, r. 467–96 / 1074–1102).[16]

The particularity of the literature of counsel from the tenth and early eleventh centuries appears in greater relief when considered in conjunction with contemporaneous forms of cultural production in the eastern Iranian region. Comparison with the historiographical writings of the period is especially profitable. Indeed, advisory literature is not always fully separable from historiography, which, as Julie Scott Meisami has elucidated in a series of studies, is frequently characterized by a striking emphasis on the moral dimensions of history.[17] Equally prevalent is the tendency among authors of 'mirrors' to articulate the lessons of past events and renew the received wisdom of the past for overtly didactic purposes. In the eastern regions in the tenth and early eleventh centuries, the parallels appear to extend beyond these general affinities. Elton Daniel has suggested that the writing of history in this locale, in Arabic and Persian, may represent the development of 'a true "school" of historiography, closely associated with the Samanid chancery and probably going back to the influence of the geographer–scholar Abu Zayd Balkhi'. In contrast to the historiography produced in western Iran, the works of the eastern regions, according to Daniel, were characterized by an exceptional attention to 'the cultural, geographical, and material dimensions of history' and to the 'affairs of non-Muslim peoples'. An additional feature of the eastern historiographical 'school' was its pattern of 'systematic and philosophical thinking about the nature of history'. Daniel perceives some evidence of this pattern in non-historiographical works, such as the *Mafātih al-'olum* of Mohammad b. Ahmad Khwārazmi (d. 387 / 997), a compendium of scholarly and technical designations dedicated to Abu 'l-Hasan Obaydallāh Otbi, vizier to the Samanid amir Nuh II b. Mansur (r. 365–87 / 976–97), and the *Jawāme' al-'olum* of Ebn Farighun, an elaborate manual for secretaries written for Abu Ali Ahmad b. Mohammad, the Mohtājid amir of Chaghaniyan and governor of Khorasan under the Samanids.[18]

The two tenth and early eleventh-century advisory works that have survived in their entirety, the previously mentioned *Nasihat al-moluk* and *Ādāb al-moluk*, suggest specific parallels between the advisory and historiographical literatures that took form in Khorasan and Transoxiana in this period. The local qualities and significance of Tha'ālebi's *Ādāb al-moluk* have been explored with skill and subtlety in a recent study,[19] and it is the (presumably) earlier of the two examples, the *Nasihat al-moluk* of (Pseudo)-Māwardi, that will constitute the primary point of reference in much of the remainder of this article. As Daniel has indicated, the historiographical sources of the region reveal an exceptionally broad historical vision. The *Nasihat al-moluk* is likewise characterized by a receptivity to numerous traditions of wisdom, derived from the past or from culturally diverse sources. The scope of the author's interests evokes his distinctive geographical–cultural setting, which, as the major regional crossroads of several intersecting commercial routes, facilitated cross-cultural encounters among Slavs, Turks, Indians, Tibetans and Chinese, as well as Muslims from western Asia and North Africa.[20] The author's cosmopolitan outlook also suggests a conviction that wisdom, especially that derived from the lessons of the past, was not the monopoly of a particular community but belonged to humanity as a whole. Given the relatively few works of advisory literature that have survived in their entirety, it is not possible to establish firmly the degree to which the *Nasihat al-moluk* was representative of or distinctive within the larger genre of its time. Situated in relation to the region's contemporaneous material and artistic culture and its contemporaneous historiography, *adab* and poetry, however, it becomes possible to surmise that the *Nasihat al-moluk* and other works of advisory literature produced in the same environment functioned as a conduit for the transmission of cultural materials of highly varied provenance into the Arabic and Persian literary traditions.

In another indication of the close relationship between the advisory and historiographical discourses of the region and time under discussion, the figure of Abu Zayd Balkhi (d. 322 / 934), linked by Daniel to the outward-looking trends in historiography, almost certainly played a significant role in the shaping of works devoted to statecraft and counsel as well. In his youth, Balkhi spent eight years in Iraq as a student of the philosopher Abu Yusof Kindi (d. *c.* 255 / 868–9); he then returned permanently to his native city in the east. Kindi's capacious sense of useful knowledge was evident in his conviction that the concerns of philosophical enquiry and the message of the prophets coincided.[21] Balkhi, a prolific author perhaps best known to posterity as a geographer–cartographer but at least as productive in the fields of philosophy, theology and *adab* was, like his teacher, a noted scholar in '[all] the ancient and the new sciences', according to Ebn al-Nadim (d. 380 / 990).[22] Like Kindi, and in the tradition of Khwārazmi, who endorsed and dignified both the *olum al-shariʿa* and the *olum al-ajam*, Balkhi sought to integrate the sciences of *shariʿa* and *hekma*, wisdom or, here, philosophy.[23] Balkhi is reported to have said, '*Shariʿa* is the greatest philosophy (*al-falsafa al-kobrā*); no man can devote himself to the pursuit of philosophy unless he also devotes himself to worship and perseveres in the fulfilment of the commands of the religious law'.[24] Among Balkhi's students, Ebn Farighun and Abu 'l-Hasan Āmeri (d. 381 / 992) likewise sought to reconcile philosophy and the religious sciences.[25]

If Balkhi's professional network provides an intellectual context for his inclusive sense of knowledge, it also links him with the composition of writings on the subject of statecraft. In his entry for Kindi, Ebn al-Nadim records twelve titles in the field of *siyāsiyāt*.[26] Ahmad b. Tayyeb Sarakhsi (d. 286 / 899), one of Kindi's most prominent students and a teacher and later boon companion to the caliph Moʿtaded (r. 279–89 / 892–902), composed a *[Ketāb] al-Siyāsa al-kabir*, a *[Ketāb] al-Siyāsa al-saghir*, a *Ketāb ādāb al-moluk* and a *Ketāb zād al-*

mosāfer wa khedmat al-moluk.[27] Balkhi likewise composed a *Ketāb al-siyāsa al-kabir*, a *Ketāb al-siyāsa al-saghir* and a *Ketāb adab al-soltān wa'l-ra'iya.*[28]

Although regrettably few of Balkhi's writings appear to have survived, several sources indicate that he, like Kindi, was inclusive in his pursuit of learning and receptive to a broad range of scholarly disciplines regardless of their cultural locations. As far as can be ascertained, his pioneering geographical and cartographical works appear to have demonstrated an exceptional interest in all regions of the known world and their peoples. In the absence of most of his writings, circumstantial factors and peripheral indications of Balkhi's interests facilitate the conjecture that Balkhi may have contributed to the transmission of South Asian materials in particular into the Arabic and later Persian intellectual and literary cultures.

First, Balkh, one of the gates to which was called the *Bāb al-hend,* enjoyed extensive historical, commercial and cultural links with South Asia. As is well known, Balkh had a particularly prominent Buddhist history, as evidenced by, among other sources, the seventh-century Buddhist pilgrim from Chang'an, Xuanzang; recent research suggests that Buddhist culture not only survived but even expanded in proximate locations throughout the ninth century.[29] A major Buddhist shrine had flourished at Nawbahār in the environs of Balkh and the Barmakids, from the same city, were descendants of an eminent Buddhist family.[30] As Ebn al-Nadim reports, the Barmakids were especially interested in knowledge pertaining to India, to which their Buddhist heritage linked them.[31] Abu Zayd Balkhi's long residence in the vicinity of his native city, to which he was deeply attached, situated him well for direct access to persons and materials, including texts, from South Asia.[32] Given his physical and cultural location, the various geographical and cultural materials assembled by envoys, travellers and scholars in his immediate environment and his pursuit of geographical knowledge, it seems likely that Balkhi had access to multiple sources of information regarding South Asia and its peoples and that the information available to him was both more plentiful and more direct than that available to many of his contemporaries.

Secondly, Balkhi's social and intellectual milieu linked him to several persons and groups who were deeply engaged in the pursuit of knowledge related to South Asia. In 249 / 863, Kindi had transcribed the report of an envoy dispatched by Yahyā b. Khāled Barmaki to study the medicinal plants (*aqāqir*) of India.[33] Kindi's transcription of the envoy's report, which from Ebn al-Nadim's account evidently included a description of Indian religions, may have been known to Balkhi, and in any case suggests an interest in South Asia among members of Kindi's circle. The Mu'tazili theologian Abu 'l-Qāsem Ka'bi (d. 319 / 931), whose friendship with Abu Zayd extended to donating a portion of his salary to him during the short administration in Khorasan (306–7 / 918–19) of Ahmad b. Sahl (d. 307 / 920), is reported by Mas'udi to have explicated Hindu religious customs in his *Oyun al-masā'el wa'l-jawābāt.*[34] It is also probable that Balkhi was familiar with the (lost) *Ketāb al-masālek* produced by the family of his contemporary Mohammad b. Ahmad Abu Abdallāh Jayhāni (vizier 301–13 / 914–25), who had a particularly strong interest in India and with whom the philosopher once enjoyed a cordial relationship.[35] The Jayhāni work is cited in several later descriptions of India created in the eastern Iranian regions. Maqdesi, whose *Ketāb al-bad' wa 'l-ta'rikh* (355 / 966) includes an informative account of 'the religions of the brahmans' (*adyān al-barāhema*), attributes his information regarding two Buddhist sects (*ferqa*) to his reading of a *Ketāb al-masālek*, possibly that of Jayhāni;[36] Abu Rayhān Biruni (362–442 / 973–1050 or later) and 'Abd al-Hayy Gardizi, both of whom wrote for Ghaznavid patrons, explicitly cite the Jayhāni work.[37]

Thirdly, apparent vestiges of Balkhi's writings suggest that he participated actively in the dissemination of knowledge related to South Asia. While Balkhi's geographical writings have not survived in their complete forms, the extant works of later tenth-century geographers associated with his school – notably, Estakhri and Ebn Hawqal – provide important information on the region.[38] Furthermore, Abu 'l-Ma'āli Mohammad Hosayni Alawi, author of the late eleventh-century *Bayān al-adyān* (485 / 1092), cites a Bu-Zayd-e Hakim, plausibly identified as Abu Zayd Balkhi,[39] as an authority on Indian religious beliefs and customs. From this source, Abu 'l-Ma'āli reports that the 'Indian' name for the Persian *bot* ('idol', or perhaps, here, 'Buddha')[40] is Qāqlit; that Hindus hold the eating of meat to be prohibited, especially the meat of the cow; that most do not drink wine and consider it prohibited; that they eat vegetal rather than animal products; that they attach extreme importance to trustworthiness and honesty and, implicitly drawing an equation with his own society, that the Brahmans constitute 'their ascetics' (sing. *zāhed*).[41] If the invoked Bu-Zayd-e Hakim is, as seems likely, Abu Zayd Balkhi, then Abu 'l-Ma'āli may have derived his account from Balkhi's geographical writings, or perhaps from his *Ketāb sharā'i' al-adyān* or even his *Ketāb al-radd alā abadat al-asnām*.[42]

Of particular interest in Abu 'l-Ma'āli's account is Abu Zayd the Philosopher's reference to *qāqlit*, possibly a rendering of *fāriqlit*, or the Paraclete, the 'Holy Spirit' or 'Comforter' announced by Jesus, according to the Gospel of John. Ebn al-Nadim and Biruni report that the prophet Mani proclaimed himself the Paraclete.[43] If this identification for *qāqlit* is accurate, it permits the hypothesis that Abu Zayd the Philosopher's information regarding Indian religious customs may have derived from a region imprinted by a mixed Buddhist and Manichaean population or, as has been proposed for some other works that flourished in the same locality, from a Buddhist source that had passed through a Manichaean intermediary.[44] This confluence of elements is of significance to the present discussion since, as will be seen below, a small portion of the materials introduced into Arabic and Persian literature through advisory texts also allows for the conjecture that they had travelled through a Buddhist or Buddhist–Manichaean milieu. Lack of adequate or definitive evidence prevents more than a preliminary venturing of this hypothesis, which perhaps finds some circumstantial support in the charge of *zandaqa* levelled against Ebn al-Moqaffaʿ, whose literary production, in the form of translation–adaptations from Pahlavi and indirectly from Sankrit as well as personal compositions, contributed greatly to the formation of an Arabic-Islamic and later Persian-Islamic advisory tradition.[45]

In the light of the scattered information available, it is possible that the ideas and writings of Abu Zayd Balkhi, whom Daniel has linked to an eastern historiographical 'school', might have been equally significant in the development of the advisory discourse produced in the Khorasanian–Tranoxianian cultural and intellectual environment of the Samanid and post-Samanid periods, and that his writings in various genres might have contributed to the diffusion of information related to South Asia in particular. That Balkhi's treatments of *siyāsa* were influential and appreciated in the eastern Iranian world is suggested by the quotations from them that appear in the *Ketāb al-saʿāda wa ʾl-es ʿād* (possibly the work of Balkhi's student Āmeri)[46] and the previously mentioned *Ādāb al-moluk* of Thaʿālebi.[47] The *Tohfat al-wozarāʾ*, an advisory work that in its present form dates from the late twelfth or early thirteenth century but that might derive from a work authored by Thaʿālebi, to whom it is attributed, also includes three extended quotations from Abu Zayd Balkhi.[48]

The markedly cosmopolitan outlook reflected in much of the historiographical, geographical, scientific and literary production of the Samanid realms was rooted in a tradition of receptivity to the cultural inheritance of the past and of regions beyond the Samanid polity. Many inhabitants of the eastern regions, such as the renowned Abu Maʿshar Balkhi (171–272 / 787–886), had participated in the preservation, transmission and adaptation of scientific knowledge as well as literary and *adab*-related materials from India and elsewhere.[49] A number of Indian medical texts were translated into Persian and Arabic in tenth-century Iran,[50] where figures such as Abu Bakr Mohammad b. Zakariyāʾ Rāzi (*c.* 250–313 or 323 /854–925 or 935) and Abu Mansur Mowaffaq b. ʿAli were active. These historical and cultural elements serve to situate the prodigious achievements, in the first half of the eleventh century, of Abu Rayhān Biruni (362–442 / 973–1050 or later), who acquired and recorded first-hand information on South Asia and produced direct translations from Sanskrit into Arabic. References in a number of ninth, tenth and early eleventh-century Arabic and Persian works indicate that in certain learned circles, India was regarded as a source not only of authoritative knowledge in the fields of medicine, mathematics and astronomy, but also of ancient wisdom. In a suggestive example, Abān-e Lāheqi (d. 200 / 815), associated with the Barmakids and credited with the versification of several books related to Persian, Indian and sometimes Greek culture, is reported by Ebn al-Nadim to have produced, among other works, a *Ketāb elm al-hend*. In the absence of the text, the kind of knowledge denoted by the title of Abān's book remains uncertain, but in the context of other compositions associated with the author, it seems quite likely that it consisted of, as D.M. Lang has inferred, 'wisdom'.[51] Moreover, Mas'udi (d. 345 / 956), who developed a particularly strong interest in India, described the ancient Indians as a people who cultivated righteousness (*salāh*) and wisdom (*hekma*).[52] By his own report, Mas'udi wrote extensively about Indian governmental practices (*siyāsāt*), reports (*akhbār*) and customs (*siyar*) in his (lost) *Akhbār al-zamān* and *al-Ketāb al-awsat*.[53] In an interesting passage, the *adib*-historian relates that when Alexander defeated Porus (Fur), ruler of the Jhelum region, he heard of a king in a remote part of India 'possessed of wisdom, discipline (*siyāsa*) and religion (*deyāna*), and (known for his) equity towards the subjects'. This ruler, to whom Mas'udi refers under the name K.n.d, was 'victorious over himself' (*kāna qāhiran li-nafsihi*), 'having eliminated his characteristics of appetite, anger and so on' (*mumītan li-sifātihi min al-shahwiya wa'l-ghadabiya wa ghayrihā*).[54]

In another example of particular interest for studies of advisory literature, it has been proposed that the work of Shānāq-e Hendī, available in Arabic as *Firdaws al-hekma fi 'l-tebb* (completed in 235 / 850) by Ali b. Rabban Tabari, a ninth-century convert to Islam, reflects a version of the *Arthaśāstra* associated with Kautilya, also known as Chānakya.[55] An extensive advisory text addressed to an Indian king and ascribed to Shānāq-e Hendi appears in a well-known later Arabic work of advice, the *Serāj al-moluk* of Turtushi (451– c. 520 / 1059–c. 1126).[56] The author of the 'Older Preface' to the *Shāhnāma* likewise groups together, as products of Indian royal initiative and patronage, *Kalila wa Demna*, *Shānāq* (listed as if it were the title of a book) and *Rām-o Rāmin* (the Ramayana).[57]

The *Nasihat al-moluk* attributed to Māwardi constitutes a particularly fruitful source for the exploration of the effective function of early advisory writing as a little recognized conduit for the transmission and integration into the literatures of early Muslim societies of a rich and diverse assortment of cultural materials. The text, which is fully and unambiguously situated within an Islamic intellectual and ethical context, is replete with quotations from Iranian traditions and literature, aphoristic materials with Greek associations, examples of Arabic poetry as well as, above all, references to a variety of figures and materials drawn from Islamic history and culture. In the present context, it is the prominence of materials associated, often explicitly, with an Indic cultural heritage that is of particular interest. It is noteworthy that, in many cases, these materials express the author's endorsement of a markedly austere model of kingship. Pseudo-Māwardi asserts the exceptional standing of kings in the divinely ordained order of things; at the same time, he urges the ruler to discipline his appetites, transcend desire and abstain from pleasures.

This ideal reflects the interest in and attraction to *zohd*, in the full spectrum of its meanings, that was prevalent in the eastern Iranian environment in the early Islamic centuries. The author found support for his ideal first and foremost in sources that were closely identified with Islamic religions and cultural values,[58] but he also sympathized with the representations of renunciation of desire in certain cultural materials that he associated with a South Asian provenance.

The collection of allegorical fables known as *Kalila wa Demna* constituted probably the central work in the process of cultural transmission under discussion. Derived in part from the *Panchatantra*, the collection had been translated and adapted into the languages of regions outside South Asia in the centuries preceding its introduction into Arabic literary culture in the versions of Ebn al-Moqaffa' (d. *c.* 140 / 757) and other translator–writers. Numerous quotations from *Kalila wa Demna* appear in Arabic works, notably in the anthologies of Ebn Qotayba (213–76 / 828–89) and Ebn Abd Rabbeh (246–328 / 860–940), where such passages are sometimes introduced explicitly but more often by the anonymous phrase 'in one of the books of the Indians'.[59] Under the Samanids, *Kalila wa Demna* was adapted into Persian forms, in both prose and poetry. At the request of the amir Nasr b. Ahmad (r. 301–31 / 914–43), Abu 'l-Fazl Bal'ami translated an Arabic version of *Kalila wa Demna* into Persian and Rudaki (d. *c.* 329 / 940–1), whose Persian verse often exhorted his listeners to moral rectitude, used Bal'ami's text as a basis for a versified *Kalila wa Demna*.[60]

The Arabic *Kalila wa Demna*, conforming to the generic requirements of *adab*, endorses the dual functions of instruction and amusement. The introductory section to the version passed down from Ebn al-Moqaffa' includes the following passage:

> He [Bidpāy]... put its [the book's] speech on the tongues of beasts, wild animals, and birds, so that its external form should be entertaining to the élites and the common people, while its internal aspect should provide exercise for the intellects of the élites... He caused its form to resemble both internally and externally that of other books that follow the model of wisdom (*hekma*), in such a way that the animals serve to provide enjoyment while their utterances convey wisdom and *adab*.[61]

The text concludes, however, with less emphasis on the entertaining aspects of the collection than on its function as a work of counsel (*nasiha*) and admonition (*maw'eza*).[62] Similarly, Ya'qubi, remarkable for his interests in varied cultural phenomena and for his affinity with the traditions of *adab*, observes the exemplary nature of the book's parables (*amthāl*), 'on which those endowed with intelligence should reflect, from which they should learn, and on which they should base their conduct'.[63] This tendency to accentuate the didactic aspects of *Kalila wa Demna* over the amusing qualities of its stories is characteristic of anthologies of *adab* materials and mirrors for princes as well.[64]

Like Ebn Qotayba and Ebn Abd Rabbeh, Pseudo-Māwardi exhibits a somewhat ambivalent attitude in his employment of *Kalila wa Demna*. He too quotes from the collection several times, sometimes acknowledging his source and sometimes identifying it only as 'one of the books of the Indians'.[65] Occasionally, Pseudo-Māwardi presents his quotations as entirely unattributed, and decontextualized, *bons mots* (*wa kāna yuqālu...*); for example, he cites, without attribution, the maxim, 'He who conceals his advice from the ruler, his illness from the doctors, and his sorrow from his friends, has betrayed himself' – an aphorism from *Kalila wa Demna*.[66] Again like Ebn Qotayba and Ebn Abd Rabbeh, Pseudo-Māwardi limits his quotations to the wise maxims contained in the work. As will be seen, the author was suspicious of diverting tales. Accordingly, he recounts relatively little narrative material of any kind, but rather extracts the aphoristic pronouncements that punctuate *Kalila wa Demna* without allusion to the collection's stories.[67] Two lengthy sets of quotations from *Kalila wa Demna* appear in the author's epilogue (*khātema*), where he felt less constrained than in the main body of his text; it is also in this section that the only passage of extended narrative occurs. Tha'ālebi's early eleventh-century Arabic work contains only four quotations from *Kalila wa Demna* and, anticipating the Persian works of the later eleventh century, it is less reticent in its use of exemplary narrative.[68]

As he avers explicitly, Pseudo-Māwardi considers entertaining stories to be not only useless, but also potentially subversive. He offers these cautionary remarks in the context of his treatment of the proper education of the king's children. In this discussion, Pseudo-Māwardi stresses the importance 'especially in this community' (*fi hādhihi 'l-milla khāssatan*) of learning the Qur'an together with the Arabic language. He proceeds to enumerate the virtues of Arabic and recommends that princes should seek to acquire the language by way of the 'lightest' and 'easiest' literary materials. Furthermore, they should concentrate on the meanings of the texts, and should not be troubled with obscure features of the language, such as details of grammar or the conventions of prosody – matters of use only to specialists. As part of his education, the prince should learn to recite Arabic poetry, as long as the verses are chosen for their wisdom, and for their effectiveness in inculcating understanding of such matters as the divine unity, religion, knowledge and self-restraint (*zohd*), bravery and generosity, and praiseworthy moral qualities.[69] Pseudo-Māwardi distinguishes between edifying and instructive Arabic poetry and poetry devoted to such worldly subjects as love and sensual pleasures; verse of the latter kind, in his view, is likely to instill pleasure-loving habits rather than firm religious conviction and upright behaviour.[70] He further advises that princes should commit to memory the accounts of the Prophet's campaigns (*maghāzi*) and conduct (*siyar*) and the reports (*āthār*) of the caliphs,[71] not the tales of lovers (*āthār al-oshshāq*) or books of stories (*kotob al-afsānaqāt*) such as the *Book of Sendbad*, the *Thousand Stories* (*Hazār afsāna*) and the like.[72] Such books will be of little use to the prince in his efforts to attain the stature of the scholars and jurists or to win precedence among the people of his realm and religious community, or to advance him in his governance (*wa laysa yanālu fī tilka 'l-kotob min hādhihi 'l-abwāb illā qalīlan*). Moreover the prince may succumb to the erroneous belief that the stories are true, a misconception that will render him ignorant of his religion and the virtues of his community; such nightly story-tellings (*asmār*) will prove of no assistance to him in his governance, in holding disputations on religious matters, in convening assemblies or in investigating the grievances of his subjects (*'alā… nazarihi fī mazālim ra'iyatihi*).[73]

Pseudo-Māwardi's use of the Persian term *afsānaqāt* instead of an Arabic word indicates that it was principally Persian stories, or stories associated with the *ajam*, that he had in mind. An extensive prose literature of entertainment had existed in the Sasanian period, largely passed on in oral form but by the end of the Sasanian period in part written down, and known in Islamic times as *khorāfāt*. The *Hazār afsān* and the *Book of Sendbad* were evidently well known and widely appreciated in the locality in which Pseudo-Māwardi produced his *Nasihat al-moluk* and, like other collections of stories in circulation in eastern Iran, including *Kalila wa Demna*, it is probable that they reflected accretions from a considerable degree of inter-cultural contact in the region that stretched from Khorasan to beyond the Indus river.[74] His evident appreciation of diverse wisdom literatures notwithstanding, Pseudo-Māwardi warns his audience against the potentially damaging effects of collections of stories on the prince's intellectual and moral formation. His discussion of the matter includes an explicit illustration of his ambivalence towards *Kalila wa Demna*. In support of his argument, Pseudo-Māwardi invokes the Qur'ān, 31:6, 'And among the people are those who purchase the diversion of tales, so that they are misled from the path of God without knowledge'. According to the views of certain commentators (*qāla ba'd ahl al-tafsīr*), he asserts, the revelation of the verse was occasioned by (al-Nadr b.) al-Hārith b. Kalada's purchase of *Kalila wa Demna*, which he read aloud to a gathering of people. When al-Nadr b. al-Hārith claimed that the collection was finer and more delightful (*aladhdh wa ahsan*) than the ancient stories (*asātir al-awwalin*) brought by the Prophet Mohammad, God revealed the verse in correction.[75]

Kalila wa Demna's transmission into languages beyond South Asia had begun before the florescence of various Muslim cultures facilitated its diffusion, from Arabic, into a plethora of languages and communities across Asia, Africa and Europe. The collection was, however, one of a number of works that made their way, directly or indirectly, into Arabic and Persian from Sanskrit. The *Nasihat al-moluk* of Pseudo-Māwardi again supplies suggestive indications of the significance of Indic-associated materials in the shaping of a distinctively 'eastern' advisory discourse. The author cites several sources, in addition to *Kalila wa Demna*, that he associates with a South Asian provenance, and in many instances, he specifies that he has examined these writings himself.[76] Occasionally, he introduces his references with generic phrases, such as *wa fi ba'di kotobi 'l-hend* (191), *wa fi hekam al-hend* (392), or *wa fi ba'd siyāsat al-hend* (395) – formulae that resemble Ebn Qotayba's invocations of the 'books of the Indians' (*kotob al-hend*), and Ebn Abd Rabbeh's introduction of citations with the formulae *wa fi ketāb lil-hend, wa min ketāb lil-hend,* or *wa qara'tu fi ketāb lil-hend.* But whereas in the case of Ebn Qotayba and Ebn Abd Rabbeh, these references almost invariably turn out to be to *Kalila wa Demna,* Pseudo-Māwardi's acquaintance with South Asian-related materials appears to have been considerably more extensive.

A large number of Pseudo-Māwardi's references to materials of South Asian provenance are drawn from a literature that the author knew as an Indian king's testament to his son. These citations are sometimes introduced by the phrases *wa qāla ba'd al-fudalā' min moluk al-hend fi ahdin lahu ilā bnihi* (65), or *wa qāla ba'd moluk al-hend fi ahdin lahu* (282). In a majority of cases, Pseudo-Māwardi specifies that he has read these materials himself: *wa laqad qara'nā fi ahdin li ba'd moluk al-hend ilā bnin lahu* (78), *wa wajadnā li ba'd al-hokamā' min moluk al-hend fi ahdihi ilā bnihi* (79), *wa qara'nā li hakīmin min moluk al-hend fi ahdin lahu ilā bnihi* (146), *wa qad qara'nā li ba'di moluk al-hend fi ahdin lahu ilā bnihi* (169), *wa laqad qara'nā li ba'di l-hokamā' min moluk al-hend fi ahdihi* (171), *wa wajadnā fi ba'di 'ohudi 'l-hind* (251), *wa laqad qara'nā fi ba'd siyar al-hend* (256), *wa qad qara'nā li ba'di moluk al-hend fi ahdihi ilā bnihi* (270). In a significant number of instances, similar, even virtually identical, sayings appear in other Arabic collections attributed to Aristotle. Pseudo-Māwardi was familiar with, and cited countless examples from, the literary corpus associated with Aristotle's advice and moral exhortation to Alexander and clearly distinguished between his 'Indian' and 'Greek' materials.[77] Although the relationship of Pseudo-Māwardi's 'Indian' sources to the Alexander Romance lies beyond the scope of the present article, it appears that the evidence of the *Nasihat al-moluk* might support the arguments advanced by Shaul Shaked and, more recently, Kevin van Bladel regarding the Pahlavi and possibly Sanskrit derivation of other pseudo-Aristotelian materials commonly thought to have arisen from Greek antecedents.[78]

On two occasions, Pseudo-Māwardi identifies as his source a royal testament 'by Sāb.t.r.m, king of India, to his son'. Again, he specifies that he has read this text himself (*wa laqad qara'nā li-Sāb.t.r.m malek al-hend fi ahdin lahu ilā bnihi* [161, 183]). This pair of citations is of sufficient interest to justify translation in full. The first passage reads:

> If you occupy yourself with pleasure (*ladhdha*), let your pleasure be in conversation with the learned and in studying their books; for the joy (*sorur*) that lies in (the satisfaction of) passions (*shahawāt*) will amount to

little, while your dedication to it [will entail considerable danger] and a hastening towards transgression and a bad end (161).[79]

The second passage reads:

> Know that through your natural dispositions (*tabā'e '*) and the trickery of your passions (*mokāyadat ahwā'eka*), you have been afflicted with a war (*harb*). There is no war in which a truce would be more advantageous (*anfa '*) to you (than this war), or in which defeat will be more damaging to you. There is no war for which the warrior does not require material provision (*mādda*), so reinforce your forebearance (*helm*) with the forebearance of the learned, your knowledge (*elm*) with their knowledge, and your reasoning (*aql*) with their reasoning, for a single intellect is not strong enough to prevail in matters pertaining to the ordinary people (*amr al-āmma*), and it is inadequate in matters pertaining to the élite (*amr al-khāssa*) (183).[80]

Textual uncertainties notwithstanding, it is apparent that the two passages ascribed to Sāb.t.r.m reflect a strongly negative view of the human passions. They admonish the prince to resist the forces of his appetites as if he were engaged in a struggle against a mortal enemy and urge him to enlist the aid of the learned in the conflict. In the case of similar texts attributed to Aristotle, scholars have often regarded such ascetic elements as signs of transmission through Stoic and Christian milieux.[81] But it may also be noted that these passages convey an attitude reminiscent of that associated by Mas'udi with the Indian king K.n.d who, in similarly martial language, 'conquered' his (lower) self and 'put to death' his appetites.

Little information regarding this source, the 'Testament of Sāb.t.r.m', has so far come to light. It is surely identical, however, to the *Ketāb Sār.t.r.m* recorded in the *Fehrest*, where it appears under the heading, 'Titles of Indian books containing legends, evening stories and sayings' (*asmā' kotob al-hend fi 'l-khorāfāt wa 'l-asmār wa 'l-ahādith*), together with other relevant works, including the *Ketāb al-Bodd*, *Kalila wa Demna*, the *Ketāb Sendbād al-kabir* and the *Ketāb Sendbād al-saghir*, the *Ketāb Budāsaf wa Bilawhar* and the *Ketāb Budāsaf mofrad*, the *Ketāb Shānāq fi 'l-tadbir* and the *Ketāb Bidpāy fi 'l-hekma*.[82] According to Ebn al-Nadim's classification, then, it seems that he knew the *Ketāb Sāb.t.r.m* (or Sār.t.r.m) as a collection of narratives and possibly aphorisms.[83] The Baghdadi bibliophile confirms, moreover, Pseudo-Māwardi's association of the work with a South Asian cultural provenance. To the information to be inferred from Ebn al-Nadim, Pseudo-Māwardi adds the identification of the 'author' as an Indian king and the information that the work included, or perhaps consisted entirely of, an exhortative 'testament' addressed to a prince.

Attempts to locate the *Ketāb Sāb.t.r.m* more precisely yield a small number of observations. In the preface to his translation of Biruni's *Tahqiq mā lil-hend*,

E.C. Sachau refers to an author Sādbrm, noting that he is 'mentioned' (presumably by Ebn al-Nadim), unfortunately without indication of the contents of his book. Sachau proposes a possible identification for this author in Satya (Stt), mentioned by Biruni as the author of a *jātaka*, and observes that the name is 'perhaps an abbreviation of that one here mentioned, *i.e. Satyavarman*'.[84] According to this hypothesis, Pseudo-Māwardi's quotations would derive from a *jātaka* known, at least by its author's name, to Biruni. The specific identification becomes less likely when it is noted that Satya, as Albrecht Weber observed, appears in Sanskrit sources as a sage rather than a king.[85]

At the present stage of research, the most likely context for Pseudo-Māwardi's 'Testament of Sāb.t.r.m' is provided, perhaps not surprisingly, by *Kalila wa Demna*. One of the stories in *Kalila wa Demna* involves a king, his vizier and his wife and features a malicious 'interpretation' of the king's dreams by 'the brahmans'. The hostile depiction of the brahmans in this tale has been taken repeatedly as an indication of its provenance from a Buddhist milieu.[86] In most Arabic versions of the narrative, the king's name appears as Biladh.[87] The Syriac translation of *Kalila wa Demna*, however, preserves a different strand of transmission: it renders the name of the Indian king as Sh.t.p.r.m, a form reflected in certain Arabic, Hebrew and Old Spanish versions of the narrative.[88] Theodor Benfey identified this figure as Chanda-Pradyota, the king who appears in the two concluding tales of a Tibetan Buddhist cycle of stories.[89] Chanda-Pradyota was a contemporary of Bimbisāra (r. *c.* 543–493 BCE), the ruler of Magadha and subject of many Buddhist and Jain narratives.[90] It seems reasonable to infer that the Arabic versions of *Kalila wa Demna* in which the king's name appears as Shādaram reflect closer contact with a South Asian environment, and with cultural materials of an Indian or Tibetan provenance, than those in which the name appears as Biladh.[91]

If Pseudo-Māwardi's Indian king Sāb.t.r.m is related, as seems probable, to the Indian king Shādaram who appears in these versions of *Kalila wa Demna*, the coincidence illustrates further the extensive cultural contact with South Asia that appears to have characterized Pseudo-Māwardi's environment, including the circulation of literary materials, almost certainly in oral as well as written form. Considerable further research will be required in order to establish the complex and diffuse processes of oral and written transmission that eventually produced the text known to Pseudo-Māwardi as the 'Testament of Sāb.t.r.m'.[92]

It is, however, apparent that Pseudo-Māwardi adduces his quotations from the 'Testament of Sāb.t.r.m' in support of his repeated point that the king should practise self-control and exercise mastery over his appetites. As noted above, the author adduces numerous wise utterances and admonitions to illustrate and lend authority to his argument for such royal austerity. Among such citations are a significant number to which he ascribes a South Asian provenance.[93] These features intensify the impression that the *Nasihat al-moluk* emanated from an environment that enjoyed a degree of familiarity with South Asian cultural materials, or materials that bore South Asian, especially Buddhist, accretions. On two occasions, the author cites *al-bodd*, 'the Buddha', offering in one instance the explanatory 'the leader (*za'im*) of the Indians who is called *al-bodd*'.[94] The possibility of Balkh as the location for the book's composition has already been mentioned. Celebrated ascetics from Balkh, notably Ebrahim b. Adham (d. *c*. 161 / 777–8), Shaqiq-e Balkhi (d. 194 / 810) and Hātem-e Asamm (d. 237 / 852) are reported to have dispensed extensive advice and admonition for the benefit of rulers and other persons.[95] Moreover, poets and authors from Balkh played a prominent role in the composition of Persian *shāhnāma*s during this period, and the unidentified author of the 'Older Preface' to Ferdowsi's *Shāhnāma* averred that 'the Chinese', possibly a reference to the Manichaean Uighurs, had added images to the text of *Kalila wa Demna*.[96] The probable expertise on Indian matters of Abu Zayd Balkhi and several of his contemporaries in the Samanid realms has also been noted, and Abu Zayd's contemporary and fellow citizen Shahid (or Shuhayd) b. Hosayn Balkhi (d. 315 / 927–8) invoked the multi-ethnic and multi-confessional environment of his city and region in his lyric poetry.[97]

As the Buddhist communities of the region receded, literary allusions to and stories associated with Buddhism continued to thrive. Stories that reflected the *vita* of the Buddha, the son of a king who, despite his father's efforts to prevent it, renounced the trappings and comforts of royalty for the life of a mendicant ascetic, circulated in Arabic and Persian (an Iranian line of transmission may have been contemporary with Rudaki).[98] At the Ghaznavid court, Abu 'l-Qāsem Hasan Onsori Balkhi (d. 431 / 1039–40), whose poetry in praise of Mahmud invokes the multi-confessional environment of *johud-o kāfer-o gabr-o mosalmān*, composed a (lost) mathnavi concerning the Buddhas of Bamiyan.[99] The physical evidence of the locality's Buddhist history, continuing contacts with South and Central Asia, a literary corpus that had passed through Buddhist and other South Asian channels and an abundant repertoire of oral traditions provide an important context for the region's cultural production in Arabic and Persian in the tenth and eleventh centuries.

A number of scholarly investigations into the dissemination of a diverse cultural repertoire in Arabic and Persian writings have explored, on the one hand, historiographical works, and particularly historians' inclusion of the traditional histories of earlier dynasties, and on the other hand, the anthologies of literary materials, which incorporated aphorisms attributed to Persian kings and Greek sages. A perhaps disproportionate preoccupation with the 'political' content of advice literature has occasionally tended to obscure its intersection with these two related genres. Not infrequently, all three types of writing issued from the pens of the same authors and were addressed to substantially the same audiences. Like historiography and the literary anthology, advisory literature functioned as a medium for the adaptation and transmission of varied cultural materials. Translations from Pahlavi into Arabic, and later Persian, including sequential translations across the linguistic boundaries of South and West Asia in which Pahlavi (and Syriac) served as intermediate languages, facilitated a cultural integration articulated first in the Arabic language and later in Persian. Indeed, Tarif Khalidi has pointed out that the systematic and extensive incorporation of the stories of other nations had occurred in works of *adab* somewhat before the ninth and tenth-century historians Dinawari (d. 282 / 895), Ya'qubi (d. 284 / 897), Tabari and Mas'udi included such materials in their works of history.[100]

The advisory discourse produced in tenth and early eleventh-century eastern Iran would eventually contribute to the formation of the remarkable Persian works of the later eleventh century, especially the *Siyar al-moluk* of Nezām al-Molk and the *Nasihat al-moluk* of Ghazāli. Several characteristics of these Persian works are already apparent in the *Nasihat al-moluk* of Pseudo-Māwardi and the *Ādāb al-moluk* of Tha'ālebi, both of which reflect their authors' familiarity with the varied cultural traditions of the region. The later eleventh-century Persian works reflect oral as well as written sources, some of which had antecedents in Arabic-language materials, while certain aphoristic and narrative elements had passed through a number of languages and cultural–historical settings before their assimilation into the celebrated Persian works of prose. In its single extended narrative sequence, the *Nasihat al-moluk* of Pseudo-Māwardi relates the story of an infidel king who was hard of hearing; he devised the stratagem of having his petitioners dress in red, so that he could identify them and invite them to voice their grievances in a quiet place. A century and a half later, the tale, variously adapted and probably reflecting oral as well as written processes of transmission, reappears in the *Siyar al-moluk* of Nezām al-Molk and Ghazāli's *Nasihat al-moluk*.[101]

Despite the limited body of identified advisory writing from the tenth and early eleventh centuries, the available materials, read in conjunction with the larger literature of eastern Iran, are consistent with the hypothesis that the region produced a literature of counsel that reflected the particular cultural character of that time and place. It is proposed that the social, cultural and intellectual environment of Khorasan and Transoxiana shaped an advisory discourse, articulated in Arabic and Persian, that embraced cultural materials of highly diverse provenance, including a substantial literature associated by local authors with South Asia. Like the historiographical branch of literary activity to which it was related, the advisory literature participated in the continuing creation of culture, not only in its construction of images and ideals of rulership but also in its transmission and shaping of a large repertoire of cultural materials amenable to varied contexts and purposes.

Notes:

1. I would like to thank Edmund Herzig, Sarah Stewart and the Soudavar Memorial Foundation for inviting me to the 'Idea of Iran' symposium at which the ideas in this chapter were first presented.

2. Ghazāli's *Nasihat al-moluk* was translated into Arabic in the second half of the twelfth century under the title *al-Tebr al-masbuk fī nasihat al-moluk* (Jalal al-Din Homa'i, 'Dibācha', ii; see Ghazāli, *Nasihat al-moluk*, i–cxcvi). The *Qābusnāma* was translated into Ottoman Turkish at least five times, see Charles-Henri de Fouchécour, *Moralia. Les notions morales dans la littérature persane du 3e/9e au 7e/13e siècle* (Paris: Institut français de recherche en Iran, 1986), 179–222, esp. 180–81.

3. Erika Glassen, *Der mittlere Weg: Studien zur Religionspolitik und Religiosität der späteren Abbasiden-Zeit* (Wiesbaden: Franz Steiner Verlag, 1981), 95.

4. Glassen, 93; Carole Hillenbrand, 'Islamic Orthodoxy or Realpolitik? Al-Ghazālī's Views on Government', *Iran* XXVI (1988), 81–94 (91–2).

5. *Qābusnāma*, ed. by Gholam-Husayn Yusofi (Tehran: Sherkat-i enteshārāt ilmi va-farhangi, 1989), 234, 237; Reuben Levy, *A Mirror for Princes. The Qābūs Nāma by Kai Kā'ūs ibn Iskandar, Prince of Gurgān* (London: The Cresset Press, 1951), 230, 234.

6. C.E. Bosworth, 'The Tahirids and Arabic Culture', *JSS* 14 (1969), 45–79.

7. The text was broadly circulated immediately after its composition; the caliph Ma'mun (r. 198–218 / 813–33) admired it and had copies made for all his provincial governors (Mohammad b. Jarir Tabari, *Ta'rikh al-Tabari = Tarikh al-rosol wa 'l-moluk*, ed. by M Abu 'l-Fadl Ebrahim (Cairo: Dār al-Ma'rif, 1960–/1977–), vol. VIII, 591).

8. Mohammad b. Eshāq Ebn al-Nadim, *al-Fehrest*, ed. by Sha'ban Khalifa and Walid Mohammad al-'Awza, 2 vols (Cairo: al-'Arabi lel-nashr wa-l-tawzi', 1991), vol. I, 211.

9. *Nasihat al-moluk al-mansub ilā Abi-l-Hasan al-Māwardi*, ed. by Fo'ad Abd al-Mon'im Ahmad (Alexandria: Mo'assasat shabāb al-jāme'a, 1988), 'Introduction', 5–33; see also, Louise Marlow, 'A Samanid Work of Counsel and Commentary: The *Nasīhat al-mulūk* of Pseudo-Māwardī', *Iran* XLIV (2007), 181–92.

10. *Nasihat al-moluk* (hereafter *NM*), 364, where the detailed nature of the account strongly suggests local knowledge. The author alludes to an encounter at Qantarat al-Sirhān (Sarjanān?) between supporters of the Abbasid *da'wa* and 'the Arabs of the Umayyad armies'. The latter are said to have numbered 40,000 cavalry, while Abu Dā'ud (probably Abu Dā'ud Khāled b. Ebrāhim, one of Abu Moslem's generals in eastern Khorasan) commanded only a small number of men. The episode in question might have taken place in 130 / 747–8, when Abu Dā'ud's men defeated large numbers of anti-Abbasid rebels on the banks of the Sarjanān (Mohammad Tabari, vol. VII, 386–8; Abdallāh Mohammad b. Hosayn Balkhi, *Fazā'el-e Balkh* ed. by Abd al-Hayy Habibi [Tehran: Bonyād-e Farhang-e Īrān, 1350 / 1971], 86; Elton L. Daniel, *The Political and Social History of Khurasan under Abbasid Rule 747–820* [Minneapolis and Chicago: Bibliotheca Islamica, 1979], 86–7). According to Pseudo-Māwardi, when the Umayyad and anti-Umayyad forces met, Abu Dā'ud overheard a cry from the opposing army: 'We are a victorious gathering' (*nahnu jamī'un muntasir*, Q. 54: 54), to which he responded with the Qur'anic answering verse, 'The entire assembly will be defeated and will turn their backs in flight' (*sa-yuhamu l-jam'u wa-yuwallūna l-dubur*, 54: 45) – and so it was.

11. As de Fouchécour has indicated with reference to Tha'ālebi's work, 'L'important est de noter qu'au moment où la littérature persane prenait son essor, il existait déjà en arabe un miroir des princes tel que celui-ci, dans lequel les sujets se trouvaient bien fixés; les conseils et les sentences étaient abondamment utilisés dans un cadre qui convenait tout à fait aux notions qu'ils véhiculaient et qui était fortement charpenté' (Charles-Henri de Fouchécour, 138).

12. See Abd al-Malek Tha'ālebi, *Ādāb ul-moluk*, ed. by J. Atiya (Beirut: Dār al-gharb al-eslāmī, 1990), 172-3; see also Tha'ālebi, *al-Tamthil wa-l-mohādara*, ed. by Abd al-Fattah Mohammad al-Helw (Cairo: Dār ehyā' al-kotob al-arabiya, 1381 / 1961), 145.

13. Abd al-Hayy Gardizi, *Tārikh-e Gardizi = Zayn al-akhbār*, ed. by 'Abd al-Hayy Habibi (Tehran: Donyā-ye ketāb 1363 / 1984), 361. See further W. Luke Treadwell, 'The Political History of the Sāmānid State', Unpublished D. Phil. Thesis, University of Oxford, 1991, 241–7, 321.

14. Abd al-Karim b. Mohammad Sam'āni, *al-Ansāb*, ed. by 'Abd al-Rahman b. Yahya al-Mu'allimi al-Yamani, 13 vols (Hyderabad: Matba'at majles dā'erat al-ma'āref al-othmāniya, 1382–1403 / 1962–82), vol. VII, 351–3.

15. *Ādāb al-moluk*, 52. In this section, Tha'ālebi cites Abu 'l-Hasan b. Mohammad b. Ebrāhim b. Simjur's work on *siyāsa* (54); presumably the reference is to Abu 'l-Hasan Mohammad b. Ebrāhim b. Simjur. It is likely that Tha'ālebi's two citations from Abu 'l-Hasan are taken from a single work. The quotation from the work on *siyāsa* appears in almost identical form in the *Ahd Ardashir* (99).

16. Robert Dankoff, *Wisdom of Royal Glory (Kutadgu bilig): a Turko-Islamic Mirror for Princes* (Chicago and London: Chicago University Press, 1983).

17. For the most comprehensive treatment, see Julie S. Meisami, *Persian Historiography to the End of the Twelfth Century* (Edinburgh: Edinburgh University Press, 1999).

18. Elton L. Daniel, 'Historiography III: Early Islamic Period', *EncIr* VIII; (2004), 330–48 (337).

19. Julia Bray, 'Al-Tha'alibi's *Adab al-muluk*, a Local Mirror for Princes' in *Living Islamic History. Studies in Honour of Professor Carole Hillenbrand*, ed. by Yasir Suleiman (Edinburgh: Edinburgh University Press, 2010), 32–46. I am grateful to the author for providing me with a copy of this article in advance of its publication.

20. W. Barthold, *Turkestan down to the Mongol Invasion* (London: Luzac, 1977), 76–9; Daniel, 'Historiography', 337.

21. See F.W. Zimmermann, 'Al-Kindī' in *The Cambridge History of Arabic Literature. Religion, Learning and Science in the 'Abbāsid Period*, ed. by M.L.J. Young, J.D. Latham and R.B. Serjeant (Cambridge: Cambridge University Press, 1990), 364–9.

22. *Fehrest*, vol. I, 251. See further Yāqut, *Ershād al-arib elā ma'refat al-adib al-ma'ruf be-mo'jam al-odabā'* = *Dictionary of Learned Men of Yāqút*, ed. by D.S. Margoliouth (London: Luzac and Co., 1923–31), vol. I, 141; Jalāl-al-Din Soyuti, *Boghyat al-wo'āt fi tabaqāt al-loḡawiyin wa 'l-nohāt*, ed. by M. 'Abd-al-Qader Ata (Beirut: Dār al-kotob al-'ilmiya, 2004), vol. I, 256.

23. Yāqut, vol. I, 125; Everett K. Rowson, *A Muslim Philosopher on the Soul and its Fate: al-'Āmirī's Kitāb al-Amadalā l-abad* (New Haven: American Oriental Society, 1988), 19.

24. Zahir al-Din Bayhaqi, *Tārikh hokamā' al-Islām*, ed. by M.H. Muhammad (Beirut: Maktabat al-thaqāfa al-diniya, 1966), 55.

25. Abu Hayyan Tawhidi, *al-Emtā' wa 'l-mo'ānasa*, ed. by A. Amīn and A. al-Zayn (Cairo: Lajnat al-ta'līf wa 'l-tarjama wa 'l-nashr, 1939–44), vol. II, 15–16; see also

Rowson, 18–20. On the various meanings of and relationships among *adab*, *falsafa*, *hekma*, *din* and *shari'a* in the discourse of Tawhidi and his predecessors, notably Kindi and his students, see Everett K. Rowson, 'The Philosopher as Littérateur: al-Tawhīdī and his Predecessors', *Zeitschrift für Geschichte der Arabisch-Islamischen Wissenschaften* 6 (1990), 50–92 and Hans Hinrich Biesterfeldt, 'Ibn Farīġūn's Chapter on Arabic Grammar in his *Compendium of the Sciences*', *Studies in the History of Arabic Grammar II. Proceedings of the 2nd Symposium on the History of Arabic Grammar, Nijmegen, 27 April – 1 May 1987*, ed. by K. Versteegh and M.G. Carter (Amsterdam/Philadelphia: Johns Benjamins Publishing Company, 1990), 49–56 (51). See also Tarif Khalidi, *Arabic Historical Thought in the Classical Period* (Cambridge: Cambridge University Press, 1994), 131–81.

26. *Fehrest*, vol. I, 526–7.
27. *Fehrest*, vol. I, 529–31.
28. *Fehrest*, vol. I, 251–2; Yāqut, vol. I, 142–3; Salāh al-Din b. Aybak Safadi, *al-Wāfi bi 'l-wafayāt = Das biographische Lexikon des Salāhaddīn Halīl ibn Aibak as-Safadī* (Wiesbaden: Franz Steiner Verlag, 1962–), vol. VI, 409–10. Safadi reports that Balkhi composed a *Ketāb al-siyāsa* for a certain Yānes al-Khādem, who was governor of Balkh; he also records under Balkhi's authorship a work entitled *Fadl al-molk* (*al-Wāfi bi 'l-wafayāt*, vol. VI, 409–10 and vol. XVII, 26. See Franz Rosenthal, 'Abū Zayd al-Balkhī on Politics', *Essays in Honor of Bernard Lewis. The Islamic World from Classical to Modern Times*, ed. by C.E. Bosworth et al. (Princeton: The Darwin Press, 1989), 287–301 (288). Ebn Hajar lists a single *Ketāb al-siyāsa* as well as an *Adab al-soltān*. See Ahmad b. 'Ali Ebn-Hajar al-'Asqalāni, *Lesān al-mizān*, ed. by G. b. A. Ghanem (Cairo: Maktabat Ebn-Taymiya, 1416 / 1996), vol. I, 283).
29. Deborah Klimberg-Salter, 'Buddhist Painting in the Hindu Kush ca. VIIth to Xth centuries', *Islamisation de l'Asie Centrale: processus locaux d'acculturation du VIIe au XIe siècle, Cahiers de Studia Iranica* 39 (2008), 131–59.
30. See Ebn-al-Nadim, vol. I, 684; Ali b. al-Hosayn Mas'udi, *Moruj al-dhahab wa ma'āden al-jawhar*, 4 vols (Beirut: Dār al-Andalus, 1404/1984); trans. by Barbier de Meynard and Pavet de Courteille as *Les prairies d'or*, 2 vols, (Paris: Société Asiatique, 1965), II, 228–9; Richard W. Bulliet, 'Naw Bahār and the Survival of Iranian Buddhism', *Iran* XIV (1976), 140–45; S.M. Yusuf, 'The Early Contacts between Islam and Buddhism', *University of Ceylon Review* 13 (1955), 1–28, (6–7, 20–1); C.E. Bosworth, 'Balkh II: History from the Arab Conquest to the Mongols', *EncIr* III (1989), 588–91, (588).
31. *Fehrest*, vol. I, 683.
32. Balkhi composed a *Book on the Virtues of Balkh* (*Ketāb Fadā'el Balkh*) (Yāqut, vol. I, 144; Safadi, vol. VI, 410; Soyuti, vol. I, 256).
33. *Fehrest*, vol. I, 683. See V. Minorsky, *Sharaf al-Zamān Tāhir Marvazī on China, the Turks and India* (London: The Royal Asiatic Society, 1942), 125–6; Bruce B. Lawrence, *Shahrastānī on the Indian Religions* (The Hague and Paris: Mouton and Co., 1976), 21; Moritz Steinschneider, 'Zur Geschichte der Übersetzungen aus dem Indischen in's Arabische und ihres Einflusses auf die arabische Literatur', *ZDMG* 24 (1870): 325–92 (347). The account of the expedition echoes the story of the physician Burzoy's return from his embassy to India with (in addition to *Kalila wa Demna*) an abundance of medical knowledge, especially related to medicinal plants (François de Blois, *Burzōy's Voyage to India and the Origin of the Book of Kalīlah wa Dimnah* [London: Royal Asiatic Society, 1990], 33, 40–43).
34. Mas'udi, vol. I, 94. See Yāqut, vol. I, 144–5, 147, 149; Safadi, vol. VI, 410–13.

35. According to Ebn al-Nadim, the vizier used to send Balkhi presents of female slaves, until Balkhi wrote a book on the subject of sacrifices (*Ketāb al-qarābin wa'l-dhabā'eh*) that displeased him (*Fehrest*, vol. I, 251, 252).

36. Maqdesi, *al-Bad' wa'l-ta'rikh*, ed. by Cl. Huart, 6 vols (Paris: École des langues orientales vivantes, 1899), 19; see Lawrence, 22. Maqdesi's source could also have been the work of Abu 'l-'Abbās Ja'far b. Ahmad Marvazi (d. 274 / 887–8), who was, according to Ebn al-Nadim, the first person to attempt a book on *al-Masālek wa'l-mamālek* (*Fehrest*, vol. I, 275).

37. Abu Rayhān Biruni, *Tahqiq mā lil-hend* (Hyderabad: Matba'at majlis dā'irat al-ma'ārif al-othmāniya, 1377 / 1958), trans. by E.C. Sachau, *Alberuni's India: An Account of the Religion, Philosophy, Literature, Geography, Chronology, Astronomy, Customs, Laws and Astrology of India about A. D. 1030* (London: Routledge and Kegan Paul, repr. Delhi: S. Chand and Co., 1964), 198; Abu Rayhān, *Āthār al-bāqiya an al-qorun al-khāliya*, ed. by C.E. Sachau (Leipzig: Otto Harrassowitz, 1923), trans. by C.E. Sachau, *The Chronology of Ancient Nations* (London 1879, repr. Frankfurt: Minerva GMBH, 1969), 264, 284. Gardizi cites Jayhāni's 'Book of Histories' (*Ketāb-e Tavārikh*), 612–13.

38. S. Razia Jafri, 'Description of India (Hind and Sind) in the works of al-Istakhrī, Ibn Hawqal, and al-Maqdisī', *Bulletin of the Institute of Islamic Studies* V (1961), 1–67.

39. Abu 'l-Ma'āli, *Bayān al-adyān*, ed. by Hachem Razi (Tehran, 1964); 430–1 (for Abu Yazid, read Abu Zayd). Cl. Huart notes the same identification in 'Annexe au procès-verbal', *Journal Asiatique* [1901], 16–21 (18). On the various sources of information regarding South Asia available to early Muslim writers, see S.M.H. Nainar, *Arab Geographers' Knowledge of Southern India* (Madras: University of Madras, 1942) where Balkhi is not mentioned as a source; Lawrence, 17–29.

40. W.B. Henning ('Sogdian Loan-words in New Persian', *BSOAS* 10 [1940], 93–106 [94 and n. 3]) observes that the word *bot* itself entered Persian through Sogdian, which was still spoken in the Samanid capital of Bukhara in Balkhi's lifetime (Ebrahim b. Mohammad Estakhri, *Masālek al-mamālek*, ed. by de Goeje [Leiden: E. J. Brill, 1967], 314). See further Lawrence, 105. A.S. Melikian-Chirvani, 'L'évocation littéraire du Boudehisme dans l'Iran musulman', *Le monde iranien et l'Islam: sociétés et culture*, vol. 2 (1974), 1–72 (34–5). On the possible conflation of *bot* with 'Buddha', see Yusuf, 21.

41. *Bayān al-adyān*, 20–21.

42. *Fehrest*, vol. I, 251–2.

43. *Fehrest*, vol. I, 654; Biruni, *Āthār*, 207. See Mary Boyce, 'On Mithra in the Manichaean Pantheon' in *A Locust's Leg: Studies in Honour of S.H. Taqizadeh*, ed. by W.B. Henning and E. Yarshater (London: Percy Lund, Humphries and Co., 1962), 44–54, (44).

44. See Sachau, *Chronology*, 191.

45. See further Gustav Richter, *Studien zur Geschichte der älteren arabischen Fürstenspiegel* (Leipzig: Hinrichs, 1932), 11–18; J.D. Latham, 'Ibn al-Muqaffa' and Early Abbasid Prose' in *The Cambridge History of Arabic Literature. 'Abbāsid Belles-lettres*, ed. by J. Ashtiany, T.M. Johnstone, J.D. Latham, R.B. Serjeant and G. Rex Smith (Cambridge: Cambridge University Press, 1990), 48–77; Shaul Shaked, 'From Iran to Islam: Notes on Some Themes in Transmission', *Jerusalem Studies in Arabic and Islam* IV (1984), 3–67. Repr. *From Zoroastrian Iran to Islam* (London: Variorum, 1995) vol. VI. , 50–59; de Blois, *Burzōy's Voyage*, 24–33.

46. Balkhi is cited twice in the *Ketāb al-Sa'āda wa 'l-es'ād* (407, 419). Minovi, who published a facsimile of the text, speculates that two additional references to an

unidentified *al-shaykh* may also denote Balkhi (224, 413). The identification of the named author Ebn Abi-Dharr with Mohammad b. Yusof 'Āmeri, though widely accepted, rests on relatively little evidence (Rowson, 'The Philosopher as Littérateur', 88).

47. Tha'ālebi, *Ādāb al-moluk*, 85–6, 97; see Fouchécour, 137. A *Ketāb al-siyāsa* of Abu Zayd Balkhi was also known to, and admired by, Tawhidi (Rosenthal).

48. *Tohfat al-wozarā' al-mansub elā Abi Mansur 'Abd al-Malek b. Mohammad b. Esmā'l al-Tha'ālebi*, ed. by H. 'Ali al-Rawi and I.M. al-Saffar (Baghdad, 1977), 62, 81–2, 89.

49. On the actual and legendary derivations of Abu Ma'shar's *Ketāb al-oluf*, see David Pingree, *The Thousands of Abū Ma'shar* (London: The Warburg Institute, University of London, 1968), 1–21.

50. Fuat Sezgin, *Geschichte des arabischen Schrifttums* (Leiden and Frankfurt: E. J. Brill, 1967–2000), vol. III, 187–202; August Müller, 'Arabische Quellen zur Geschichte der indischen Medizin', *ZDMG* 34 (1880), 465–556 (esp. 474–5). On translations from Sanskrit into Arabic, see also the account of Ebn Ezra, in Steinschneider, 353–6.

51. *Fehrest*, vol. I, 214–15 (reading with [Mohammad Mohammadi, *al-Tarjama wa 'l-naql 'an al-fāresiya = La traduction des livres pehlevis en arabe dans les premiers siècles de l'Islam* (Beirut: Manshurāt qesm al-logha al-fāresiya wa ādabihā fi 'l-jāme'a al-lobnāniya, 1964), 44] *Ketāb 'elm al-hend;* taken by Lang to be a work on the 'Wisdom of the Hindus' [D.M. Lang, *The Wisdom of Balahvar: A Christian Legend of the Buddha* (London: George Allen and Unwin, 1957), 34]). Among the works that Abān is reported to have versified are *Kalila wa Demna*, the *Book of Sendbad* and *Bilawhar wa Budāsaf*, a work that reflects a Buddhist derivation (D.M. Lang, 'Bilawhar wa-Yūdāsaf', *EI²* I (1986), 1215–17).

52. Mas'udi, *Moruj al-dhahab*, vol. I, 91. See further S. Maqbul Ahmad, 'Al-Mas'ūdī on the Kings of India', *Al-Mas'ūdī: Millenary Commemoration Volume* (Aligarh, 1960) 97–112 (99); Tarif Khalidi, *Islamic Historiography: The Histories of Mas'ūdī* (Albany: State University of New York Press, 1975), 103, 104.

53. *Moruj al-dhahab*, vol. I, 100.

54. *Moruj al-dhahab*, vol. I, 324–32. The passage reflects a version of the Alexander Romance (Armand Abel, *Le roman d'Alexandre, légendaire médiéval*, Brussels: Office de publicité, S. A. Éditeurs, 1955). It is possible that Mas'udi's reference is to Chandragupta Maurya, reputed in Jain sources for his abdication in favour of his son, his pursuit of asceticism and his eventual death by the honoured means of voluntary starvation (Romila Thapar, *A History of India. Volume One* (London: Penguin, 1966. Reprinted 1990), vol. I, 70–71; R.C. Majumdar, *Ancient India,* sixth revised edition (Delhi: Motilal Banarsidass, 1971), 99, 103, 104). The figures of Alexander and Chandragupta were linked in certain strands of ancient folklore. See further Thomas R. Trautmann, *Kautilya and the Arthaśāstra: A Statistical Investigation of the Authorship and Evolution of the Text* (Leiden: E.J. Brill, 1971), 48–67, esp. 64. Barbier de Meynard and Pavet de Courteille also noted the possibility that Mas'udi's reference was to Chandragupta (*Les prairies d'or*, vol. II, 257). Related accounts, though lacking Mas'udi's attention to the Indian king's asceticism, appear in the *Ghorar al-siyar* sometimes attributed to Tha'ālebi and Ferdowsi's *Shāhnāma* (in both cases the king's name is recorded as K.i.d: *Ghorar al-siyar*, 424–30; Abel, *Le roman d'Alexandre*, 85). Ya'qubi follows his description of Alexander's conquest with a description of a wise man named K.i.h.n. whom Alexander made ruler of the whole of India (vol. I, 87–8).

55. Trautmann, 10; see *Sezgin*, vol. III, 188, 193–7. Ebn Rabban's text includes a section devoted to 'admonitions that I found in their books' (*mawā'ez wajadtuhā fi kotobihim*) (*Ferdaws al-hekma*, 397-8). Ebn Rabban, a secretary to Māzyār b. Qārin and, following the latter's execution in 225 / 840, a member of the retinues of Mosta'sim (r. 218–27 / 833–42) and Motawakkel (r. 232–47 / 847–61), is also reported to have composed a *Tohfat al-moluk*, from its title possibly a work of counsel (*Fehrest*, vol. I, 593).

56. *Serāj al-moluk*, vol. II, 742–8 (Shābāq al-Sindi). The king's name appears as Ebn Qamāyes (see n. 7).

57. M.M. Qazvini, *Bist maqāla*, 2 vols, Tehran: Sharq, 1332/1943), vol. II, 31; V. Minorsky, 'The Older Preface to the *Shāh-nāma*', *Iranica: Twenty Articles* (Tehran: University of Tehran, 1964), 260–73. First published in *Studi Orientalistici in onore di Giorgio Levi Della Vida* (Rome: Instituto per l'Oriente, 1956), 159–79 (167).

58. L. Kinberg, 'What is Meant by *zuhd*', *SI* 61 (1985), 27–44.

59. For examples, see A. b. M. Ebn Qotayba, *Oyun al-akhbār*, 4 vols (Cairo: Matba'at dār al-kotob al-mesriya, 1343–8 / 1925–30), vol. I, 3, 18, 19, 22, 25, 27, 30, 45, 92 (from Book I, *Ketāb al-Soltān*); see further Gérard Lecomte, *Ibn Qutayba (mort en 276/889). L'homme, son oeuvre, ses idées*, 2 vols (Damascus: Institut français de Damas, 1965), vol. I, 184 and n. 3, and Walter Werkmeister, *Quellenuntersuchungen zum Kitāb al-Eqd al-farīd des Andalusiers Ibn Abdrabbih (246 / 860–328 / 940)* (Berlin: Klaus Schwarz Verlag, 1983), 142–5, esp. 143, where parallels with the *Oyun* are also indicated. Noting the discrepancies between the extant version of *Kalila wa Demna* and the citations in the *Eqd al-farid*, Werkmeister suggests that Ebn Qotayba and Ebn Abd Rabbeh may have drawn from common sources, some of which were modified in the process of their transmission to al-Andalus (143–5).

60. Treadwell, 183, 185; Meisami, *Persian Historiography*, 17; de Blois, *Burzōy's Voyage*; Richter, 22–38.

61. *Kalila wa Demna*, 53–4. Unless otherwise indicated, references to *Kalila wa-Demna* are to the text given in *Āthār Ebn al-Moqaffa'*, ed. by Omar Abu 'l-Nasr (Beirut: Manshurāt Dār al-Hayāt, 1966).

62. *Āthār Ebn al-Moqaffa'*, 276.

63. *Ta'rikh al-Ya'qubi*, vol. I, 88–9. See Khalidi, *Arabic Historical Thought*, 115–18; Chase F. Robinson, *Islamic Historiography* (Cambridge: Cambridge University Press, 2003), 136–7.

64. See de Blois, *Burzōy's Voyage*, 12–17, esp. 15–17, for a summary of the collection's growth in size through the accretion of additional tales and its transformation in character through the mitigation of the 'decidedly amoral' quality of the *Pañcatantra*.

65. On two occasions, Pseudo-Māwardi cites and praises the author's introductory section to *Kalila wa Demna*, *NM*, 220, 234. He also includes several extended quotations, for which the source is acknowledged (231–2, 387–8, 392–3). Occasionally, Pseudo-Māwardi cites the text without acknowledgement (44, 146 [n. 14]).

66. *NM*, 44. See also *Oyun*, vol. I, 92; *al-Eqd al-farid*, vol. I, 18. In the two anthologies, the text appears at the end of a longer extract introduced with the phrase *wa fi ketāb lil-hend*. See *Āthār Ebn al-Moqaffa'*, 120, where the aphorism appears as an internal quotation, introduced by *fa innahu yuqālu*.

67. As Lecomte observed, Ebn Qotayba deliberately excluded the apologues of *Kalila wa Demna* and cited only the work's moral points, in the form of the maxims that

almost always conclude the apologues. Lecomte suggested that perhaps in Ebn Qotayba's day there existed a separate epitome in which the moral maxims from *Kalila wa Demna* were collected, and that the existence of such a collection might account for Ebn Qotayba's references sometimes to *Kalila wa Demna* and sometimes to 'one of the books of the Indians', as if they were separate works, when in both cases the citations derive from *Kalila wa Demna* (*Ibn Qutayba*, vol. I, 184– 6). Ebn al-Nadim records a *Ketāb Jawāmeʿ Kalila wa Demna* under Ebn al-Moqaffaʿ's name (*Fehrest*, vol. I, 214), and the *Ādāb al-saghīr*, probably not the work of Ebn al-Moqaffaʿ, consists largely of aphorisms drawn in part from *Kalila wa Demna*, Latham, 57; see Ihsan Abbas, 'Nazra jadida fi baʿd al-kotob al-mansuba l-Ebn al-Moqaffaʿ', *RAAD* 52 (1977), 538-80 (578).

68. *Ādāb al-moluk*, 58, 173, 228, 229.
69. Pseudo-Māwardi's work is replete with lengthy quotations of verse, and he cites a succession of Prophetic hadith in praise of poetry: 'Poetry contains wisdom' (*inna min al-sheʿr al hekma*), and 'Poetry is the record of the Arabs' (*al-sheʿr diwān al-arab*) (*NM*, 217).
70. *NM*, 214–15.
71. In his recommendations of reading and listening materials for the young prince, the author probably has in mind the works of Wāqedi (130–207 / 747–822) and Madā'eni (d. c. 228 / 843), both of whom he cites elsewhere (*NM*, 153, 390; see *Fehrest*, vol. I, 173–4, 177–86). (On Ebn Qotayba's use of these sources, see Lecomte, vol. I, 78–80.) In the same period and region as Pseudo-Māwardi, Ebn Farighun, a student of Abu Zayd Balkhi, also noted the importance of studying these subjects, see Franz Rosenthal, *A History of Muslim Historiography*, second revised edition (Leiden: E.J. Brill, 1968), 35, 540; Julie S. Meisami, 'Why Write History in Persian? Historical Writing in the Samanid Period' in *Studies in Honour of Clifford Edmund Bosworth,* vol. II, ed. by C. Hillenbrand (Leiden: E.J. Brill, 2000), 348–74 (359–60).
72. *Fehrest*, vol. I, 609–12. Ebn al-Nadim records two versions of the *Book of Sendbad* (*Ketāb Sendbād al-kabir, Ketāb Sendbād al-saghir*); furthermore, a Pahlavi *Sendbādnāma* was translated into Persian, probably commissioned by Nuh b. Nasr in 339 / 950 (Treadwell, 181, n. 147). Ebn al-Nadim knew of many books that recorded the stories of lovers (*Fehrest*, vol. I, 615–21).
73. *NM*, 216.
74. See A. Berriedale Keith, *A History of Sanskrit Literature* (London: Oxford University Press, 1920) 352–71, esp. 357–65.
75. *NM*, 216–17, and see nn. 56, 57, 58.
76. *NM*, 78, 79, 146, 169, 171, 251, 256, 270, 395.
77. For quotations attributed to Aristotle, see *NM*, 55, 58, 81, 97, 108, 117, 122, 129, 134, 146, 152, 157, 162, 167, 168, 177, 182, 184, 185, 197, 208, 231, 236, 238, 262, 268, 269, 273, 289, 296, 297, 336, 340, 341, 352, 353, 355, 359, 364, 366, 386, 394. I plan to explore the relationship between the 'Indian' and 'Greek' materials in the *NM* in a future publication.
78. Shaked, 'From Iran to Islam'; Kevin van Bladel, 'The Iranian Characteristics and Forged Greek Attributions in the Arabic *Sirr al-asrār (Secret of Secrets)*', *Mélanges de l'Université Saint-Joseph* 57, (2004), 151–72.
79. The text is unclear; see 161, n. 75; compare *NM*, ed. by Kh. M. Khedr (Kuwait: Maktabat al-falāh, 1983); Shahrazuri, *Nozhat al-arwāh wa rawdat al-afrāh fi tā'rikh al-hokamā' wa 'l-falāsefa*, ed. by Khurshid Ahmad (Hyderabad: Matbaʿat majlis

dā'erat al-ma'āref al-othmāniya, 1976), 127. In other sources, the passage is attributed to Aristotle, for example, see *Nozhat al-arwāh*, vol. I, 199.

80. There are again some uncertainties in the text; see 183, n. 155; compare *NM Kh*, 145. See also Mohsen Zakeri, *Persian Wisdom in Arabic Garb* (Leiden: Brill, 2007).

81. Miklós Maróth, *The Correspondence between Aristotle and Alexander the Great: An Anonymous Greek Novel in Letters in Arabic Translation* (Piliscsaba: The Avicenna Institute of Middle Eastern Studies, 2006), esp. 30–38.

82. *Fehrest*, vol. I, 612. On the *Ketāb al-Bodd*, the *Ketāb Budāsaf wa-Bilawhar* and the *Ketāb Budāsaf mofrad*, see Lang, *Wisdom of Balahvar*, 32–6.

83. Gustav Flügel, without indicating his sources, listed the *Ketāb Sādiram* (*Sārdum*, *Sārirm*) as a collection of stories (G. Flügel, 'Zur Frage über die Romane und Erzählungen der mohammedanischen Völkerschaften', *ZDMG* 22 (1868), 731–7, (732, n. 25)).

84. Sachau, *Alberuni's India*, vol. I, xxxiii. See *Tahqiq*, 122 = Sachau, *Alberuni's India*, vol. I, 157.

85. Albrecht Weber, *The History of Indian Literature*, trans. from the Second German Edition by John Mann and Theodor Zachariae (Boston: Houghton, Osgood, and Co., 1878), 260, n. 290.

86. I.G.N. Keith-Falconer, *Kalīlah and Dimnah or the Fables of Bidpai* (Cambridge: Cambridge University Press, 1885), lv; Thomas B. Irving, *Kalilah and Dimnah* (Newark, Delaware: Juan de la Cuesta, 1980), 197, n. 1; de Blois, *Burzōy's Voyage*, 13.

87. *Āthār Ebn al-Moqaffa'*, 247 ff., where the story forms the fifteenth chapter of the collection. Ya'qubi knew the story as the fourth chapter (*Ta'rikh*, vol. I, 88), and in the edition of de Sacy, *Calila et Dimna*, 247–65, the story forms the fourteenth chapter. On the chapters and their order in the various versions of the collection, see de Blois, *Burzōy's Voyage*, 61–5.

88. Keith-Falconer, xlix, 302–05; Ignazio Guidi, *Studii sul testo arabo del libro di Calila e Dimna* (Rome: Libreria Spithöver, 1873), 72; Theodor Benfey, 'Einleitung', *Kalilag und Damnag. Alte syrische Übersetzung des indischen Fürstenspiegels. Text und deutsche Übersetzung von Gustav Bickell. Mit einer Einleitung von Theodor Benfey* (Leipzig: F. A. Brockhaus, 1876), V–CXLVII, esp. L–LI. Irving's translation, based on Spanish and Arabic versions, renders the name Shādaram, Thomas B. Irving, *Kalilah and Dimnah* (Newark: Juan de la Cuesta, 1980), 126ff.

89. A. Schiefner, *Mahâkâtjâjana und König Tshanda-Pradjota. Ein Cyklus buddhistischer Erzählungen*, Mémoires de l'Académie Impériale des Sciences de St Pétersbourg, VIIe série, XXII (1875), no. 7, 47–53. Versions of the story in Pali and Chinese have also survived (*The Jātaka or Stories of the Buddha's Former Births*, 6 vols, ed. by E.B. Cowell (London: Luzac and Co., 1957), vol. I, 187–94; Édouard Chavannes, *Cinq cents contes et apologues extraits du Tripitaka chinois*, 3 vols (Paris: Librairie d'Amérique et d'Orient, 1910–62), vol. III, 102–13.

90. *Vinaya Texts Translated from the Pali* by T.W. Rhys Davids and H. Oldenberg in *The Sacred Books of the East*, ed. by F. Max Müller, Oxford University Press, vol. XVII (1882), (Reprinted Delhi: Motilal Banarsidass, 1982), 171–95. See Majumdar, 95–7; Narendra K. Wagle, *Society at the Time of the Buddha*, second revised edition (Bombay: Popular Prakashan, 1995), 38–9.

91. Where the name appears as Bilādh, the name of the vizier has been substituted for that of the king; the process of substitution continues with the name of the king's wife being transferred to the vizier (Benfey, LI–LII).

92. In a similar example, the Indian king who asks his 'philosopher' to relate instructive narratives in the frametale of *Kalila wa Demna* is frequently given the name Dabshalim; the same name is often given to the Indian king who sends a chess set as a challenge to the sages of Sasanian Iran (de Blois, *Burzōy's Voyage*, 18–21).

93. See Kautilya's *Arthaśāstra*, Chapters V and VI of Book I (T.N. Ramaswamy, *Essentials of Indian Statecraft, Kautilya's Arthaśāstra for Contemporary Readers* [New York: Asia Publishing House, 1962], 50–51).

94. *NM*, 78, 395. The first quotation, introduced by the phrase rendered above, reads: 'With fine words but no action, a thousand men will never achieve the improvement (*eslāh*) of a single man; whereas a single man, by way of good action, will improve a thousand men.' The second example is apparently the first of two internal quotations *fi ba'd siyāsat al-hend*: 'The Buddha said to one of our kings, when he asked him about justice, 'When you consider every child as if he were a child of yours, every old man as if he were a father to you, every old woman as if she were a mother to you, every peer among men as if he were a brother of yours, and similarly every woman as a sister, and then treat them with the appropriate kindness and generosity – then you will have practised justice'.

95. Mohammad 'Awfi, *Pānzdah bāb-e Javāme' al-hekāyāt*, ed. by M. Ramazani (Tehran: Chāpkhāna-ye khāder, 1335/1957), 195–217.

96. Qazvini, vol. II, 33, nn. 14, 15; Minorsky, 168; de Blois, *Burzōy's Voyage*, 28, n. 2.

97. Heshmat Moayyad, 'Lyric Poetry' in *Persian Literature*, ed. by E. Yarshater (Albany, New York: Bibliotheca Persica, 1988), 120–46 (120). See further François de Blois, 'Shuhayd al-Balkhī, a Poet and Philosopher of the Time of Rāzī', *BSOAS* 59 (1996), 333–7.

98. Jes P. Asmussen, 'Barlaam and Iosaph', *EncIr* III (1989), 801; Lang, 'Bilawhar wa-Yūdāsaf', 1215–17. Henning proposed and then discarded the hypothesis that Rudaki was the author of a *Bilauhar u Būdīsaf* in Manichaean Persian, but still attributed the work to a contemporary of Rudaki (W.B. Henning, 'Persian Poetical Manuscripts from the Time of Rūdakī' in *A Locust's Leg: Studies in Honour of S.H. Taqizadeh*, ed. by W.B. Henning and E. Yarshater (London: Percy Lund Humphries and Co., 1962), 89–104). See also Gimaret, 'Traces et parallèles'.

99. Mohammad 'Awfi, *Lobāb al-albāb*, (Tehran: Ketābkhāna-ye Eba Sinā, 1335 / 1957), vol. II, 265, 269; Melikian-Chirvani, 497.

100. Khalidi, *Islamic Historiography*, 82–3; Richter, 33–92.

101. *NM*, 397–9; *Siyar al-moluk*, 19 = Darke, *The Book of Government*, 14; Ghazāli, *Nasihat al-moluk*, 31–2 (cf. 310–11); = Bagley, *Ghazālī's Book of Counsel for Kings*, 21. See also Glassen, 91–2.

7

The Expression of Power in the Art and Architecture of Early Islamic Iran

Jonathan M. Bloom

(Boston College and Virginia
Commonwealth University)

The Arab conquest of Iran in the seventh century introduced to the Iranian plateau not only a new form of government but also new institutions and a new visual language. The conquest by Arab Muslim armies began in 632 CE with the conquest of Ctesiphon in modern-day Iraq; Sasanian forces retreated towards Merv in Central Asia and the Sasanian empire collapsed nearly two decades later in 651 CE. Arab governors immediately replaced the Sasanian rulers, although the population slowly converted to Islam.[1] The Sasanians, of course, had been great royal patrons of architecture and the arts, for it was through such media that they projected their power in the capital and throughout their realm. For example, the remains of the great palace at Ctesiphon, rock-cut reliefs at Tāq-e Bustān and Naqsh-e Rostam, gold and silver crowns and vessels, silk textiles and coins all testify to the dissemination of a royal iconography of power in the Sasanian period.

Arab rule in the eighth and ninth centuries led to the emergence of new institutions, such as the mosque, and the *locus* of power was transferred from greater Iran to the caliphs' capitals elsewhere, whence authority was then delegated to local representatives of the central government. At the same time much of the wealth produced in Iran drained out in the form of tribute and taxes to Damascus in Syria under the Umayyads (661–750) and then to Baghdad and Samarra in Iraq under the Abbasids (r. 749–1258). This wholesale transfer of wealth in the early Islamic period in Iran seems to have left few if any patrons and little money for the patronage of architecture and the arts. Nevertheless, there is some evidence for construction and patronage under the early Arab governors. For example, the early Abbasid supporter Abū Muslim built a palace at Merv, now in Turkmenistan. According to literary sources, it had a domed chamber surrounded by four *iwan*s facing in four directions.[2] At Sarvestan in Fars, a mysterious structure survives that has been thought to have been a palace or a garden pavilion (Fig. 7.1). Long attributed to the Sasanian or even Achaemenid period, it was studied in the 1970s by Lionel Bier, who suggested that it had been a fire temple. But structural similarities to Islamic buildings in

Fig. 7.1 Sarvestan, Fire Temple (?) 8th century.
Photo:Jonathan M. Bloom and Sheila S. Blair.

Iraq, such as the palace at Ukhaidir, indicated to him that it was built after the Islamic conquest, which would indicate that structures continued to be built for Zoroastrian purposes.[3] Although this building does not preserve any decoration, artisans continued to decorate buildings, to judge from a series of stucco plaques discovered at the site of Chal Tarqān-Ishqābād near Rayy in northern Iran.[4] Again, they were once thought to be Sasanian, but Deborah Thompson ascertained that they dated from the late seventh century or the early eighth, well after the region had been conquered by Muslim forces. Some of the plaques bear geometric and vegetal ornament but others have figural ornament. For example, a plaque in Los Angeles depicting a Sasanian king on horseback shows that some wealthy patrons still wanted or appreciated figural relief decoration, despite the coming of Islam.[5]

Similarly, some rich Iranians must also have maintained their taste for silver dishes. There are many examples of 'Post-Sasanian' silver dishes that can be ascribed to the seventh century or eighth. In contrast to earlier Sasanian silverwares, the relief is flat and low, the outlines and details are strongly emphasized, the rendering of costumes and other motifs is conventionalized and the background, rather than the figures, is gilded.[6] One well-known example in the Museum für Islamische Kunst in Berlin depicts a popular story about Bahrām V (r. 420–38; 'Bahrām Gur') who was remembered for his prowess in hunting.[7] In this example, the artist neglected, however, to show the weapons with which the hero killed the animals and also added an extraneous winged figure bearing a necklace – probably borrowed from an investiture scene – to a traditional depiction of a hunt.

An octagonal gilded silver dish also in Berlin, which is decorated with representations of *simurghs* and blossoms, shows a new approach to decoration that is thought to be characteristic of the Islamic period.[8] Rather than a single scene, as in the previous example, the field is divided by a continuous band into a series of geometric compartments, each containing a motif. This kind of design is more characteristic of arrangements seen in stucco carving or on textiles. It suggests that in the Islamic period artisans were becoming freer to transfer motifs from one medium to another

Silk textiles continued to be luxury items. We know from textual sources that great lengths of brightly-coloured Iranian silks were exported to the Ka'aba in Mecca where they were used to drape the shrine with the *kiswa,* its traditional cloth covering.[9] Between 1969 and 1975 at Moschevaya Balkha, an extremely remote site in the northern Caucasus, Soviet archaeologists excavated the tomb of a local prince who had died in the eighth century or ninth, to judge from the coins buried with him. He was buried in an emerald-green long-sleeved robe, which was decorated with rows of medallions each enclosing a yellow *simurgh*, the legendary Iranian bird–lion and closed with gold buckles. Silks in other patterns were used for the linings and facings of the robe.[10] All this evidence indicates that Iranians continued to weave fancy silks in Iran in the Islamic period and that traditional iconography continued to express luxury and power, despite the passing of the old Sasanian regime.

Local rulers continued to strike silver coins as they had before, but now they minted them in the name of their Abbasid overlords. These coins were inscribed in Arabic with verses from the Qur'an and information about the place and date of issue, rather than with portraits of Sasanian rulers. We know from historical accounts that the new Muslim rulers also erected mosques for congregational worship in the principal cities but very little, if any, monumental evidence for these buildings has survived, apart from the Abbasid mosque at Balkh, usually dated to the first half of the ninth century (Fig. 7.2).[11] It comprises a square brick and *pisé* structure with four internal supports that once supported nine domes (now destroyed). The interior walls, supports and arches are decorated with stucco, intricately carved in patterns comparable to those found on buildings in Abbasid centres in Iraq, although it remains unresolved whether these stucco techniques were originally developed in Iraq or in Central Asia. The Balkh mosque is also one of the earliest surviving examples of a type of mosque plan found from Spain to Central Asia in the ninth and tenth centuries, although in this case too it remains unresolved whether or not this type of mosque was an innovation of the central Islamic lands that was disseminated to east and west.[12] In short, for the earliest period of Muslim rule in Iran there is some tantalizing but inconclusive evidence about how traditional forms were maintained and the slow emergence of a new visual language associated with the Arab Muslim conquerors.

Fig. 7.2 Balkh, Abbasid Mosque, 9th century.
Photo: Jonathan M. Bloom and Sheila S. Blair.

In the ninth and tenth centuries Abbasid central power waned as several regional dynasties emerged in the years before the emergence of the Saljuq Turks in the mid-eleventh century, a period first characterized by Vladimir Minorsky as the 'Iranian Intermezzo'.[13] It was also, by all accounts, a period of increasing conversion to Islam. Five dynasties of local rulers emerged: the Taherids (r. 821–73) in Khorasan; the Saffarids (r. 861–1003) in south-eastern Iran, with their capital at Zaranj; the Samanids (r. 875–999) in Central Asia and Khorasan, centred on the cities of Balkh and Bukhara; the Buyids (r. 932–1062) in Daylam and eventually Iraq, where they established a protectorate over the Abbasid caliphs; and the Sallarids (r. 942–79) in Iranian Azerbaijan and Armenia.[14] Of these, the Samanids and the Buyids have left the most notable visual record, as they reconfigured Arab, Islamic, Iranian and Central Asian artistic ideas to meet the needs of the evolving Muslim society in Iran.

The most notable Samanid monument is their dynastic mausoleum in Bukhara (Fig. 7.3).[15] The building is popularly associated with Isma'il b. Ahmad (r. 892–907), the most successful member of dynasty, but it was probably erected as a family tomb after his death. The building comprises a cubic chamber covered by a dome and decorated on the exterior and interior with intricate brickwork patterns. The extraordinary quality of brickwork decoration shows that although this is the only building to survive from this

Fig. 7.3 Bukhara, Mausoleum of the Samanids, 10th century.
Photo: Jonathan M. Bloom and Sheila S. Blair.

time, there must have been a sophisticated architectural tradition in Bukhara during the Samanid period. Fragments of an Arabic inscription survive on one of the wooden lintels over one of its doorways (Fig. 7.4), but it was principally the building's form that was meant to preserve the memory of the Samanid rulers. It is one of the first surviving funerary structures in Islam, and stands in stark contrast to the Prophet Muhammad's prohibition of erecting monumental tombs over grave sites. It also represents a broader trend throughout the Islamic lands of the tenth century to monumentalize the grave sites of local rulers and revered religious figures.[16]

Quite a different aspect of Samanid art is preserved in the textile known as the Shroud of St Josse (Fig. 7.5).[17] These two silk fragments, now in the Louvre, were made for a general in service to Samanids; the Arabic inscription reads: 'Glory and prosperity to the commander Abū' l-Mansūr Bukhtekīn, may God perpetuate his happiness'. We know that Abū' l-Mansūr Bukhtekīn was put to death by the Samanid sovereign Abd al-Malek b. Nuh in 961; the

*Fig. 7.4 Bukhara, Mausoleum of the Samanids, detail of inscription over
the portal. Photo: Jonathan M. Bloom and Sheila S. Blair.*

wording of the inscription indicates that the textile had to have been made
while the commander was still alive, presumably in the mid-tenth century. The
two surviving pieces, which show elephants, dragons, phoenixes and Bactrian

*Fig. 7.5 Silk textile made for Abū'l-Mansūr Bukhtegīn (d. 961), known
as the 'Suaire de Saint-Josse'. Paris. Louvre. OA 7502.*

camels, can be reconstructed as coming from a rectangular cloth measuring some 2 x 3 metres that probably served as a saddle-cloth. Such silks were produced on a drawloom, a complex machine that made it possible to weave intricate patterns in multiples. The immense labour of setting up the loom made sense only when many pieces were to be woven; the Shroud of St Josse had to have been made not as a one-off piece, but as one of set. The textile represents the continuation of pre-Islamic traditions of silk weaving combined with the introduction of the Arabic script. One can imagine that Abū' l-Mansūr Bukhtekīn showed off his power by having all his troops decked out with matching saddle-cloths proclaiming his name and titles.

The other major Samanid art form was ceramics, represented by many examples associated with the cities of Nishāpur and Samarqand.[18] Several varieties of Samanid ceramics have been identified, but none appears to have had anything to do with power or even royal patronage. The most notable are the epigraphic wares: earthenware plates and bowls covered with a white slip and decorated with Arabic inscriptions written in dark brown (and red) slips under a transparent glaze. Such ceramics represent a presumably urban taste with a deep knowledge of and appreciation for Arabic. Typically, such vessels bear witty aphorisms such as 'Blessing to its owner: It is said that he who is content with his own opinion runs into danger' or 'He who believes in a reward [from God] is generous with gifts' (Fig. 7.6).[19]

Fig. 7.6 Earthenware bowl from Nishapur or Samarqand, 10th century.
Copenhagen, David Collection, 22.1974.

The Buyids were the other dynasty in this period that is known to have been a major patron of the arts, particularly once they had left the highlands of Daylam for the Iranian plateau. In addition to constructing such buildings as the Jurjir Mosque in Isfahan (Fig. 7.7)[20] and restoring ones such as the Friday mosques of Isfahan[21] and Nā'in, inscriptions and stylistic evidence show that work was done during the Buyid period on the octagonal pavilion now incorporated in the Friday mosque of Natanz[22] and on the mosque at Ardestān[23], both in central Iran. Contemporary sources note that the Buyids and their associates constructed lofty royal mausoleums at Rayy and a multi-storied 360-room palace at Shiraz.[24] Neither the tombs nor the palace survives, however, so we are left with an incomplete picture of Buyid architecture.

Like his pre-Islamic forebears, the Buyid ruler Adud al-Dawla added inscriptions to the ruins of Persepolis.[25] This inscription (Fig. 7.8) reads 'In the name of God. The exalted *amir* Adud al-Dawla Fannākhusraw b. al-Hasan was present in the year

Fig. 7.7 Isfahan, Portal to the Jurjir (Hakim) Mosque, c. 1000. Photo: Jonathan M. Bloom and Sheila S. Blair.

344 (955–6) on his return, victorious, from the conquest of Isfahan, his capture of Ibn Makan, and his rout of the army from Khorasan. He fetched someone who read the inscriptions in these ruins'. Adud al-Dawla's interest in the pre-Islamic Persian past represented more than just a tourist's visit to the ruins. In this inscription he cited his Persian name *Fannākhusraw* (Refuge of Khusraw) to evoke to his Daylamite followers his Sasanian antecedents. Nevertheless, the inscription was composed in Arabic and uses Arab titles, although he later would adopt the old Persian title *shāhanshāh* (king of kings).[26]

Fig. 7.8 Persepolis: Inscription of Adud al-Dawla, 955-6.
Photo: Jonathan M. Bloom and Sheila S. Blair.

The Buyids also struck commemorative coins.[27] The historian Ibn al-Athir states that on New Year's Day, 1 Muharram 378 / 21 April 988 the vizier Ibn Abbad presented Fakhr al-Dawla, the Buyid ruler of Rayy, with a gold coin weighing 11 *mithqal* (perhaps as much as 47g).[28] On one side it had seven lines of Arabic poetry likening the *dinār* to a sun and the ruler to the king of kings; on the other side it was inscribed just like an ordinary coin with Sura 112 (*Ikhlas*), as well as the names of the caliph, the Buyid ruler and the mint, Gorgān, where it was struck. Significantly, the decoration of this coin was entirely epigraphic, like virtually all Islamic coins. No such commemorative coin survives, but several smaller coins bearing Buyid names and dates are known, although their authenticity has been questioned. One bears the name of Rukn al-Dawla and the date 962; it has a coin-like obverse and a neo-Sasanian reverse. A gold medallion in Tehran claims to have been struck by his son Adud al-Dawla at Fārs in 969–70; it bears two neo-Sasanian portraits. Three gold presentation pieces were supposedly issued at Baghdad in the name of Izz al-Dawla between 973 and 976: one shows a lion attacking a stag or an ibex, another shows an eagle seizing a duck or a gazelle, and the third depicts a seated king and a lutenist. The most accessible is the gold medallion in the Freer Gallery of Art, which depicts an enthroned prince drinking on one side and a mounted falconer on the other. Although it has no inscription, its authenticity has also been questioned.

Several decades ago it would have been far easier than today to speak about how the Buyids expressed their power through art because there was so much art to discuss.[29] In late 1925 and early 1926, thirteen medieval Islamic and three Byzantine silk textiles were excavated at a site known as Bibi Shahr Banu near Rayy south of Tehran. The site was supposedly the grave of a daughter of the last Sasanian ruler who had been one of the wives of Husayn, the Prophet's grandson. Some of the textiles quickly passed into private hands in Tehran, and, as early as March 1926, dealers in Paris began to offer some of them to British, French and American museums and collectors, who began to publish their acquisitions. It was not until the 1931 International Exhibition of Persian Art at the Royal Academy in London, however, that these textiles came to public notice, when some twenty examples attributed to Iran in the eleventh and twelfth centuries were exhibited. Seven more examples were exhibited at the Third International Congress for Persian Art and Archaeology at Leningrad in 1935–6 and dozens more published in 1939 in A.U. Pope and Phyllis Ackerman's *A Survey of Persian Art.*

In the *Survey*, Pope and Ackerman published fifty-two different textiles from Rayy; they contrasted the embarrassing richness of documentary information about the medieval textile industry in Iran with the heretofore scanty physical remains.[30] But, Ackerman noted, this situation had changed now that 'fifty-odd patterned pieces, in addition to plain and striped silks, [had been] excavated in 1925 in a group of tombs in the vicinity of Rayy'. Indeed, in her catalogue of sixty early silks in the *Survey*, forty-three were said to come from that site.

In January 1943, in the midst of the Second World War, Pope and Ackerman published an article in the *Illustrated London News* entitled 'The Most Important Textile Ever Found in Persia'.[31] It described an unusually large double-faced silk dated 384 / 994 along with an account of the finds at Rayy.[32] Their account of one of the 'momentous discoveries in the history of textiles' is both dramatic and romantic: ignorant grave robbers searching for gold thought they had only found rags, but these rags turned to riches when discerning collectors and museums recognized their true value.

In 1948 the French scholar Gaston Wiet published a group of related textiles, many of which bore historical inscriptions, while others had explicit dates, specific historical information which allowed them to be dated precisely, or poetry that suggested dates in the Buyid period.[33] Wiet's publication, was, however, demolished by the American scholar Florence Day, who challenged the textiles' authenticity on historical, epigraphic, iconographic and technical grounds.[34] In subsequent years, scholarly opinion was sharply divided between the 'believers' and the 'unbelievers' in the 'Buyid' silks.[35] About twenty years ago, Sheila Blair, Ann Wardwell and I studied these textiles from epigraphic, technical, and historical perspectives and submitted several for Carbon-14 analysis.[36] Not only did we find that virtually all had not been produced in medieval times, but we also found that several had been made after the nuclear explosions of the 1940s and 1950s!

The overabundance of information characteristic of the 'Buyid' textiles was coincidentally found on several pieces of supposedly Buyid woodwork, including a pair of doors or window shutters, formerly in the Rabenou collection and now in Cairo, and a door leaf in the Freer Gallery of Art. The pair of panels bears an inscription stating that it was ordered by Tāj al-Milla al-Shāhanshāh Abū Shujā Fannākhusraw, 'may he ever be the support of the empire' (adud al-dawla) and dated 363 (974 CE), but the authenticity of this piece (and others) has been questioned because, as we have seen from the undoubtedly authentic Persepolis inscription, Adud al-Dawla did not take on the title shāhanshāh until later in his career.[37]

The Buyids are also supposed to have had gold vessels. A ewer in the Freer Gallery of Art is inscribed with blessings to Abū Mansur Bakhtiyār (d. 978), the son of Mu'izz al-Dawla.[38] Raised from a single sheet of gold and weighing half a kilo, the 13 cm high jug has an unusual curvaceous profile with little of the distinction between body and neck characteristic of other genuine (but undated) examples of the type. The decoration on the body is worked in relief and consists of three pairs of confronted sphinxes, peacocks and horned animals, each figure enclosed in a medallion formed by unusual three-dimensional, almost-Baroque swags of foliage which join above in two tiers of trefoil fleurs-de-lis.

Another gold jug in Cleveland, also 13 cm high, has the more traditional squat body and flaring neck. Wide bands on the neck and body displaying birds within medallions formed by interlaced bands are bordered by narrower bands inscribed with a poem dedicated by Abū Ishāq Ibrāhīm Sābī to the Buyid ruler Samsām al-Dawla Abū Kālījār Marzubān, the son of Adud al-Dawla, who ruled in Baghdad between 983 and 987 and in Fars between 990 and 998. For historical reasons, the poem can be dated to Baghdad between 983 and 985, thereby suggesting an extraordinarily precise date for the ewer. Wiet first published the Cleveland ewer in 1947 as part of the same private collection that included eighteen Persian textiles which all later were discovered to be forgeries.[39]

Finally, the manuscript of the Andarznāma, which had appeared in 1950 purporting to be the earliest Persian illustrated manuscript, was shown to be a crude forgery because of the presence of Prussian blue, the ferric ferrocyanide pigment discovered only in 1710.[40] Once the Andarznāma was proved to be a forgery, no other such manuscripts appeared on the market. Similarly, after our definitive publication of the Buyid silks as forgeries, no new ones have appeared. In short, much of what we thought we knew about Buyid art was a fantasy, created by scholars, dealers and forgers who tried to imagine what the art of this intriguing period should have looked like.[41] So what is left that is genuine?

A weft-faced compound silk twill in the Textile Museum, Washington, D.C. (Fig. 7.9), is inscribed in Arabic: 'Glory and Prosperity to the King of Kings,

Fig. 7.9   Silk twill inscribed with the names of Zādānfarrūkh and Bahā al-Dawla, c. 1000. Washington, DC, Textile Museum, no. 3.116.

Bahā' al-Dawla, Light of the People, Strengthener of the Nation, Father of Victory, son of Adud al-Dawla, Crown of the People, may his life be long'. Underneath this line of monumental angular script a smaller text reads 'for the use of Abū Sa'īd, Zādānfarrūkh ibn Āzādmard, the Treasurer'. Technical analysis, including Carbon-14 testing, has determined that this textile is genuine.[42] In 1001 Zādānfarrūkh was ambassador to Bahā' al-Dawla, Buyid ruler of Mesopotamia 989–1012. Unlike earlier textiles, such as the Shroud of St Josse, this piece is exclusively epigraphic. Writing makes up the entirety of its decoration.

A second example of genuine Buyid art comprises a hoard of eleven silver objects discovered in Iran – three bowls, two saucers, a ewer, a bottle, a vase, a jar, a cup and a dish – inscribed in niello (a black sulphide mixture) to Abū'l-'Abbās Valgīr (or Valgīn) b. Hārūn (Fig. 7.10).[43] This individual is identified in the inscriptions as the (something) of the Commander of the Faithful. His name indicates that he was a Muslim but, despite that, everything about this hoard seems connected to the consumption and enjoyment of wine. Despite the Arabic inscriptions and Muslim names and titles, the set shows that the ancient

Persian traditions of wine-drinking continued despite Islamic disapproval.[44] One could imagine that the otherwise unknown Valgīr was a Buyid officer from Daylam. The style of the Arabic script suggests a date *c*. 1000, and, in comparison to earlier pieces, the figural motifs have been superseded by writing.

Fig. 7.10   Set of silver vessels inscribed with the name of Valgīr b. Hārūn, c. 1000. Tehran, Museum of Islamic Art (after Pope and Ackerman, Survey*).*

Many of these trends can be seen in a series of minarets attached to mosques at such sites as Fahraj (to the west of Zāhedān), Nā'in (in central Iran) and Dāmghān (in northern Iran). The mosque tower or minaret had not been a feature of the earliest mosques but seems to have been invented in the late eighth or early ninth century; they became increasingly common in the tenth century.[45] Although some scholars have tried to connect tall towers with Indo-Aryan ideas of worshipping pillars, etc., there is no evidence that such towers existed in pre-Islamic Iran. Rather, the mosque tower was popular not only because it served as a generalized sign of Islam but also as a particular sign of local power. It should be remembered that the tower served not only as the place of the call to prayer but also as the place from which the ruler's name was proclaimed. According to the historian Muhammad b. Abd al-Jabbār al-Utbī, when the caliph al-Qādir (991–1031) gave ceremonial robes to Sultan Mahmud of Ghazna (998–1030) sometime in the first decades of the eleventh century, 'Khorasan submitted to his authority and his name was mentioned from the top of the minarets'.[46] Towers were especially attractive, moreover, because it was far cheaper to build a tower than an entire mosque, and they were gratifyingly visible.

The oldest datable tower still standing in Iran is the one adjacent to the Tarik Khane mosque, Damghan, which was built by the local governor Abū Harb Bakhtiyār, sometime between 1026 and 1032, probably in 1028 (Fig. 7.11).[47] Standing more than 30 metres tall, it represents the work of a team of highly skilled and experienced masons who had previously worked on a series of similar projects, only one of which has survived: they had just completed work on the tomb he had built for his father, the Pir-e Alamdār.[48] Both structures show a mastery of bricklaying techniques that produced the inventive and attractive relief patterns and inscriptions that encircle the structures. The inscription on the tower reads 'the exalted governor, Bakhtiyār ibn Muhammad ordered the construction of this *man-mad* [minaret] under the sovereignty of the *amir*, the most exalted lord, Falak-al-Ma'āli Abū Man-sūr, may his victory be glorified'.[49] The builder's overlord was the Ziyarid Manuchehr ibn Qābus, who recognized the

Fig. 7.11 Damghan, Minaret of the Tarik Khane mosque, 1026–32. Photo: Jonathan M. Bloom and Sheila S. Blair.

authority of both the Abbasid caliph and the Ghaznavid Mahmud. Minuchihr's father Qābus was himself famed for his tomb tower at Gorgān of 1006–7.[50] The same Abū Harb Bakhtiyār also built another tower, this one attached to the Friday mosque nearby at Semnān, dated 1031–5.[51] In the inscription on this tower Abū Harb Bakhtiyār calls himself 'client [*mawlā*] of the Commander of the Believers', which probably represents a newly-received title. In these works, Abū Harb Bakhtiyār used the relatively new architectural form of the tower to advertise not only the general presence of Islam but also his new specific position of power. In short, the mosque tower presented Iranian patrons with a new way of expressing power through architecture.

In conclusion, although the Islamic conquest of Iran was accomplished relatively quickly in the seventh century, it took several centuries for Iran to become Islamic and for the old Persian artistic traditions to reflect this change. We have seen that in the first centuries of Islam, many of the traditional Iranian artistic media such as luxury textiles or gilded silverware continued to be produced, and one may assume that many of the practices associated with these media (i.e. the ritual consumption of wine) continued despite the coming of Islam. By the late tenth and early eleventh century, however, Iranian patrons adopted new Islamic architectural forms, such as the mosque tower/minaret or the tomb tower, as a means of expressing power. In all the art forms of this period in Iran, whether architecture or ceramics, the traditional decorative use of representation declines in popularity as it is replaced by an extensive use of Arabic writing as the major means of expression of power and authority. In short, the Arabic word replaced the Persian image, providing evidence of the increasing use of the language of Islam throughout the Iranian lands. Oddly enough, this was also the very moment when Persian was reemerging as a literary language, a development represented most notably by Ferdawsi's composition of the *Shāhnāma* one thousand years ago. These developments in the arts of the last of the Persian dynasties in Iran are all foretastes of what would continue to happen in the coming decades under the domination of the Saljuq Turks.

Notes:

1. Richard W. Bulliet, *Conversion to Islam in the Medieval Period: An Essay in Quantitative History* (Cambridge, MA: Harvard University Press, 1979).
2. K.A.C. Creswell, *Early Muslim Architecture*, vol. II (Oxford: Clarendon Press, 1940), 3–4.
3. Lionel Bier, *Sarvistan: A Study in Early Iranian Architecture* (University Park, PA and London: College Art Association of America, 1986).
4. Deborah Thompson, *Stucco from Chal Tarkhan-Eshqabad Near Rayy*, Colt Archaeological Institute Publications (Warminster: Aris and Phillips, 1976).
5. Linda Komaroff, *Islamic Art at the Los Angeles County Museum of Art* (Los Angeles: Los Angeles Country Museum of Art, 1998), accession no. M.76.174.250.
6. Oleg Grabar, *Sasanian Silver: Late Antique and Early Mediaeval Arts of Luxury from Iran: August–September 1967, the University of Michigan Museum of* Art, exhibition catalogue (Ann Arbor: The Museum, 1967); Prudence O. Harper, *Silver Vessels of the Sasanian Period* (Princeton: Princeton University Press, 1981).
7. Harper, 68–70; Musée Ceruschi, F. Demange, *Les Perses sassanides: fastes d'un empire oublié (224–642)* (Paris: Editions Findakly, 2006), no. 68.
8. Janine Sourdel-Thomine and Bertold Spuler, *Die Kunst Des Islam*, Propyläen Kunstgeschichte (Berlin: Propyläen Verlag, 1973), 238, no. 149.
9. Maurice Gaudefroy-Demombynes, 'Le Voile de la Ka'ba', *Studia Islamica* 2 (1954), 9–14.
10. A. Jeroussalimskaja, 'Le cafetan aux simourghs du tombeau de Mochtchevaja Balka' (Caucase Septentrional), *Studia Iranica* 7 (1978): 182–212.
11. Barbara Finster, *Frühe iranische Moscheen, vom Beginn des Islam bis zur Zeit salğūqischer Herrschaft*, Archaeologische Mitteilungen Aus Iran: Ergänzungsband 19 (Berlin: Reimer, 1994); Lisa Golombek, 'The Abbasid Mosque at Balkh', *Oriental Art* 15 (1969), 173–89.
12. Bernard O'Kane, 'The Origin, Development and Meaning of the Nine-Bay Plan in Islamic Architecture' in *A Survey of Persian Art*, vol. XVIII, *From the End of the Sasanian Empire to the Present, Studies in Honor of Arthur Upham Pope*, ed. Abbas Daneshvari (Costa Mesa: Mazda, 2005), 189–244.
13. Vladimir Minorsky, 'The Iranian Intermezzo' in *Studies in Caucasian History* (Cambridge: Cambridge University Press, 1953).
14. Clifford Edmund Bosworth, *The New Islamic Dynasties: A Chronological and Genealogical Manual* (Edinburgh: Edinburgh University Press, 1996), 148–9.
15. Sheila S. Blair, *The Monumental Inscriptions from Early Islamic Iran and Transoxiana*, Supplements to *Muqarnas* (Leiden: Brill, 1992), 25–9.
16. Thomas Leisten, *Architektur für Tote: Bestattung in architektonischem Kontext in den Kernländern der islamischen Welt zwischen 3./9. und 6./12. Jahrhundert*, Materialien zur Iranischen Archäologie (Berlin: D. Reimer, 1998).
17. M. Bernus, H. Marchal, and G Vial, 'Le suaire de Saint-Josse', *Bulletin de Liaison du Centre International d'Etudes des Textiles Anciens* 33 (1971), 1–57; '"The Saint-Josse Shroud'."
18. Lisa Volov (Golombek), 'Plaited Kufic on Samanid Epigraphic Pottery' *Ars Orientalis* 6 (1966): 107–34; Charles K. Wilkinson, *Nishapur: Pottery of the Early Islamic Period* (New York, 1973); Oya Pancaroğlu, 'Serving Wisdom: The Contents of Samanid Epigraphic Pottery', in *Studies in Islamic and Later Indian Art from the Arthur M. Sackler Museum, Harvard University Art Museums* (Cambridge, MA: Harvard University Art Museums, 2002), 58–75.

19. Esin Atıl, *Ceramics from the World of Islam*, [in the Freer Gallery of Art] (Washington, DC: Smithsonian Institution, 1973), no. 12; Sheila S. Blair and Jonathan M. Bloom, *Cosmophilia: Islamic Art from the David Collection, Copenhagen*, with essays by Kjeld von Folsach, Nancy Netzer, and Claude Cernuschi (Chestnut Hill, MA: McMullen Museum of Art, 2006), 94, no. 29.

20. Blair, *Monumental Inscriptions*, 52–3.

21. Eugenio Galdieri, *Isfahan: Masgid-i Jum'a*, III (Rome: IsMEO, 1984).

22. Sheila S. Blair, 'The Octagonal Pavilion at Natanz: A Reexamination of Early Islamic Architecture in Iran', *Muqarnas* 1 (1983), 69–94.

23. Jonathan M. Bloom and Sheila S. Blair, eds., *The Grove Encyclopedia of Islamic Art and Architecture* (New York City: Oxford University Press, 2009), see 'Ardistan'.

24. Blair, 'The Octagonal Pavilion at Natanz: A Reexamination of Early Islamic Architecture in Iran', 84.

25. Ibid., 32–5.

26. Ibid., 34–5.

27. M. Bahrami, 'A Gold Medal in the Freer Gallery of Art', in *Archaeologica Orientalia in Memoriam Ernst Herzfeld*, ed. George C. Miles (Locust Valley, NY: J. J. Augustin, 1952), 5–20.

28. Ibn al-Athir, *al-Kāmil fi'l-ta'rīkh* (Beirut: Dār Sadr, 1402/1982), IX, 59.

29. Jonathan M. Bloom, 'Fact and Fantasy in Buyid Art', *Oriente Moderno* XXIII (LXXXIV), n.s. (2004), 387–400; *Kunst und Kunsthandwerke in Im Frühen Islam, 2. Bamberger Symposium der Islamischen Kunst 25.-27. July 1996*, vol. XXII (LXXXIV), n.s., ed. by Barbara Finster, Christa Fragner and Herta Hafenrichter.

30. A.U. Pope and P. Ackerman, eds, *A Survey of Persian Art from Prehistoric Times to the Present*, reprint, 1938–9 (Tehran: Soroush Press, 1977).

31. Arthur Upham Pope and Phyllis Ackerman, 'The Most Important Textile Ever Found in Persia', *Illustrated London News*, 9 January 1943, 48–9.

32. Washington, D.C., Textile Museum, inv. no. 3.230.

33. Gaston Wiet, *Soieries Persanes* (Cairo: Institut Français d'Archéologie Orientale, 1948).

34. Florence E. Day, 'Review of *Soieries Persanes* by Gaston Wiet', *Ars Islamica* 15–16 (1951), 231–44.

35. Mechthild Lemberg, 'The Buyid Silks of the Abegg Foundation, Berne', *Centre International d'Études de Textiles Anciens, Bulletin de Liaison* 37 (1973), 28–43; Gabriel Vial, 'Technical Studies on the Buyid Silk Fabrics of the Abegg Foundation—Berne', *Centre International d'Études de Textiles Anciens, Bulletin de Liaison* 37 (1973), 70–80; Judith H. Hoffenck-De Graaff, 'Dyestuff Analysis of the Buyid Silk Fabrics of the Abegg Foundation, Bern', *Centre International d'Études de Textiles Anciens, Bulletin de Liaison* 37 (1973), 120–33; Dorothy G. Shepherd, 'In Defence of the Persian Silks', *Centre International d'Études de Textiles Anciens, Bulletin de Liaison* 37 (1973), 143–5; Dorothy G. Shepherd, 'Medieval Persian Silks in Fact and Fancy (A Refutation of the Riggisberg Report)', *Bulletin de Liaison du Centre International d'Étude des Textiles Anciens* (1974) 39–40, no. i–ii.

36. Sheila S. Blair, Jonathan M. Bloom and Anne E. Wardwell, 'Reevaluating the Date of the "Buyid" Silks by Epigraphic and Radiocarbon Analysis', *Ars Orientalis* 22 (1992), 1–42.

37. Jonathan M. Bloom, 'Fact and Fantasy', 388.

38. Glenn D. Lowry, 'On the Gold Jug Inscribed to Abu Mansur al-Amir Bakhtiyar Ibn Mu'izz al-Dawla in the Freer Gallery of Art', *Ars Orientalis* 19 (1989), 103–15.

39. Wiet, *Soieries Persanes*, 91–8.

40. Rutherford J. Gettens, 'Andarz Nama. Preliminary Technical Examination' in *A Survey of Persian Art from Prehistoric Times to the Present*, ed. Arthur Upham Pope, asst. ed. Phyllis Ackerman, Volume XIII-Fascicle, Addendum A—The Andarz Nama (London: Oxford University Press, 1971), A/53-A/63.
41. Jonathan M. Bloom, 'Fact and Fantasy'.
42. A.U. Pope and P. Ackerman, *Survey*, 2009, 2031 no. 12; *The Arts of Islam*, exhibition catalogue, Hayward Gallery (The Arts Council of Great Britain, 1976), no. 75; R. W. Ferrier, *The Arts of Persia* (New Haven and London: Yale University Press, 1989), 158.
43. *The Arts of Islam*, 161–2; Eva Baer, *Metalwork in Medieval Islamic Art* (Albany: State University of New York Press, 1983), 211; R.W. Ferrier, *The Arts of Persia*, 171.
44. Assadullah Souren Melikian-Chirvani, '*Rekāb:* The Polylobed Wine Boat from Sasanian to Saljuq Times' in *Au Carrefour Des Religions: Mélanges Offerts à Philippe Gignoux* (Bures-sur-Yvette: Groupe pour l'étude de la civilisation du moyen-orient, 1995), 187–204; A.S. Melikian-Chirvani, 'The Wine-Birds of Iran from Pre-Achaemenid to Islamic Times', *Bulletin of the Asia Institute* 9 (1997), 41–97.
45. Jonathan Bloom, *Minaret: Symbol of Islam*, Oxford Studies in Islamic Art (Oxford: Oxford University Press, 1989).
46. Ibid., 151.
47. Blair, *Monumental Inscriptions*, 96–7; Jonathan Bloom, *Minaret*, 153.
48. Ibid., 93–5.
49. Ibid., 96.
50. Ibid., 63–5; for further discussion of the Gunbad-i Qābus, see Melanie Michailidis's contribution to this volume.
51. Blair, *Monumental Inscriptions*, 99–100.

8

The Lofty Castle of Qābus b. Voshmgir

Melanie Michailidis
(University of California, Davies)

The soaring tomb tower known as the Gonbad-e Qābus is the only prominent architectural remnant of the Ziyarid dynasty, which ruled the area around Gorgān in northern Iran from 927 to 1090 CE (see Fig. 8.1). Visible even from the air, and located on the main road from Gorgān to Khorasan, the monument has garnered attention from admiring travellers since the medieval period. It appears in every survey of Islamic art and architecture, classed as something of an anomaly because it is one of the earliest extant examples of Islamic funerary architecture and yet displays such dramatic assurance and a stark, almost modern, simplicity. Removed from all contemporary context, it is usually categorized awkwardly with the Saljuq tomb towers which followed over half a century later. Constructed in 397 AH (1006–7) by the Ziyarid ruler Qābus b. Voshmgir, this magnificent structure can only be understood through its own historical context, by examining the aims and aspirations of its patron and by placing it in its architectural context, a series of tomb towers built high in the Alborz mountains for relatives of Qābus, the rulers of the Bavandid dynasty. This funerary architecture not only served as to commemorate individual rulers in a very particular and visible way but also formed the architectural dimension of a broader legitimizing programme in politics, literature, art and other arenas. While the type of detailed examination of a local context that I will present in this chapter runs counter to the essentializing notions frequently encountered in the study of early Islamic funerary architecture, it does provide a richer background to help us to understand particular buildings and to build up a much more nuanced appreciation of architectural developments over time. Placing the Gonbad-e Qābus in its historical and cultural context is important beyond the creation of architectural typologies, however, as it helps to illuminate the choices available to the patrons of canonical buildings and enhances our understanding of the societies which created these monuments by using the structures as historical documents.

Fig. 8.1 Gonbad-e Qābus

The Building and its Setting

Both the Ziyarids and the Bavandids were relatively minor players during the time when the larger regional actors were the Buyids in western Iran and Iraq and the Samanids in Transoxiana and Khorasan. The Bavandids ruled a small, mountainous region in eastern Tabaristān, while the Ziyarids controlled the coastal plain to the east of the Alborz, sandwiched between the mountain range, the Caspian Sea and Khorasan. The culture of this region was, not surprisingly, somewhere between that of neighbouring Khorasan and Tabaristān. Excavations at the Ziyarid capital, Gorgān, have revealed fragments of architectural decoration datable to a tenth-century context consisting of stucco related to that of the mosque at Nā'in,[1] showing how Gorgān participated in wider Iranian trends, while the ceramic production of the Ziyarid era overlapped with that of Sāri and Nishāpur, both of which produced their own unique local styles of pottery as well as styles which enjoyed a wider degree of circulation in the eastern Islamic world, such as epigraphic ware. Like Khorasan, Gorgān had been a *locus* of much early Islamic intellectual activity. The city enjoyed both intellectual ties and trading connections with Yemen; Moqaddasi mentions that the silk for which Gorgān was famous was exported to Yemen in the form of veils.[2] Ebn Hawqal states that the climate of Gorgān was perfect for silkworms, so that all the silk of Tabaristān was actually made from Gorgān worms.[3] In addition to the trade with Yemen, the silk was also exported northwards, through the port of Abaskun on the Caspian, to the realm of the Khazars and beyond. The city of Gorgān was divided into two parts by a river, with the most populous areas on the eastern bank;[4] Moqaddasi informs us that the population was comprised of Hanafis, Shi'is and *dhimmī*s.[5]

The Gonbad-e Qābus is located on a flat plain near Gorgān, towering over the surrounding countryside at a height of 51 metres, further accentuated by its placement on a ten-metre high artificial mound. The exceptional height of the building and the flat terrain on which it is situated would have combined to render the building readily visible from the city of Gorgān and from the main road between Gorgān and Khorasan. It is composed of baked brick, which at this time was still only used for the most important buildings.[6] Baked brick would therefore have implied wealth and lavish consumption, given the number of kiln-fired bricks needed for this enormous structure, as well as the importance of the building to its patron and a desire to construct something with a far greater degree of permanence than the unbaked brick used for most buildings. The height of the structure is emphasized with ten flanges which extend from the enlarged base of the tower all the way up to the base of the dome, and the very simplicity of the building highlights its expensive material. The only decoration consists of two inscription bands which encircle the building, one just under the conical dome and one above the doorway, each repeating the same foundation inscription in Kufic script composed of cut bricks. This aesthetic, where form and quality are of the utmost importance and the only decoration is the severe yet well-executed Kufic script, recalls the epigraphic ware which was produced at Gorgān as well as at Nishāpur and Samarqand. The dramatic upward thrust of the tomb tower is pierced only by a single entrance facing east–southeast and a single, small window in the dome facing east. The interior is a single dark chamber which extends all the way up to the inner dome; there is no decoration and no trace of any plaster revetment.

The building is exceedingly well-preserved, having sustained damage only at the base due to the depredations of local builders over the centuries; this damage was restored in the mid-twentieth century. In 1899, a Russian team excavated the building, and found that the foundations extended all the way to the bottom of the artificial mound, and that there was no body buried within it. According to a legend recounted by Jannābi, Qābus was placed in a glass or crystal coffin, which was suspended from the roof by chains. This story has been taken as evidence of lingering 'Avestan' practices,[7] although this in no way accords with Zoroastrian funerary practice, as such a coffin would serve to preserve the flesh contained within it, whereas the intention of the Zoroastrian practice of exposure was to dispose of the flesh quickly. Moreover, this was purely a legend, since the Russian excavators found no evidence of chains having ever been fastened to the apex of the interior chamber.

Oleg Grabar has suggested that perhaps the tower was never meant to function as a mausoleum *per se*, but was instead more of a victory symbol, akin to the Ghaznavid towers of indeterminate function farther to the east.[8] The inscription on the Gonbad-e Qābus refers to the building as a 'lofty castle' or *qasr al-'ali*; it does not call the building a grave (*qabr*) or a dome (*qobba*), a term frequently used to refer to mausoleums by their most distinguishing feature. This exceedingly monumental tower had, however, garnered attention long before its inclusion in the canon of Islamic architectural history and its function as a mausoleum has always been taken as a given. Ebn Esfandiyār, the thirteenth-century court chronicler of the Bavandids and the most authoritative source for the Caspian provinces, says that Qābus 'was buried beneath a dome outside Gorgān on the road to Khorasan'.[9] This statement clearly indicates not only that the building was considered to be a mausoleum but also that an actual burial was assumed to be contained within it. Moreover, the historical and architectural links between the Gonbad-e Qābus and the Bavandid tomb towers, including the terminology of the inscriptions, further underscores the clear funerary purpose of this structure.

The Gonbad-e Qābus has entered into the canon of Islamic architecture as an early masterpiece of the funerary genre. It was first published by Diez in 1918[10] and since then has appeared in every major survey of Islamic and Persian art and architecture,[11] as well as the catalogues of funerary architecture and eastern Islamic inscriptions.[12] But in spite of the universal admiration for the building (no doubt greatly enhanced by the frequent comparisons of its dramatic simplicity to that of modern architecture), it has received little more than the superficial treatment typical of the surveys. And in the surveys in particular, enthusiastic descriptions of the building's aesthetic qualities have generally far outweighed any concern with historical accuracy: in the volume edited by Michell, for example, Hutt describes it as 'one of the first buildings in Iran that can be associated with the advent of the Central Asian Turks',[13] while Dickie described it as embodying the 'sense of power [which] is the first impression to be conveyed by a Seljuq building',[14] despite the fact that Qābus was a member of the Iranian Ziyarid dynasty and died several decades before the first arrival of the Saljuqs in Iran. Others, however, have noted that the building is a very Iranian one, with dates given in both the Arabic lunar and the Persian solar calendars; this fact, combined with the legend of the glass coffin, led Ettinghausen and Grabar to assert the following:

> we may very tentatively suggest that its background may be sought in some Mazdean commemorative monument or in the transformation into permanent architecture of a transitory building such as a tent.[15]

This linking of tomb towers, including the Gonbad-e Qābus, with the tents of Turkic nomads has characterized the historiography of Islamic funerary architecture ever since Diez.[16] While it is still an open question whether the nomadic tents may have influenced the Saljuq and later tomb towers, this idea definitely does not apply to the Gonbad-e Qābus. It is an argument that blatantly ignores the historical and architectural context of this particular structure and it is an example of the tendency to draw sweeping, essentializing conclusions about Islamic architecture without regard to their actual applicability to a particular historical setting. An examination of the life of Qābus and the historical and geographical milieu of the Ziyarid dynasty shows that the building can only be understood in an eleventh-century Iranian context.

Qābus b. Voshmgir

Qābus b. Voshmgir is a figure who features prominently in the regional sources. The Ziyarid dynasty was founded by Qābus's paternal uncle, Mardāvij b. Ziyār, an adventurer from Daylam. The entire Alborz mountain range, including Daylam, was a very remote and inaccessible area which had never been militarily conquered by Arab armies during the early Islamic period; it was only with the advent of Tāherid rule in Khorasan in the ninth century that the petty dynasts of the region became increasingly tempted to involve the larger outside powers in their squabbles with one another. Mardāvij amassed an enormous amount of territory in the early 930s, which included Tabaristān, Gorgān, Rayy, Qazvin, Qom, Hamadān and Isfahan. Like other Iranian dynasts of this era, he claimed descent from pre-Islamic royalty (in this case from Arghosh Farhādān, a ruler of Gilān), and modelled his court upon that of the Sasanians.[17] He was an exceptionally ardent Iranian partisan who aimed to re-establish the Sasanian empire, but was murdered by his slaves before he could attempt to achieve this ambition. He was succeeded by his brother, Voshmgir, who married a Bavandid princess from Tabaristān.[18] Due to simultaneous Buyid advances from the south and Samanid incursions from the north east, Voshmgir lost most of the territory conquered by his brother and only regained Gorgān and the coastal strip of Tabaristān with help from a Samanid army. He was killed on a boar hunt in 967 and succeeded by his eldest son and Qābus's elder brother, Bisutun. Qābus gained the throne in 977 after Bisutun's death, he advanced his claim over that of his nephew with help from the Buyid ruler 'Adud al-Dawla and Qābus's maternal uncle, the Bavandid *espāhbod* Rostam b. Sharvin. Following Buyid orders, the caliph bestowed the title 'Shams al-Ma'ali', or 'Sun of Eminences', on Qābus; this title appears in the rhyming prose of the foundation inscription on his mausoleum, rhyming with *qasr al-'ali*. His rule was the high point of the Ziyarid dynasty both culturally and economically, and Ziyarid coins have been found in eastern Europe and Scandinavia.[19]

There was, however, a long interregnum in Qābus's reign. When Fakhr al-Dawla, the Buyid ruler of Rayy, fell out with his brothers in 980 and was attacked by them, he fled to Gorgān and was given refuge by Qābus. This enraged 'Adud al-Dawla, who attacked Gorgān, forcing both Fakhr al-Dawla and Qābus to flee. The pair found refuge in Nishāpur, which at that time was part of the Samanid realm. The Samanids, always eager to thwart the Buyids, attempted to restore Qābus to his throne but failed. Fakhr al-Dawla regained his throne after the death of his brother, Mu'ayyad al-Dawla, in 984, but he then turned on Qābus, perhaps fearing a strong rival at Gorgān. So Qābus stayed in exile in Nishāpur for a total of eighteen years and only regained his throne in 998, long after the death of Fakhr al-Dawla in 986, when his minor son Majd al-Dawla inherited the throne at Rayy and his widow, the Bavandid princess Shirin, best known by her title of 'Sayyeda', took over as queen regent.

Qābus ruled until 1012, when he was overthrown by a group of nobles who were exasperated by his harsh treatment of their class; the last straw was apparently his execution of his chamberlain, whom he had made governor of Astarābād, on charges of embezzlement. The rebels enlisted Qābus's son, Manuchehr, who feared losing his own right to the throne if he did not co-operate. Due to the participation of his son in the conspiracy, Qābus abdicated in his favour and retired to a castle at Janashk. Despite his reputation as a tyrant, this rather poignant episode shows a very human side of Qābus, with strong familial attachments. The rebels, however, still feared him and conspired to have him locked out of the castle in winter, so that he froze to death. Manuchehr did manage to retain the Ziyarid throne, but only by pledging allegiance to Mahmud of Ghazna and ruling as his vassal, a course of action his father had been strong enough to avoid. The Ziyarids ruled until the end of the eleventh century, but only as vassals of the Ghaznavids and then the Saljuqs.

In addition to his political life, the sources also comment extensively on Qābus's character. Biruni (973–1048), for example, who dedicated his *Āsār al-bāqiya* to Qābus, compares his patron's character to that of the Prophet himself and then continues:

How wonderfully has he, whose name is to be exalted and extolled, combined with the glory of his noble extraction the graces of his generous character, with his valiant soul all laudable qualities, such as piety and righteousness, carefulness in defending and observing the rites of religion, justice and equity, humility and beneficence, firmness and determination, liberality and gentleness, the talent for ruling and governing, for managing and deciding, and other qualities, which no fancy could comprehend, and no human being enumerate![20]

Biruni clearly knew how to appeal to his patron's vanity, a quality noticeably absent from his list, which reflects the panegyrics typical of literary dedications to a patron during this period. A more balanced view is given by Ebn Esfandiyār, who wrote his *Tā'rikh-e Tabaristān* two centuries after the death of Qābus for a Bavandid patron, utilizing contemporary sources such as the *Bāvandnāma* and the *Tārikh-e Yamini* of 'Utbi, the chronicler of Mahmud of Ghazna. Ebn Esfandiyār praises Qābus's positive attributes, such as his learning, piety, munificence, magnanimity, wisdom, prudence and intelligence, but also tells us that Qābus was arrogant, harsh and sometimes cruel.[21] He enumerates the fields in which Qābus particularly excelled as manly exercises (such as hunting, riding, archery and the like), philosophy, astronomy, astrology and the Arabic language,[22] all of which fulfill qualities expected of rulers not only in the Iranian world but in the *dār al-Islām* as a whole.

Qābus does seem to have been generally magnanimous in at least one respect: he seems to have given shelter to almost anyone seeking refuge at his court. In the case of Fakhr al-Dawla, this cost him dearly, yet he never turned against his erstwhile ally. Another example is Ebn Sinā (980–1037), the prominent polymath whose work in medicine, philosophy and other fields was of world importance. He left the court of the Khwārazmshāh and came to Gorgān in order to avoid being taken into the service of Mahmud of Ghazna; in taking him in, Qābus risked incurring the wrath of the formidable Ghaznavid. He also disregarded the opinion of the religious classes by sheltering the poet Divārvaz, who had been persecuted by them for staggering drunk past the shrine of the Zaydi imam Nasr-e Kabir in Amol. He seems to have particularly enjoyed the poem in Tabari which Divārvaz composed to relate his misadventures, and dubbed the poet '*Mastāmard*', or 'Drunk Man'.[23]

In one case, however, he did turn against one of his asylum seekers, Montaser, the last Samanid. Montaser had been defeated by an alliance of the Qarakhanids and Ghaznavids and taken prisoner by the latter. He escaped and sought refuge with Qābus and this was granted. He wished to regain his kingdom, but Qābus advised him that it would be impossible for him to defeat either the Qarakhanids or the Ghaznavids, and that a more realistic target would be Majd al-Dawla at Rayy. Montaser duly set out for Rayy with two of Qābus's sons, but was betrayed by members of his own entourage and hence did not have sufficient forces to carry out a siege. Montaser, also abandoned by Qābus's sons, decided to attempt to wrest Nishāpur away from Mahmud of Ghazna. When this inevitably failed, Qābus prevented the Samanid from reentering Gorgān, effectively sealing his fate. Understandably, Qābus could not have risked the ire of Mahmud on that occasion.

In addition to Ebn Sinā, Biruni and the poet Divārvaz, Qābus also patronized al-Thaʿālebi, who composed his *Yatima al-Dahr* at the Ziyarid court in Gorgān. Other poets at Qābus's court included Qomri and Sarakhsi; their panegyrics and al-Thaʿālebi's dedication echo the type of lavish praise produced by Biruni, and hence reveal little about Qābus himself. Sarakhsi composed verses in both Arabic and Persian, a skill which was common at that time and appealed to sophisticated patrons such as Qābus. While Persian was the *lingua franca* throughout the eastern Islamic world, the educated classes used Arabic with equal facility. In addition to Persian, other Iranian languages were still used in several regions, such as Sogdian in Transoxiana and Tabari in Tabaristān. Qābus's enjoyment of the poetry of Divārvaz indicates that he at least understood Tabari, even if he did not compose in it. Indeed, his correspondence with his learned contemporaries, such as the Buyid vizier Esmāʿil b. ʿAbbād and his Bavandid uncle Rostam b. Sharvin, was in Arabic.[24] The foundation inscription of his mausoleum was also in Arabic:

> In the name of God. This is the lofty castle for the Amir Shams al Maʿali, the amir son of the amir, Qābus b. Voshmgir. He ordered it built during his lifetime in the lunar year 397 and the solar year 375 [1006–7].

Due to the sophisticated rhyming prose and the careful placement of the inscription, with the phrase describing the building located directly over the doorway, Sheila Blair has suggested that he was probably responsible for the design of the inscription.[25] Both the terminology of the inscription and the use of Arabic were typical of the period; the earliest extant example of a foundation inscription in Persian was the Qarakhanid mausoleum known as Shāh Fazl, constructed between 1055 and 1060 at Sefid Boland in the Farghāna valley. However, Qābus's Iranian heritage is highlighted in the use of the Persian solar calendar dating back to Yazdgerd, the last Sasanian shah, as well as the Arabic lunar calendar.

Qābus was far more than an enlightened patron; he himself authoured a treatise on the use of the astrolabe and composed poetry in both Arabic and Persian. His surviving works include love poems in both languages, as well as a poem in which he laments the misfortune of rulers, perhaps composed in exile at Nishāpur. One of his Persian poems hints at other ways in which he passed his time in Khorasan:

> The things of this world from end to end are the goal of desire and greed,
> And I set before this heart of mine the things which I most do need,
> But a score of things I have chosen out of the world's unnumbered throng,
> That in quest of these I my soul may please and speed my life along.
> Verse, and song, and minstrelsy, and wine full-flavoured and sweet,
> Backgammon and chess, and the hunting ground, and the falcon and

cheetah fleet,
Field and ball, and audience hall, and battle and banquet rare,
Horse and arms, and a generous hand, and praise of my Lord and prayer.[26]

Qābus enumerates here the standard pastimes associated with Persian kingship, and in all likelihood he did actually engage in many of them, particularly during his years of enforced leisure in Nishāpur. His father, who was known to be an excellent rider, was killed on a boar hunt, a pastime frequently associated with the tropes of kingship. Through his poetry, Qābus appears to be keenly aware of his own position and of the long tradition of *javānmardi* associated with that position.[27] To a much greater extent than any other Persian dynast, he had first-hand knowledge of the courts of his contemporaries, through his exile in the Samanid realm, through the time he spent with Fakhr al-Dawla and his long correspondence with Esmā'il b. 'Abbād, and through his many close connections with the Bavandids. Qābus therefore knew of the New Persian literary renaissance promoted by the Samanids as well as the cultural conservatism of Tabaristān. His kingdom was positioned between those two areas geographically, just as he himself culturally participated in both.

The Bavandids and their Tomb Towers

The Bavandids had ruled in Tabaristān since the late Sasanian period and were extremely proud of their Sasanian connections. In an era when Persianate dynasties proliferated throughout the eastern Islamic world and the major regional powers, the Samanids and Buyids, were eager to claim Sasanian descent and even arrogated Sasanian titles such as *shāhanshāh,* the Bavandids stubbornly clung to the title '*espāhbod*', or military governor, which the Sasanians had given them. Given the early start of their dynasty, their claims of early intermarriage with Sasanian princesses were plausible and conferred a certain status upon them which their rivals lacked. In all aspects of their public identity, Sasanian descent was stressed as the primary element of their legitimacy: this public identity was forged through their literary and artistic patronage, their coronation rituals and dynastic foundation myths and in their architectural patronage, which consisted primarily of their funerary architecture. As I have argued elsewhere, the Bavandid tomb towers appear to be modelled on contemporary perceptions of Sasanian funerary practice in order to emphasise the Bavandid claim to Sasanian descent in the most visible way possible.[28] Although there is no archaeological evidence of actual royal Sasanian funerary practices, it is the emulation of what these practices were believed to have been which is important in the eleventh-century context. Piecing together the descriptions of royal Sasanian funerals and funerary monuments contained in contemporary literary texts such as the *Shāhnāma* and the *Qābusnāma* gives a vivid picture of how the Bavandids would have imitated the practices of their eponymous ancestors. This would have entailed embalming and wrapping the body in an expensive textile, placing it on a platform composed of an impermeable material located inside the single chamber of the tomb tower and sealing up the entrance. Such a ritual would account for a combination of features which is unique in the context of Islamic funerary architecture: high and inaccessible entrances, lack of windows, lack of interior decoration, lack of burial chambers containing bodies and bilingual foundation inscriptions in both Arabic and Pahlavi, the language of the Sasanians.[29]

The earliest of the extant Bavandid tomb towers, known as the Mil-e Rādkān, was constructed in 1016–21 as the tomb of Abu Ja'far Mohammad b. Vandarin Bāvand, who terms himself both 'Espāhbod' and 'Amir' in the inscriptions (see Fig. 8.2).

Fig. 8.2 Mil-e Rādkān

Like that at the Gonbad-e Qābus, the inscription reveals that it was built during the lifetime of the patron. The tower is not located on or near a main road (or on any trading route described by tenth-century geographers), but is instead situated on a relatively low hill in an isolated valley in the Alborz mountains. At 35 metres high, it is the highest of the Bavandid towers but is still considerably shorter than the Gonbad-e Qābus. Like the earlier building, it is a cylindrical structure composed entirely of baked brick and topped by a conical roof. It also has a single entrance, approximately one and a half metres off the ground, without any staircase to provide access. The interior chamber, which reaches all the way to the inner dome, is dark and undecorated. The foundation inscription is located over the doorway, in a now fragmentary terracotta plaque framed with a star border; there is also an inscription band below the roof with another foundation text repeated in both Arabic and Pahlavi. It is quite likely that either Mohammad b. Vandarin or his architect had seen the Gonbad-e Qābus, particularly since the inscription on the terracotta plaque over the doorway echoes both the terminology of the earlier building (referring to the building as a *qasr*) and the location of the word *qasr*. The Mil-e Rādkān differs from the Gonbad-e Qābus, however, in its usage of stucco, its band of decoration under the dome and its bilingual foundation inscription – features which it shares with the other Bavandid towers.

The Bavandid tomb tower at Lājim was constructed just a few years later, in 413 AH (1022–3), and shares the same basic features with the Mil-e Rādkān (see Fig. 8.3). It is also a double-domed conical structure composed of baked brick laid in a single bond and widely spaced with mortar, with a single interior chamber and a high entrance which originally lacked a staircase. Although the interior lacks decoration, there is now a cenotaph inside which is associated with an eighteenth-century caretaker of the building, who is now the object of local veneration. Restorations of the building in the 1950s and 1970s have shown, however, that like the Gonbad-e Qābus, there was no body buried inside.[30] The exterior has rows of small blind niches in the tympanum over the doorway and a band of blind niches immediately under the dome. The foundation inscription is contained in two bands underneath and, just as at the Mil-e Rādkān, the inscription is in Pahlavi as well as Arabic. In Arabic the building is referred to as *qobba* and *qabr*; in Pahlavi it is called a *gonbad*. The incumbent is named as Abu'l Favāris Shahriyār b. 'Abbās b. Shahriyār, who is called a great prince in the inscription but is otherwise unknown in the historical sources. This individual may have died prematurely, as the tomb tower was not constructed by him. Instead, the inscription names the patron as his mother, Chehrāzād; the builder's name, Hosayn b. 'Ali, is also given.[31] The tower is situated on top of a hill surrounded by deep ravines at the edge of the remote village of Lājim, in the central Alborz mountains; in the eleventh century, the village was probably farther away since there are remains of an earlier settlement at the opposite end of the village, approximately one kilometre from the tomb tower. Although this village was not on any trade routes, the tower is visible from some distance away.

Fig. 8.3 Tomb Tower, Lājim

The third Bavandid tower not only shares the same basic features of the other two, but is closely modelled on the nearby Lājim tower (see Fig. 8.4). It is situated on an isolated outcrop of rock and the nearest village, Resget, is just visible in the distance. Like the other two towers, it is constructed of baked brick, with a dark, windowless interior chamber entirely lacking in decoration. The entrance is approximately five feet off the ground, without any staircase to provide access. In size and profile it is very similar to the Lājim tower, although it does have more elaborate decoration in the band under the dome. Based on this decoration, the building has been dated stylistically to the early twelfth century. The foundation inscription is in both Arabic and Pahlavi, but is too badly damaged to read the date. This inscription is contained within a

Fig. 8.4 Tomb Tower, Resget

terracotta plaque over the doorway, just as at the Mil-e Rādkān. It names the incumbents as Hormozdiyār and Habusiyār, the sons of Masdarā.[32] Although these individuals are otherwise unknown in the sources, the area was still under the control of the Bavandids until the early thirteenth century. There is another inscription band in Arabic beneath the dome, with several Qur'anic verses which deal with the theme of death and hence are frequently seen on mausoleums.[33] The Arabic inscription refers to the building as a *qobba*, but despite these clear funerary allusions, restoration excavations have not revealed a body buried underneath.[34]

The Gonbad-e Qābus shares several of the features which make the Bavandid tomb towers anomalous in the history of Islamic funerary architecture, primarily the lack of a body underneath. It was constructed away from the town of Gorgān, on a mound which resembles the outcrops of rock on which the Bavandid towers are sited. It has a single, dark, undecorated chamber and although there is a window at the very top, this only lets in light at one certain time of day. It also has a single entrance high off the ground, albeit not quite as high as the Bavandid towers (the current step belongs to the early-twentieth-century restoration of the base of the building). It repeats the Arabic foundation inscription twice and lacks a translation in Pahlavi, but it does give the date of construction in both the Sasanian and Arabic calendars. The similarities in the content of the foundation inscriptions, particularly between the Gonbad-e Qābus and Mil-e Rādkān, show a definite connection between the buildings, a connection that is echoed in the life of Qābus himself.

His Bavandid connections were both familial and political: as noted earlier, his mother was a Bavandid princess; his father, Voshmgir, married her while seeking refuge at the *espāhbod*'s court. Given the reasonable Bavandid claim to Sasanian descent and the eagerness of other Persianate dynasties to assert their own claims, this would have been a coveted liaison: marriage to a Bavandid princess would unarguably confer a strong claim to Sasanian descent upon any offspring. This can be seen in their prominent position in genealogies, such as the Ziyarid genealogy given in the *Qābusnāma*.[35] Nevertheless, the name of Qābus's mother is unknown and it is somewhat difficult to discern her precise position in the Bavandid family since there are discrepancies between the histories of the region, numismatics and the inscriptions on the tomb towers. These discrepancies can be resolved, however, by accepting that several *espāhbod*s would have ruled simultaneously whilst acknowledging the overlordship of one member of the family, a type of system also practised by the Buyids, with their three separate capitals at Shiraz, Rayy and Baghdad. It was a system which naturally led to disagreements over successions and over who precisely should be regarded as the senior family member; this is also well attested in the Buyid realm.[36] With his close ties to the Bavandids, Qābus was deeply involved in such struggles amongst them, just as they were involved in the succession struggles of the Ziyarids.

As mentioned earlier, Qābus first came to power with Buyid support as well as the support of his uncle, Rostam b. Sharvin, who pushed Qābus's claim over that of his nephew, the son of his deceased brother Bisutun. Another Bavandid relative who was close to Qābus was his second cousin Shahriyār b. Darā b. Shahriyār, who willingly accompanied Qābus into exile in Nishāpur. At that time, Shahriyār's grandfather was still the *espāhbod* and head of the family. After regaining his kingdom, Qābus encouraged him to attack another Bavandid cousin, Rostam b. Marzbān, who was ruling the area of Shahriyār-kuh and is referred to as a maternal uncle of Majd al-Dawla by Ebn Esfandiyār.[37] Majd al-Dawla's mother was the Sayyeda Shirin, the wife of Fakhr al-Dawla, who had turned on Qābus after he had regained his throne in 984. A coin exists that was minted at Firim in 986 by Shahriyār on which he pledges loyalty to Fakhr al-Dawla,[38] indicating that an alliance with Shahriyār continued after the Buyid left Nishāpur; after Fakhr al-Dawla died that year, the long struggle began which pitted Qābus and Shahriyār against Shirin, her brother Rostam and her son Majd al-Dawla.

Rostam had taken over Shahriyār-kuh while Shahriyār was in exile with Qābus in Nishāpur; hence Shahriyār was re-asserting the right of his branch of the Bavandids to rule that region and head the family. The two cousins succeeded and Qābus and Shahriyār continued to expand their respective kingdoms in alliance with one another, fighting against Nasr b. Hasan b. Firuzān and Majd al-Dawla. The former was defeated and the latter had no choice but to make peace with Qābus and Shahriyār. Later, however, towards the end of Qābus's reign, Rostam attacked and defeated Shahriyār, after which the main Bavandid branch was deprived of power for several generations.[39]

Conclusion

Throughout both his reigns and his period in exile, during which he partook of the turmoil of not only Caspian politics but also the wider regional political stage, Qābus emerges as a man with strong familial loyalties who was also a shrewd manipulator. In all his political maneuvering, his greatest triumph was undoubtedly his ability to keep Mahmud of Ghazna at arm's length without becoming his vassal. He also managed not only to expand his realm to encompass Gilān, Ruyān and parts of Daylam, but also to hold firm to his capital, Gorgān, which neither his father nor his uncle had managed to do. Both Mardāvij and Voshmgir had ruled from Gorgān only briefly, whereas Qābus succeeded in making the city his own during his second reign and successfully repelled several sieges by his Caspian rivals.

Gorgān fell between Khorasan and the Caspian region politically and culturally as well as geographically, and its inhabitants participated in the artistic and intellectual trends of both areas. Qābus mirrored this, with his strong family ties to Tabaristān and his years in exile in Nishāpur. His mausoleum, however, took the form of the towers of Tabaristān, rather than the domed squares popular in Khorasan and Transoxiana. Although it is the earliest extant tomb tower, it is highly unlikely to have been the first in the series, given the accomplishment of the building.[40] But despite the early date and the exceptional nature of the building, it cannot be understood when extracted from its architectural and historical context and grouped with later buildings also deemed seminal enough to be included in the canon of Islamic architectural history. The Bavandid towers may be remote, unknown and excluded from the canon, but they are key to understanding the Ziyarid building acclaimed as a masterpiece. The Gonbad-e Qābus should be seen as an interpretation of the Bavandid type of tower with the unmistakable stamp of Qābus himself. He almost certainly designed the inscription; it is difficult to imagine that the enormous size and dramatic appearance of the building were not also due to his bidding. The inscription clearly states that it was designed during his lifetime and the grandiosity of the building accords well with what the sources tell us about Qābus. Its monumentality made it visible from a great distance, forever inscribing the memory of Qābus himself on the landscape, while its lavish use of expensive baked brick proclaimed Qābus's wealth and importance. Its more unusual features match those of the corpus of extant towers constructed by the Bavandids, a family who were not only relatives of Qābus but also closely associated with him throughout his life. Hence the Gonbad-e Qābus is an enlarged and majestic version of a Bavandid tomb tower, and alludes to the same Sasanian connection so prized by the Bavandids while simultaneously presenting Qābus as a more important regional player than his cousins. Through his Bavandid mother, Qābus had the same claim to Sasanian descent, and through his geographical proximity and close relations with his cousins, he had a clear understanding of the visual language they used to assert their claims and justify their right to rule. It was this visual language which he emulated in his own inimitable way.

Notes:

1. M.Y. Kiani, *The Islamic City of Gurgan* (Berlin: D. Reimer, 1984), 34.
2. Mohammad b. Ahmad Moqaddasi, *The Best Divisions for Knowledge of the Regions,* trans. by B.A. Collins, (Reading: Garnet, 1994), 322. Tha'ālebi also mentioned that the city was famous for black cloth: see Tha'ālebi, *The Book of Curious & Entertaining Information: The Lata'if al-Ma'arif of Tha'alibi,* trans. by C.E. Bosworth, (Edinburgh: Edinburgh University Press, 1968), 131. On the scholarly connections between Gorgān and Yemen, see Richard Bulliet, *Islam: The View from the Edge* (New York: Columbia University Press, 1994), 85.
3. Ebn Hawqal, *Configuration de la terre (Kitab Surat al-Ard),* trans. by J.H. Kramers and G. Wiet (Paris: G.P. Maisonneuve & Larose, 1964), 372.
4. Ibid.
5. Moqaddasi, 320–22.
6. For example, the Friday mosque in the Samanid capital of Bukhara (which was more of a metropolitan centre than Gorgān) was only partially composed of baked brick: see Abu Bakr Mohammad Narshakhi, *Tārikh-i Bukhārā,* ed. Modarres Ridavi (Tehran: Bonyād-i Farhang-i Iran, 1972), 35, 70, 71, 72.
7. Diez in *Survey of Persian Art,* vol. III: *The Architecture of the Islamic Period,* ed. Arthur Upham Pope (Ashiya: SOPA, 1964), 927; see also Godard in *SPA* vol. II, 970–71. Godard does not mention any Avestan associations, but does support Diez's contention that the body was in a coffin suspended from the ceiling, as detailed by Jannābi.
8. Oleg Grabar, 'The Earliest Islamic Commemorative Structures', *Ars Orientalis* 4 (1966), 7–46, 44.
9. Mohammad b. Hasan Ebn Esfandiyār, *Tā'rikh-i Tabaristān,* ed. by Abbas Iqbal (Tehran: Mohammad Ramazāni, 1941–2), 233.
10. Ernst Diez, *Churasanische Baudenkmäler* (Berlin: D. Reimer, 1918), 39–43.
11. André Godard, *SPA,* 970–74, pl. 337–8; Godard, 'Voûtes Iraniennes', *Athar-é Iran,* vol. IV (1949), 330; David Talbot Rice, *Islamic Art* (London: Thames and Hudson, 1965), 61; Antony Hutt, 'Iran' in *Architecture of the Islamic World,* ed. by George Michell (New York: Morrow, 1978), 253; Richard Ettinghausen and Oleg Grabar, *The Art and Architecture of Islam 650–1250* (New Haven and London: Yale University Press, 1987), 221–2; Robert Hillenbrand, 'Architecture', *The Arts of Persia,* ed. by Richard Ferrier (New Haven and London: Yale University Press, 1989), 81–107, 84; Robert Hillenbrand, *Islamic Architecture: Form, Function and Meaning* (Edinburgh: Edinburgh University Press, 1994), 28, 269, 276, 280, 283; Robert Hillenbrand, *Islamic Art & Architecture* (London: Thames & Hudson, 1999), 101, 105.
12. Grabar, 22; Sheila Blair, *The Monumental Inscriptions from Early Islamic Iran and Transoxiana* (Leiden: Brill, 1992), 63–5; Thomas Leisten, *Architektur für Tote* (Berlin: D. Reimer, 1998), 169–70.
13. Hutt, in Michell, 253.
14. James Dickie, 'Allah and Eternity: Mosques, Madrasas and Tombs' in Michell, 39.
15. Ettinghausen and Grabar, 221–2.
16. Ernst Diez, *Die Kunst der Islamischen Völker* (Berlin: Akademische Verlagsgesellschaft Athenaion, 1915), 73; Ernst Diez, *Persien, Islamische Baukunst in Churāsān* (Hagen: Folkwang-Verlag, 1923), 51–5; Diez in *SPA,* 926–7; Talbot Rice, 61–3; Katharina Otto-Dorn, *L'Art de l'Islam* (Paris: A. Michel, 1964), 137–40; Guitty Azarpay, 'The Islamic Tomb Tower: A Note on its Genesis and Significance'

in *Essays in Islamic Art and Architecture in Honor of Katharina Otto-Dorn,* ed. by A. Daneshvari (Malibu: Undena, 1981), 9–12; Emel Esin, 'Al Qubbah al-Turkiyya: An Essay on the Architectonic Forms of the Islamic Turkish Funerary Monument' in *Atti del Terzo Congresso di Studi Arabi e Islamici* (Naples: Istituto universitario orientale, 1967), 281–313.

17. Abu'l Hasan Mas'udi, *Moruj al-zahab,* ed. by C.A. Barbier de Maynard and A.J. Pavet de Courteille (Paris: Imprimerie impériale, 1861–77), vol. IX, 19–30. See also Vladimir Minorsky, *La Domination des Daylamites* (Paris: E. Leroux, 1932), 10, 18; Wilferd Madelung, 'The Minor Dynasties of Northern Iran' in *Cambridge History of Iran, vol. 4: From the Arab Invasion to the Saljuqs,* ed. by Richard Frye (Cambridge: Cambridge University Press, 1975), 212.

18. Although both the Ziyarids and Bavandids claimed descent from rulers who were vassals of the Sasanians, this gave them by extension a claim to Sasanian descent as well through intermarriage between the imperial family and the local rulers in the Caspian regions. See Abū Rayhān Muhammad b. Ahmad Bīrūnī, *The Chronology of Ancient Nations,* trans. by C. Edward Sachau (London: W.H. Allen, 1879), 47–8.

19. C.E. Bosworth, 'On the Chronology of the Ziyarids in Gurgan and Tabaristan', *Der Islam,* xl (1965), 25–6.

20. Biruni, 2.

21. Ebn Esfandiyār, 232.

22. Ibid., 92.

23. Ibid., 89.

24. Ibid., 92. Since Ebn Esfandiyār used a Bavandid library at Rayy, he may well have had access to this correspondence.

25. Blair, 65.

26. Edward G. Browne, *A Literary History of Persia,* vol. 1 (Cambridge: Cambridge University Press, 1928), 471.

27. *Javānmardi* is a concept encompassing all of the pastimes enumerated in Qābus's poem, as well the code of conduct and chivalry expected of the nobility.

28. Melanie Michailidis, 'In the Footsteps of the Sasanians: Funerary Architecture and Bavandid Legitimacy' in *Persian Architecture and Kingship: Displays of Power and Politics in Iran from the Achaemenids to the Pahlavis,* ed. by Sussan Babaie and Talinn Grigor, (London: I.B.Tauris, forthcoming 2012).

29. The Gonbad-e 'Ali in Abarquh, constructed in 448 AH (1056–7) for a local dynast and his wife with connections to Tabaristan, shares many of these features but is composed of rubble and mortar and lacks a translation of the foundation inscription in Pahlavi.

30. R. Soleiman, Vezārat-i Farhang (Ministry of Culture of Iran), personal communication, July 2003.

31. Blair, 89.

32. The vowelling of 'Habusiyār' and 'Masdarā' is uncertain as these are otherwise unattested Iranian names: see Blair, 208–9.

33. 21:36, 3:185 and 29:57.

34. R. Soleiman, Vezārat-i Farhang, personal communication, July 2003.

35. Kaykāvus Ebn Eskandar, *Qābusnāma* (Tehran: Amir Kabir, 1992), 5.

36. Islamic Turkish rulers later practised a similar system, although in the pre-Islamic period the Turkish division of power amongst a ruler and sub-rulers was different, with individuals changing position in an orderly fashion (albeit a confusing one, as titles changed with position) and the practice of a clear territorial division between eastern and western portions of a realm: see Richard Frye, *The Heritage of Central*

Asia: From Antiquity to the Turkish Expansion (Princeton: Markus Weiner, 1996), 206–7.

37. Ebn Esfandiyār, 228.
38. Madelung, 217; see also Blair, 89. The coin indicates a date of 376 AH (986–7), but since the date of Fakhr al-Dawla's death falls in 986, it must have been minted before then.
39. Ebn Esfandiyār, 239.
40. Diez referred to a pre-Islamic tomb tower composed of stone at Lartale; his line drawing of the building does indeed bear a strong morphological resemblance to the Bavandid towers, and he may well have found a Sasanian prototype for this genre. However, no photograph of this monument exists, and no other scholar has visited the site or mentioned it: see Diez 1923, 52.

9

Authority and Identity in the Pahlavi Books

Alan Williams
(University of Manchester)

Although certain scholars in previous symposia have mentioned aspects of the Pahlavi books, and even discussed them in some detail as did Shaul Shaked in the volume on the Sasanian period,[1] it seems to me that something has been left out so far in a series entitled *The Idea of Iran*. If one is permitted for a moment to consider the series title, there is, I think, an ambiguity. Is one to take the meaning as implying the question 'what is the Idea of Iran?' And is it to be understood as connoting something equivalent to the idea (A) of Iran (B), i.e. an (A) originated from, or located in, (B), such as the flora and fauna of Britain? Or has it another connotation, namely 'The Idea of Iran' as the (A) that is (B), as in 'the Idea of Truth', or 'the Idea of Democracy', viz. 'The Idea that is Iran'? Those who chose the title were perhaps attracted by the ambiguity of the connotations of the phrase, not to mention that such is the reputation Iran presently enjoys on the world stage that the title could more ironically have been 'The Very Idea of Iran'. More seriously, one of the great ideas of Iran derives from the fact that the name of the divinity of Iran's oldest religion, Ahura Mazda, is not a personal or mythological name but the personification of wisdom and moreover that Zarathushtra proclaimed that the correct ministration of justice in society must derive directly from this wisdom. Such wisdom is based upon a principle of choice both at the macrocosmic level of divinity and at the microcosmic level of human moral and psychological individuality, between good and evil.[2] Mary Boyce and many others have written about the influence such a doctrine had upon other religious and philosophical traditions. You may sense that we are on track for a theological, rather than a historical, chapter, but I base the theology on good sources, on the last of the great Zoroastrian books, the *Dēnkard*, and it will be for you to decide whether this idea was such a good one after all. The idea on which I focus is given its most coherent theological expression in the Pahlavi books, as it was the basis of an entire apologetic argument directed against the rival faiths of Judaism, Christianity and Islam in newly islamicized Iran: it is nevertheless also an idea that takes on ethical, philosophical, social and political dimensions. It is the idea of the integrity of goodness and the incorruptibility of true nobility. However, this has been a subject which has been obscured by a misleading theological term, namely 'dualism'. In Late Antiquity and the early medieval period Jews, Christians and Muslims fought shy of this term in their defense of their own 'monotheisms'; in Iran and India in modern times, Zoroastrians have themselves often distanced themselves from the term, believing it to have been a theological corruption wrought by overzealous priests in the Pahlavi books. In fact the term 'dualism' as a summary definition of Zoroastrian theology is misleading: it is a misunderstanding of Zoroastrian theology based upon an outsider's theological standpoint: whether Christian, Jewish, Muslim, and in modern times, western thought and Indian Vedanta. Insufficient attention has been paid to the greatest treatise on Zoroastrian theology, the *Dēnkard*. Admittedly, such texts which best develop Zoroastrian arguments for the integrity of goodness and the absolute otherness of evil are obscured by the troublesome script of Middle Persian. The *Dēnkard* has been seen as Zoroastrianism's last gasping breaths of theology, and no more; but its theological disquisition is not remote from social, historical and human life. The theological perspective of the Pahlavi books is a subject that needs re-examination, but well away from the cross-fire of *inter*-religious theological disputation – between the *behdin*s and *juddin*s of a thousand years ago, or, as is the case today, from *intra*-religious theological controversy between Irani and Parsi Zoroastrian, 'reformist', 'liberal', 'neo-conservative' and 'orthodox' Zoroastrians. Here I wish to look briefly at this central theme of the Pahlavi books from another perspective, not as a scholastic, theological position, but rather as a fundamental and characteristic conception among the ideas of Iran. This expression took its final form in Iran slightly earlier than the period we are considering today, in the ninth and tenth centuries, but the effect was to last for several centuries afterwards, and into posterity in the texts that have survived in the tradition. Iran has experienced Islamic monotheism for 1,450 years and Abrahamic monotheists everywhere, Jewish, Christian and Muslim, are acutely sensitive to 'dualism' as a heretical form of religion. They hold the unicity, omnipotence and integrity of their divinity as utterly sacred, and countenance no possibility of a second, equal, opposing principle or partner: there is none like unto Him. 'Dualism' (a term used only by the Abrahamic thinkers) is thus considered an abomination. The epistemological prejudice against dualism is so ancient and deep that it is only by an act of will that modern readers can begin to take seriously the so-called 'dualist' arguments of the writers of the Pahlavi books. It is conceived as exalting the devil to the status of divinity and of allowing a second creator: this is a hostile understanding of Zoroastrianism and was not what was intended by the writers of the Pahlavi books. (Similarly modern readers have a problem dealing with equally misleading terms such as 'polytheist', 'atheist', 'absolutist', 'pantheist' and 'monist' when variously applied to Hindus,

Buddhists and Sufis.) In fact the authors of the *Dēnkard* themselves condemned the Manichaeans as confused heretics who preached a false dualism.

The ninth and tenth-century Zoroastrian books in Pahlavi were composed by Zoroastrian priests for apologetic purposes: to consolidate and defend the religious tradition that struggled to survive under early Islamic domination. They were written in the cryptic system known as *uzvarishn,* mixing Semitic ideograms and Iranian phonetic spellings. Difficult enough as this is to read, it is compounded by the tortuous grammar of Pahlavi, particularly in the hands of the three principal writers, Manushchihr, Ādurfarnbag ī Farrokhzādān and Ādurbād ī Ēmēdān. Some of the texts, such as the *Zand-āgāhīh* or *Bundahishn,* the *Wizīdagīhā ī Zādspram,* parts of the *Dēnkard,* the *Vīdēvdād* and the Pahlavi *Yasna,* are translations with exegetical glosses of Avestan mythological and liturgical texts. The non-mythological, non-scriptural texts of the ninth and tenth-century books, excluding certain short texts and fragments, fall into several main categories, namely:

1. the description of priestly lore, and ritual practice (for example, *Shāyist nē Shāyist, Nāmagīhā ī Manushchihr*),
2. miscellanies of different religious subjects, such as the *Dādestān ī Dēnīg* and the *Pahlavi Rivāyat* accompanying the *Dādestān ī Dēnīg,*
3. apocalyptic texts such as the *Ardāy Wīrāz Nāmag, Zand ī Wahman Yasht* and *Ayādgār ī Jāmāspīg,*
4. *Handarz* or wisdom texts, such as the sixth book of the *Dēnkard* and the *Dādestān ī Mēnōg ī Khrad,*
5. The sole surviving treatise on law, the *Mādayān ī Hazār Dādestān,*
6. Theological disquisitions, such as the *Shkānd Gumānīg Wizār* and the third and fourth books of the *Dēnkard.*

Various strategies of presentation were used, according to the particular genre of each work, but in all these texts the polarity of *weh-dēnīh* (good religion) versus *ag-dēnīh* (evil religion) obtains. I first became aware of this systemic polarity in preparing an edition and translation of the *Pahlavi Rivāyat*[3] (hereafter *PRDd.*) which contains chapters on most, if not all, of the genres mentioned above. Throughout the text the author emphasizes the stark polarity of *weh-dēnīh* and *ag-dēnīh.* Though Islam is never mentioned by name in the work, the term *ag-dēnīh* clearly refers to it, and Muslims are known by the term *druwandān* 'the wicked'; *anērān* also seems to refer to Arabs, as in the phrase:

gōsht az anērān ud agdēnān wesh ku ēwbār nē pādikhshā khrīdan ud agdēn bē ka pad ēd dārē kū be mīrēd ēnyā-sh tis-iz nē abāyēd dād

It is not permitted to buy meat from non-Iranians and infidels more than once (i.e. if your life is in danger); and unless you think that otherwise *he* will die, you must not give anything at all to an infidel *(PRDd.* 14.7).

It appears that this quoted section, which is the last in chapter 14, has been appended to the previous sections which deal with the more ancient Zoroastrian problem of reconciling the eating of animals with the belief in the sacredness of the *gōspand* creation (grazing animals). Abhorrence of contact with Muslims pervades much of the text. It is expressed not only in terms of the explicit opposition *weh-dēnīh* and *ag-dēnīh*, but also in many other of the usual theological and ritual dualisms of the Zoroastrianism of the Pahlavi books. Seen theologically, the hardships imposed upon the Zoroastrian community by Muslim authorities only compounded the difficulties of a world already under attack from other forms of evil. The resolution of such problems constitutes the underlying religious imperative of *PRDd.* and is provided by two means: (1) by righteousness (purity) and (2) by eschatological hope. Both types of resolution put the evils of the day into a greater perspective, i.e. that of a cosmic struggle, and at the same time urge the strengthening of religious commitment. The practical result of righteousness in all its forms (ritual, moral, spiritual, etc.) is to protect the community from hostile, outside influence. Eschatological hope is expressed in many ways in the text, most explicitly in the long chapter 48, and most succinctly in 49.18, which announces the restoration and triumph of the good religion in Ērānshahr.

> When Pishyōtan comes, then there will be 150 men with him, and they will keep enemies away from Ērānshahr, and (he), the Lord of the Religion, will again sit on the throne; and he will make the religion supreme. And then he will go back to Kang, and everyone who is needed to restore the supremacy of the Religion will come and will restore it, and will then go back to Kang, until the time of *Frashegird* is here, the victory of Ohrmazd and the *amahraspand*s and the smiting and conquering and destroying of Ahriman and the miscreations of the demons.[4]

The religious tradition was suffering in two direct ways from the ascendancy of Islam: conversion to Islam diminished the numbers of the priesthood and laity; consequently the remaining priesthood was impoverished. In the course of sixty-five chapters, the *PRDd.* mentions many different ways in which solidarity and survival of the community can be maintained in spite of the evils of this world. Most call for restraint and moderation. One chapter, devoted to religious *handarz*, defines moderation thus:

> moderation is he who plans everything according to the (right) measure, so that more and less should not be therein, for the (right) measure is the completeness of everything, except those things in which there is no need for moderation: knowledge and love and good deed.[5]

That the hostility towards the *anērān ud ag-dēnān* is a defensive strategy for the sake of religious self-preservation, and not merely bigotry, is suggested by the testimony of another *handarz* that follows in the same chapter, which again extols love as a fundamental Zoroastrian virtue:

> love for people is he for whom the benefit and well-being of all good men is just as necessary as his own; that which does not seem good for himself he does not do to anyone else. Benevolence is he who considers the faults and virtues of other people only after he strives to correct his own faults; as regards good men he tells them of the manifest good qualities and the faults which they have, then not aggressively but lovingly for the sake of correcting them.[6]

It is in the theologically weightier disquisitions of the third book of the *Dēnkard* that one finds fuller explanation of the nature of what ancient and modern 'outsiders' have termed as 'dualism'.

The *Dēnkard* is a defence of Zoroastrianism in nine books. Of the *Dēnkard* Books III to V are devoted to rational apologetics, Book VI to moral wisdom, and Books VII to IX to exegetical theology. As Philippe Gignoux has said,

> the work was the product of a Persian milieu already largely islamicized and was thus intended both as a reply to Muslim attacks upon dualism and as a compendium of what could be saved of the scriptures. The main task at such a late date was to produce an encyclopaedia of the religious sciences as known in the 9th-10th centuries. The *Dēnkard* is not, however, a systematic treatment; it is, rather, a compilation of preserved materials, no doubt carried out under the direction of an official master. Authors are said to have had information from the 'ancient sages'; the *pōryōtkēshān*, clearly of the Sasanian period.[7]

Book III is much the longest book, comprising almost half the whole work, in more than 400 chapters, some of them very short, of varied content and without any overall plan.[8] What lends it at least some semblance of unity is the polemic against the 'bad religions', whose practitioners (*kēshdārān*) are clearly identified when they are Manicheans or Jews but not, on account of understandable precaution, when they are Muslims. It is noteworthy that when Christian doctrine of the Trinity is rejected as absurd, Christians are not named (ch. 40). Almost every chapter begins with the phrase 'From the exposition of the good religion' (*az nigēz ī weh dēn*). As Gignoux has said, although Book III does not contain a systematic description of the revelation, thematically it is loosely arranged in relation to a tiered structure of cosmic, social and individual psychological order. Thus the development, through argumentation, of the theme of cosmic dualism in a rational and philosophical manner and the explanation of the situation of mankind in the world of 'mixture' (*gumēzishn*) corresponds to the social level of reality in the complementarity of religion and kingship. Thirdly, on the level of the individual, it includes an analysis of the virtues and vices and the final destiny of the soul.[9] From the fifty chapters dealing with the refutation of false doctrines, three Islamic principles are most disputed:

1. the notion of the 'seal of prophecy' claimed by Muhammad,
2. the debate over idolatry (veneration of the stars as sacred entities being no more idolatrous in the eyes of a Mazdean than the Quranic claim that God had ordered the angels to adore Adam), and
3. belief in an eternal hell, which contradicts the Mazdean belief in divine mercy and the separation of the principles of good and evil.

The Italian historian and comparative religionist, Ugo Bianchi attempted in several works to define different types of religious dualism, not solely in the religions of antiquity with their written scriptures, but also in those that have come to light through ethnographic study, from Californian native American societies to the Maui of Polynesia.[10] Bianchi expounded a brief taxonomy of dualism, as it is found across the world:

> In our terminology dualism means the doctrine of the two principles. More precisely articulated; dualistic are all those religions, systems, conceptions of life which admit the dichotomy of the principles which, co-eternal or not, cause the existence of that which does [exist] or seems to exist in the world.[11]

Bianchi applies a categorization according to which, he says, all dualistic positions, whether systematic, mythological or otherwise, are bound to give an answer to each of these three alternatives. The categorization depends on answers to three questions.

Question 1:

Is it a) radical dualism or b) softened dualism?

He defines radical dualism as the admission of two principles from metaphysical beginnings; examples of radical dualism, he says, are Catharism, Manichaeism, Orphism, Platonism, Empedocles, Heraclitus and Plato, and, of course, Zoroastrianism. By contrast, softened dualism exhibits only one principle in the beginning, while a second principle – somehow deriving from the first – acts in the coming into existence of the world or of constituent parts of the world, for example, matter, or body, or the inferior soul deriving from an inferior demiurge: for example, as in Bogomilism, Plato's *Timaeus* and some Cathar trends.

Question 2:

Is it c) dialectical dualism or d) eschatological dualism?

Definitions:

c) Dialectical dualism admits two principles whose relation is productive and eternally irreducible, although one of them is often conceived as 'good' and the other as 'evil' in the ethical or metaphysical sense of the word. Again the philosophy of Plato, Heraclitus and Empedocles saw dualism in this way, as did Orphism and Theosophy, but not Zoroastrianism.

d) Eschatological dualism admits that the evil is to be evacuated at the end of history, as in Bogomilism, Catharism, Gnosticism Manichaeism and Zoroastrianism.

Question 3:

Is it e) anti-cosmic dualism or f) pro-cosmic dualism?

Definitions:

e) Anti-cosmic dualism contends that the evil comes from inside the world, from a substance essentially negative, or illusory, intrinsic to this world, such as matter or body, or the inferior soul, as in Manichaeism, Catharism, Orphism, Bogomilism, Gnosticism and Hindu dualist systems.

f) Pro-cosmic dualism contends that the creation is good, and evil comes from outside into it. Zoroastrianism is the only form of this type of dualism.

Thus, Zoroastrianism emerges in Bianchi's taxonomy as a unique form of dualism: it is the only religious tradition to be characterized by radical, eschatological, pro-cosmic dualism (a,d,f). He found that the first two alternatives, radical or softened, are the least important, and that from the metaphysical point of view the second pair of alternatives is the most relevant, i.e. whether the dualism is dialectical or eschatological. However, he notes that

the most salient in relation to the conception and the practice of life is the third [pair of oppositions], that between pro-cosmic and anti-cosmic dualism. Here… the position of Zoroastrianism between all the possible forms of dualism is the most specific one…[12]

In the past theologians and historians of religions not only confused Zoroastrian dualism with the above anti-cosmic forms, they also understood it as a form of ditheism, i.e. two principal, competing divinities: this is a doctrine refuted by the Zoroastrian authors of the Pahlavi books. Ohrmazd (Ahura Mazda) is opposed not by a rival divine *being*, but rather by Ahriman, a malevolent *non-being*, whose nature is the antithesis of existence, yet who is present in the material universe, having invaded it out of lust for the existence of Ohrmazd's creation, and on which he now feeds parasitically. In one *handarz* of *Dēnkard* VI it is put bluntly: *ahreman hamē nē būd ud nē bawēd*, 'Ahriman never existed and does not exist'.[13] Another explains Ahreman's parasitic presence as entirely dependent on human complicity in allowing him a place in the world:

It is possible to put Ahriman out of the world in this manner: every person, for his own part, must chase him out of his body, for the dwelling of

Ahriman in the world is in the body of humans. When he has no dwelling in human bodies he is annihilated from the whole world; for in this world so long as there is a dwelling for a small demon in just one single person, then Ahriman is in the world.[14]

This radical, eschatological, pro-cosmic dualism is expressed consistently in a long line of tradition from antiquity to early, pre-colonial modernity.[15] The language of the most important religious texts is very precisely worded to specify the theological principles and imperatives of this theological understanding. In *Dēnkard* III all propositions, and their constituent terms, are juxtaposed with their conceptual opposites; every proposition is examined in terms of a counter-proposition, which is objectified just as black is opposed to white.[16] A proposition is formed as the rational, correct formulation of the truth: the contradictory term is nothing more than a lie. The structuring of Zoroastrian thought is amplified in liturgical and personal ritual practice of strict purity codes, which include all of life from birth to beyond death: there is seldom a neutral area between what is coded as 'good / true' and 'evil / false': for their doubt and hesitancy would be entertained. I have written several articles about the structure of Zoroastrian purity codes as reflecting a cosmic and social ordering of time and space.[17] The priestly authors struggled to find resolutions to the dilemmas posed by the contingencies of the physical and social world, which the hostile spirit Ahriman had invaded. Muslims in particular are described in epithets of Ahriman himself, as *druwand* 'wicked', *dēw* 'devilish', opponents of the 'good religion'; yet because they were in positions of power, they could never be named, only cursed anonymously in these terms. All of the ninth-century Pahlavi books, and even the Persian Zoroastrian books that followed them,[18] are written in this lexicon and register of polarization. Pahlavi texts have a spatial and dynamic metaphorical scheme that is strongly characteristic of the thought they express.[19] Many types of nominalization of abstract notions into moral, spiritual and other religious reifications are based upon a spatial, polar opposition between here / there; up / down; high / low; inner / outer etc. This is, of course, not unique to Zoroastrian thought,[20] but it is the type and intensity of the polarization that is so characteristic. The religious system posits the invisible 'mental' (i.e. spiritual)[21] existence of good spiritual agencies that are characterized as being spatially, as well as conceptually, opposed to their counterpart reifications. This is, I suggest in a bold generalization, a profoundly different way of writing from that, in general, of mainstream writers in Jewish, Christian and Islamic religious discourse. Generally speaking, in both Biblical and Quranic discourse, the omnipotent divine being seems most often to be theologically central: the focus of the discourse is the will and speech of God in relation to human moral and actual response. This interaction and complex relationship between God and 'Man', may even be said to dominate the discourse of the Abrahamic religions. This is expressed by setting greatest emphasis on the *verbal*, i.e. dynamic and interactive, components of language, as distinct from emphasis in Zoroastrian texts on the substantive, nominalized forms that are so typical of their discourse. Sometimes in the Abrahamic traditions there *is* an emphasis on reification of abstractions (an obvious example is the Muslim names of God and named angelic presences), but both their existence and independence as entities are limited by the strictly monotheistic cast of the respective theologies. Zoroastrian theology has few such constraints, if any, and hence we have the pantheon of autonomous divine *amahraspand*s 'blessed immortals' and *yazad*s 'worshipful ones' who collaborate with their creator Ohrmazd and who are opposed by an equivalent pandemonium of evil spirits.

Just as the sacred liturgy and its precincts must be kept in a state of high purity, so the words used in the religious texts had to remain pure of all that was deemed to be foreign. There was a special demonic (*daēvic*) vocabulary comprising nouns and even verbs, which was only ever used of demons and their wicked cohorts of the sinful demon-worshippers. There was even an inverted orthography used for the name of the arch-demon Ahriman, which was literally a graphic attempt to keep the language of religious utterance as pure as possible from the pollution of evil. The priests, as guardians of the religion, seem to have availed themselves of every device to keep separate notions of the good and pure from evil in the present age of the *gumēzishn* 'mixture' of good and evil in this world. Other, intrusive philosophies and religions, whether they be Christian, Jewish, Muslim, Buddhist, Manichaean or other 'false doctrines', all have in common the fact that they confuse and contradict the truths revealed in the Avesta and Zand: they distort Zoroastrian epistemology. The form of language in the Pahlavi books is an exercise in meticulous speech: verbal moderation and observance of the rule of purity in words. The practitioner of bad *zand* ('interpretation, exegesis') is with good reason called a *zandīk*, a heretic.[22]

Dēnkard III established the defence of Zoroastrian theology and attacked Jewish, Christian and particularly Islamic theologies as misconceived and destructive of the truth. The underlying argument is arranged around two central foci, the first negative, the second positive:

a) an elaboration of the rational arguments of Zoroastrian dualism and correction of errors made by Judaism, Christianity and Islam and

b) an explanation of the cosmogony and anthropology of Zoroastrian lore, which is intended to integrate the current understanding of physical nature into the dualistic metaphysics of the religious tradition.

In spite of the writer's insistence on the traditional nature of this exposition from the ancient sages,[23] passages in *Dēnkard* III appear to be a vigorous rearguard action and response to attacks on specific Zoroastrian doctrines by Muslim clerics and theologians. Muslims were not mentioned by name for fear of reprisal and punishment under Islamic law. They and those of other faiths are referred to as *kēshdārān* 'religious teachers'; but this is not nearly so polite as it sounds: the *kēshdārān* are those who hold, or profess *kēsh,* derived from a much older Avestan word,[24] which occurs as early as *Yasna* 49 in the *Gāthās* to mean the false profession of faith, as in 49.3: 'however it has been fated for this world that the truth is to be saved for its good preference, that deceit is to be destroyed for its false profession'.[25] The *kēshdārān* are members of other religions (*jud dēnān*). Again, 'other religions' does not quite translate *jud dēnān* because *jud* means other in the sense of 'anti-', so *jud-ristag* (*ristag* = 'sect') does not mean just 'another sect', but rather 'heretical, schismatic'. The foundation upon which everything is said to rest throughout *Dēnkard* III is the principle of the 'good religion' revealed to Zarathushtra and transmitted through the ages by the *pōryōtkēshān.* Central to the philosophy of the *Dēnkard,* is the unity of three notions prized as quintessentially Zoroastrian: 'the Good Religion', 'right measure', i.e. the mean between excess and deficiency, and 'innate wisdom'.[26]

Paradoxically, in view of the closed nature of the Pahlavi language to outsiders, the discussions of the *Dēnkard* seem to be addressed to the circumspectly named *kēshdārān* (false) religious teachers of other faiths. They are 'interlocutors' of the text. Islamic doctrines are the most energetically disputed of all subjects, without any direct reference to the name of either Islam or of Muslims, for certain of these were felt to be not just offensive to Zoroastrian sensibilities but illogical, impossible (because self-contradictory) and devilish (in their power to corrupt). The writer does not restrict himself to attacking these thinly disguised doctrines of the Islamic faith. There is a deeper cause, which implicates not just the Christian faith but also, and fundamentally, Judaism as culpable. Ādurbād, the writer, is no respecter of the Jewish prophets. He is extremely rude about them, including Abraham and Moses, pillars of the tradition, because they are said to have inherited the teachings of a demon, Dahāg. The author also attacks the doctrine that Muhammad is the last of the prophets. The *Dēnkard* objects that in the very terms of the Muslim doctrine of prophecy, the last of the prophets would announce and inaugurate an age of immortality and justice. But such is not the case, since Islam has inaugurated a regime of conquests and violence. The main targets for the *Dēnkard*'s attack are the Islamic doctrines of divine omniscience and omnipotence in connection with human sin and their chastisement of the fires of hell. On this subject the argument of the *Dēnkard* tends to simplify and vulgarize the logic of the theology under attack, along the following lines: if man must suffer eternal hell for the sake of his conduct, which is within the foreknowledge of God, then God is effectively the cause of what has led man to his downfall, if God is, as Zoroastrians understood Muslim belief, the author of the evil desire (*varan*) as much as of its contrary, wisdom. The alleged illogicality of the Muslim belief is that the ruin of men seems to have been brought about by the divine will itself. As Ādurbād sees it, in Islam God seems to allow evil to exist and thereby he participates in it; this is incompatible with the Zoroastrian understanding of the supreme creator-divinity. Islam is therefore referred to as an 'evil religion', as distinct from 'the good religion' of Zoroastrianism.

Several chapters of the *Dēnkard* explain that the spiritual world is not comprised of beings and forces that are *mixed* good and evil: the spiritual good is purely good, and evil is not mixed into it. This is most true of Ohrmazd and it is a fundamental mistake to teach that he is mixed up in suffering and evil, as much as it would be for a Muslim to teach that Allāh belongs to a pantheon of many divinities. In this sense what the 'false teachers' call dualism is actually the Zoroastrian insistence on the integrity of divine goodness as absolutely separate from evil: on this depends the integrity of the good society and the good individual. Wisdom is innate in human beings but attains its fullness in the Wise Lord Ohrmazd. For Zoroastrians, there is little of wisdom in the Jewish, Christian and Islamic conception of God, as their God appears to be a torturer lacking the most elementary mercy, which is itself well established in the human experience of fatherhood and motherhood of children. The Abrahamic God appears to punish those who would not know how to act otherwise, and is seen by the *Dēnkard* tradition as cruel, unjust and inhumane. The *Dēnkard* does not refrain from finding such a doctrine guilty of making God the supreme and eminent cause of evil; such a god cannot be God for, in the Zoroastrian view, he lacks all the very attributes which are of the order of good and which define God: it better describes that which is in Zoroastrianism deemed to be the antagonist of God, Ahriman. The author of the *Dēnkard* finds no similarity or common ground between the Zoroastrian and the Abrahamic views of God, most obviously in the Zoroastrian doctrine of dualism. Theological dualism has been mistakenly interpreted as a great theological stumbling block by outsiders to the Zoroastrian religion. In the *Dēnkard* it is handled with utmost confidence and adroitness. Ignorance of the radical eschatological pro-cosmic dualism of the two principles of good and evil is explained as arising from too sensual an understanding of things. A purely sensual appreciation of reality is incapable of comprehending the Zoroastrian doctrine of first principles, which can only be clearly perceived by one who is able to see beyond appearances, through innate wisdom (*asn khrad*). This supreme intellectual human faculty is damaged and eventually destroyed by a surfeit of sensuality and by other vices:

> That it is the will of the creator Ohrmazd for mankind to know him is thus manifest in that all men share in the ability to know the creator and that in the religion to know the creator is the first and most excellent commandment. And the will of the majority of men is not only to know the creator but is drawn to know those other things which it does not know. As a result of the destruction of these two capacities, by the fact that man is defiled by lust and desire and heresy and laziness and negligence and other

demons, the innate wisdom which preserves the capacity to know God is harmed, and thereby the energy of mankind's innate wisdom to learn. And the Creator of innate wisdom has prescribed the energy for learning for mankind. The innate wisdom and energy for learning should not be harmed and destroyed by desire and other vices. And the false teachers whose doctrine is that it is God who has put lust, and the other vices that suppress and destroy the capacity of innate wisdom to learn with energy, into mankind, and who has put ignorance and the need to commit sin, their god is a maleficent God, which means that he prevents mankind's knowledge of God and the practice of virtue and wills mankind's ignorance and sinfulness.[27]

Wisdom (*khrad*) and lust (*āz*, also translated as 'sensuality' 'and 'concupiscence') are opposites in the spiritual psychology of the *Dēnkard*, just as the blessed immortals (*amahraspand*s) and demons (*dēw*s) are opposed in the cosmology of the religion. Through the notion of 'innate wisdom', the *Dēnkard* explains the continuity between individual moral, spiritual action and religious cosmology, depicting the benevolent and malevolent spiritual entities as participating in an eschatological drama which is both individual and cosmic in scale:

> the innate intellect is at once the greatest and the most sure messenger from the creator to the creatures of the visible world. It is by it that men know the creator, see God as God, demons as demons.[28]

Excess of lust in the minds of those of false religions absolutely prevents their knowledge and understanding of God, because it makes them incapable of differentiating good from evil; all the vices of this world are instruments of the opposite of wisdom, supremely in the hostile spirit Angra Mainyu/Ahriman. Most importantly, *Dēnkard* III repeatedly emphasises the connections between the agencies of the invisible spiritual world, the intermediate realm of society and community, the psychological realm of our human nature and the external visible world of physical creatures. At all levels of reality, therefore, the same struggle between order and chaos takes place, and always Ohrmazd, the personification of wisdom, is seen as the source of all spiritual, moral and material good in the world.

This is perhaps the greatest idea that comes out of the third book of the *Dēnkard*.

Notes:

1. Shaul Shaked, 'Religion in the Late Sasanian Period: Eran, Aneran, and Other Religious Designations' in *The Sasanian Era*, The Idea of Iran, vol. 3, ed. by Vesta Sarkhosh Curtis and Sarah Stewart (London: I.B.Tauris, 2008), 103–17.
2. For example, *Yasna* 30.1–6, see S. Insler, *The Gāthās of Zarathustra* (Leiden: E.J.Brill, 1975), 33.
3. A.V. Williams, *The Pahlavi Rivāyat Accompanying the Dādestān ī Dēnīg* (Copenhagen: Royal Danish Academy of Sciences and Letters, 1990).
4. Edited and translated by Alan Williams, see Williams, text vol. 1, 193, translation vol. 2, 89.
5. *PRDd.* 62.18, see Williams, text vol. 1, 225, translation vol. 2, 108.
6. *PRDd.* 62.25, see Williams, text vol. 1, 227, translation vol. 2, 109.
7. P. Gignoux, 'Dēnkard', *EncIr.*
8. See the chapter titles in Pahlavi transcription in Jean de Menasce, *Une Encyclopédie Mazdéenne Le Dēnkart* (Paris: Presses Universitaires de France, 1958), 82–116 and in French translation in the same scholar's *Le troisième livre du Dēnkart* (Paris: Librairie C. Klincksieck, 1973), 443–65.
9. Gignoux *Dēnkard*.
10. For example, Ugo Bianchi, 'The Category of Dualism in the Historical Phenomenology of Religion' *Temenos*, 16 (1980), 10–25.
11. Bianchi, 15.
12. Bianchi, 16f.
13. *Dēnkard* VI.278 edited and translated in S. Shaked, *The Wisdom of the Sasanian Sages (Dēnkard VI) by Āturpāt ī Ēmētān* (Boulder, CO: Westview 1979), 108.
14. *Dēnkard* VI.264, see Shaked, 103; my translation.
15. Mary Boyce wrote many books in which she argued for the continuity of the tradition of Zarathushtra's pro-cosmic, ethical dualism which is so clearly distinguished from, and yet misunderstood by, the monotheisms of Judaism, Christianity and Islam. See, for example, her *Zoroastrianism: Its Antiquity and Constant Vigour*, Columbia Lectures on Iranian Studies, 7 (Costa Mesa California and New York: Mazda Publishers / Bibliotheca Persica, 1992).
16. French translation by J. de Menasce O.P., *Le troisième livre du Dēnkart*.
17. See A.V. Williams, 'The Body and the Boundaries of Zoroastrian Spirituality', *Religion* 19 (1989), 227–39; A.V. Williams 'Zoroastrianism and the Body' in *Religion and the Body*, ed. by S. Coakley (Cambridge, England: Cambridge University Press, 1997), 155–66; A.V. Williams, 'Zoroastrian and Jewish Purity Laws: Reflections on the Viability of Sociological Interpretation' in *Irano-Judaica III,* ed. by S. Shaked and A. Netzer (Jerusalem: Ben-Zvi Institute, 1994), 72–89; 'Purity, Pollution and the Body' in *The Blackwell Companion to the Study of Zoroastrianism*, ed. by Michael Stausberg and Yuhan S.-D. Vevaina (London: Blackwell, 2012 forthcoming).
18. For example, *Sad Dar Nasr, Sad Dar Bondahesh* and the *Revayats,* down to the late sixteenth-century Persian poem *Qesse-ye Sanjan.*
19. For a more detailed discussion of this and what follows see my article 'Lexicography and Zoroastrian Meanings in the Pahlavi Books' in *Middle Iranian Lexicography* eds by Carlo G. Cereti and Mauro Maggi, Serie Orientale Roma XCVIII, Orientalia Romana 8 (Roma: Istituto Italiano Per L'Africa E L'Oriente, 2005), 387–98.

20. See, for example, the work of George Lakoff on metaphor, particularly George Lakoff and Mark Johnson, *Metaphors We Live By* (Chicago: University of Chicago Press, 1980).
21. Pahlavi *mēnōg*.
22. Heinrich Schaeder, *Iranische Beiträge* I, *Schriften der Königsberger Gelehrten Gesellschaft*, 6 (5), (Halle 1930), 274 f.
23. Pahlavi *pōryōtkēshān*.
24. *tkaēsha*.
25. Avestan *atcā ahmāi varənāi...nidātəm/ ashəm sūidyāi tkaēshāi rashayenhē drukhshi*.
26. Pahlavi *weh dēn, paymān, asn khrad*.
27. *Dēnkard* III, ch. 294.
28. *Dēnkard* III, ch. 77.

10

The Idea of Iran in the Buyid Dominions

Roy Parviz Mottahedeh
(Harvard University)

At the beginning of the tenth century CE fierce spear-carrying warriors from the Caspian provinces, that great reservoir of Iranian identity, began to establish dynasties on the Iranian plateau.[1] The most successful of these warriors were the Buyids who came from the region of Daylam, a name that, by extension, came to be used for most of the southern Caspian region. It is important to remember that, according to the legends of Tabarestān, the sons of Qāren, a great Sasanian family, ruled much of this area from the time of their appointment as governors in the reign of Chosroes I, or Khosraw Ānushiravān. Ebn Esfandiyār gives some members of the Qarenid dynasty the title *pādeshāh*, which they may well have assumed after the Muslim conquest of the Iranian plateau.[2]

From the seventh to the ninth century the Muslim conquest of the Caspian provinces was never complete and, in most cases, temporary. Right through the ninth century Qazvin was considered a garrison city that faced the dangerous Daylamis.[3] The conversion of the province to Islam may have happened at the hands of Zaydi imams who ruled in the ninth century. In any case, the history of the local dynasties of the Caspian provinces such as the Bavandids, the Badospanids and their respective titles would be the work of another article. Here I discuss the Daylami Buyids, who controlled Rayy, Isfahan, Shiraz, Baghdad and Basra.

The Buyids are seen as having revived the Iranian tradition of kingship, an interpretation that is partly true. Azod al-Dawla revived the ancient Persian title of *shāhanshāh*, which was written on his coins and used in many other contexts.[4] In conscious imitation of the Sasanian monarchs he founded a city in Fars named 'Kard-e Fannā Khosraw', Fannā Khosraw being his given name.[5] According to Biruni he revived the Persian festivals of Sadah and Mehregān.[6]

Azod al-Dawla's most moving tributes to the Iranian past are his inscriptions at Persepolis inscribed over the doorway of the Palace of Darius. The longer of his two Arabic inscriptions reads:

In the name of God: The illustrious amir, Azod al-Dawla Fannā Khosra, son
of al-Hasan, was present here in the year 344 on his victorious return from
the conquest of Isfahān, the capture of Ibn Mākān, and the defeat of the
army of Hurāsān. He ordered that there be brought before him one who read
the inscriptions on these ruins.[7]

A second short inscription, engraved at the same time as the first, names the
mubad who read the writing on the ruins for Azod al-Dawla as Mārasfand of
Kāzerun, a known Zoroastrian scholar of the time. These inscriptions are placed
next to the inscription written for the infant Shāpur II who was brought on a
visit to Persepolis in 311 CE. In his inscription Shāpur wrote that: 'He prayed
for the one who had this building constructed'.[8] The Buyids claimed royal
Iranian lineage.[9] That Azod al-Dawla and later his son Baha' al-Dawla placed
their inscriptions next to that of one of the great Sasanian kings is totally fitting.

The third Buyid inscription, written for Bahā' al-Dawla, is significant in
that it explicitly mentions the Iranian title 'king of kings' in its Sasanian form,
shāhānshāh, but only after it has given the Arabic equivalent, *malek al-moluk*.
Bahā' al-Dawla, moreover, seems to have been equally interested in giving the
multiple Arabic titles granted him by the caliph, *diyā' al-milla* and *ghiyāth al-
umma*, which are repeated twice in the inscription. The inscription is dated to
392 AH (1001–2 CE).[10]

Yet Azod al-Dawla also displayed the limitation of the Buyids in their self-
Iranization. He commissioned a would-be definitive Arabic grammar, the
famous *al-Edeh al-'azodi*, so named by the author Abu Shojā' al-Fāresi, as a
tribute to the ruler. Abu Shojā' al-Fāresi also composed a work on grammatical
questions asked of him while at the Buyid court in Shiraz called, amusingly, *Al-
Masā'el al-shirāziyāt*. One manuscript of this work introduces the book by
quoting Abu Shojā' al-Fāresi as saying, 'I have written it for our master, the
glorious king Azod al-Dawla, may God prolong his reign and perpetuate his
rule and make his royal sovereignty firm'.[11] The very distinguished
grammarian Ebn al-Jenni is said by Yāqut to have written a fifty-page book
entitled *Al-Bushrā wa 'l-zafar* as a commentary on a single (in my view, rather
mediocre) verse of Arabic poetry by his patron Azod al-Dawla.[12] As far as I
know, this mighty ruler never showed any interest in New Persian.

Richard Frye has argued persuasively that western Iran under the Buyids
was still dominated by the Zoroastrian clergy who specialized in Avestan and
Pahlavi texts and therefore had little interest in using New Persian.[13] This
estimate seems generally correct for south-western Iran. In his late tenth-
century geography Ebn Hawqal writes:

They speak three languages. [First, there is] Farsi, which they all understand
and speak to each other. However, they use expressions that differ, without
making their speech incomprehensible to the majority of the people. There
is, moreover, the language in which the works of the Persians as well as
their annals, including the correspondence of Zoroastrians among each other

is composed: this is Pahlavi, which needs to be explained to be accessible to Persians. [Finally,] there is Arabic, which is used in all documents of state and ministries as well as for people in general.[14]

It should be noted that the Buyids of Iraq and their viziers were great patrons of literature and learning in Arabic. Al-Muhallabi, the vizier at the Buyid court in Baghdad for decades before his death in 352 AH (963 CE) was surrounded by a brilliant circle of poets and literary scholars including Ebn al-Hajjāj, Ebrāhim al-Sābi and Abu al-Farāj al-Esfahāni, the author of the *Ketāb al-aghāni*.

The Buyid court at Rayy was dominated for a long time by the celebrated vizier Sāheb b. Abbād, who is said to have preferred Arabic to his native Persian and who, as far as I know, wrote only in Arabic. Ebn Abbād certainly accepted panegyrics directed to him in New Persian. Mohammad Awfi, an admittedly later source, as he wrote in the early seventh/thirteenth century, mentions Mansur-e Ali al-Mantiqi al-Rāzi as a Persian poet who praised Ebn Abbād, but almost all of the surviving poetry about this vizier is in Arabic.[15] Ebn Abbād even supported claims to the superiority of Arabic literary culture as against the *sh'ubiya* movement, which emphasized the equality of all cultures embraced by Muslims.[16]

Buyid courts in south-western Iran both co-operated and competed to give similar patronage to Arabic letters. The well-known story of the enthusiastic reception of Mutanabbi, the greatest of the medieval Arabic poets, at the court of Azod al-Dawla in Shiraz is one striking example of Buyid patronage of Arabic literature in western Iran.[17] All the preceding, and much more, is to say that although the Buyids had a sentimental attachment to the Iranian past and, in particular, to an Iranian tradition of kingship, they were not attracted to the New Persian learning of eastern Iran.

Now I will discuss briefly a largely contemporaneous phenomenon, by no means confined to the Buyid kingdoms, namely, the revival of interest in the concept of 'Irānshahr'. The idea of Irānshahr is present in the works of geographers writing in Arabic from the beginning of that discipline. Most of these geographers happened to be Iranian. Estakhri, from the province of Fars as his name implies, was a subject of the Buyids during the late fourth century AH (late tenth century CE) for at least some of his lifetime. He writes:

> The best cultivated (*ma'mur*), fairest and most fertile part of the world, and the most established in its political life is the kingdom of Irānshahr...[18]

Irānshahr at that time was understood to include southern Iraq, called Babylon (Bābel) in these sources, and it is tempting to see the union under the Buyids of western Iran with southern Iraq as an encouragement to this ancient geographical unit.

Somewhat unexpected is the exaggerated version of the claim as to the paradisiacal character of Irānshahr combined with distasteful racism found in the famous *Kitāb al-bad' wa'l-ta'rikh* by al-Motahhar b. Taher al-Maqdisi, a Samanid official writing around 355 AH (966 CE):

> They say the most temperate and delicious clime of the world is Irānshahr, the clime of Bābel, between the river Balkh up to the Euphrates longitudinally and between the Caspian down to the Persian Ocean and Yemen then to Makrān and Kābol and Tokharestān and the confines of Azerbayjān. It is the choicest part of the earth, the *omphalos*, because of the balanced nature of the colours of its people and the proportions of their bodies and the soundness of their intellect. They are free of the 'ruddiness' of the Romans and the 'harshness' of the Turks and the 'unseemliness' of the Chinese and the 'short stature' of the Gog and Magog and the 'blackness' of the Ethiopians and the 'stupidity' of the Zanj and therefore it is called Irān, meaning the 'heart of lands', since *irān* meant 'heart' in ancient Babylonian. [Iran is the land] of the wise and the learned and the home of generosity, mercy, subtle distinguishing, and apprehension [as well as] every praiseworthy characteristic the absence of which distinguishes [other] people on earth... acquaintance with these lands is sufficient for you so that anyone who visits from elsewhere must feel in his soul [a wish] to return there, their own lands not being like that at all. But God knows best.[19]

An extremely expansive definition of Irānshahr is offered by the mid-tenth-century author Abu Mansur Mahmud b. Abd al-Razzāq al-Tusi, who, according to the great Iranian scholar Mohammad Qazvini, wrote one of the oldest passages in New Persian prose that survives. In his introduction to a lost *Shāhnāma* Tusi says that Irānshahr 'extends from the Oxus River to the Nile'.[20] Incidentally, his Islamic warrant for transmitting knowledge of the ancient Iranians is a famous *hadith* considered to be the warrant for the Esrā'iliyāt. Tusi writes:

> Those who are the enemies of knowledge consider these stories of the ancient Persians unseemly, but in this world amazement finds abundant cause. As the Apostle of God said: 'Transmit accounts from the Israelites without hesitation'. [Tusi then translates this saying into Persian as]: 'Everything you hear from the Israelites, listen to all of it, for all of it actually happened and is not a lie.'[21]

We should remember that a large number of writers of this period considered the Persians to be descendants of Isaac or Ishaq.[22]

It is not surprising that the most perceptive definition of Irānshahr comes from the nearly incomparable Abu Rayhān Biruni, who is thought to have died in 442 AH (1050 CE). In the *Tahdid nehāyāt al-amāken* he writes:

> First, I say that for political reasons and for fixing the demarcation lines between kingdoms, the inhabited world was partitioned into seven circular parts, like the six circles which encircle (tangentially) a seventh circle, when

all circles are equal. The reason for this division is that the great kings were natives of Irānshahr which consists of 'Erāq, Fārs, Jebāl, and Khorāsān... This partition has nothing to do with natural climatic conditions, nor with astronomical phenomena. It is made according to kingdoms which differ from one another for various reasons – different features of their peoples and different codes of morality and customs.[23]

It is important at this point to consider the kind of Persian spoken in the Buyid kingdoms of western Iran. There are a number of examples of Persian prose and poetry translated into Arabic. We have an example of the great Arabic prose stylist from Hamadan, Badi ' al-Zaman, spontaneously translating Persian verses into Arabic in a Buyid court setting.[24] Furthermore, we know from Māfarrokhi's Arabic *History of Isfahan*, of which we have the medieval Persian translation, that an Isfahani insulted Rokn al-Dawla 'in the Isfahani tongue' (*be zabān-e esfahani*).[25]

This and much other evidence indicates that, when not cultivating Arabic, the Buyid courts of western Iran spoke western dialects of Persian, the famous *fahlaviyāt*, which continued to be used into the Saljuk period. The area called *Fahla* included Isfahan, Rayy, Hamadān, Nihāvand and Azerbaijan, almost all of which were ruled by the Buyids. There was a genre of poetry in the western Iranian dialects of this area that may have competed with the New Persian of eastern Iran.[26] It is significant that Asadi Tusi, writing at the very end of the Buyid period, introduces his dictionary of Persian, *Loghat-e fors*, by saying that, 'It is the tongue of the people of Balkh and Transoxiana and elsewhere'.[27] Specialists have always considered New Persian to be the language of Fars, as spoken by the people of eastern Iran, somewhat analogous to the famous formulation of Italian as 'la lingua Toscana in bocca Romana'.

Considered together the preceding materials offer important clues to the question of Iranian identity under the Buyids. In the first instance we have rulers who are unashamedly Iranian and who sought by genealogy, title and homage to Persepolis to show their connection with the pre-Islamic Iranian past. At the same time, the inhabitants of the Buyid kingdoms and eastern Iranians showed a sometimes embarrassingly high level of self-esteem as the people of Irānshahr.

Then why did the Buyids fail to cultivate New Persian, which they undoubtedly understood? First, as I have mentioned, the Buyids were influenced by their presence in Baghdad and were in competition to be great patrons of Arabic letters. Secondly, the influence of the *mubad*s, Zoroastrian priests who wrote in Pahlavi in provinces such as Fars, might have deterred the use of New Persian. A third reason could be that the New Persian of eastern Iran was still at variance with the Persian dialects of western Iran, such as the Isfahani dialect mentioned above, and was not yet widely accepted outside of eastern Iran.

Yet another reason for the lack of interest of the Buyids in New Persian might be religion. This suggestion is highly speculative. The true beginning of the dissemination of New Persian as a prose medium is associated with a Samanid programme to create a popular Islamic literature in New Persian, which is widely associated with the Persian adaptation of the great world history of Tabari.[28] A somewhat neglected part of this programme was the translation into New Persian in 370 AH, at the order of the Samanid ruler Nuh, of a strongly Sunni creed by the Hanafi scholar from Transoxiana, Abu Ishāq b. Mohammad al-Samarqandi.[29] The Buyids were Shiʻi without belonging to any specific Shiʻi group. They were not interested in converting their Sunni Muslim subjects to Shiʻism and probably realized they would rouse resistance among their subjects by a translation project favouring Shiʻism. They did, however, patronize Shiʻi learning, which was largely centred in Iraq at that time and therefore written in Arabic.

It would await the coming of the Saljuq Turks and their many eastern Iranian officials in the mid-eleventh century CE before western Iran would openly delight in the beautiful New Persian language. Paradoxically, New Persian, which was so ably promoted in the Turkish court of Mahmud of Ghazna, continued to be cultivated by the Turkish rulers of their successor state, the great Saljuqs. All these Turkish rulers hoped to connect themselves with the kingly tradition represented by the *Shāhnāma* which offered an ideal of rulership that they could easily and happily embrace.

Notes:

1. The weapon associated with the Daylamis is the *zubin* or *zhubin* according to the dictionary *Loghatnāma* ed. by Ali-Akbar Dihkhuda (Tehran: Tehran University, 1373 AH), vol. V, 11, note 453.
2. Mohamed Rekaya, 'Kārinids' in *EI²* (Leiden: Brill, 1978) , 644–7.
3. 'Abd al-Karīm b. Muhammad Rāfe'ī, *al-Tadwin fī akhbār Qazwīn* (Tehran: Atārid, 1374 AH) passim.
4. On the assumption of the title *shāhānshāh* see the learned articles by Lutz Richter-Bernberg, *'Amir-Malik-Shāhānshāh:* 'Adud ad-Daula's Titulature Re-examined', *Iran* 18 (1980), 83–102 and Wilfred Madelung, 'The Assumption of the Title Shahanshah by the Buyids and "The Reign of the Daylam (Dawlat Al-Daylam)"', *Journal of Near Eastern Studies* 28, 2 (1969), 84–108.
5. Richter-Bernberg, Titulature, 89 gives this place name with an *ezāfa*, but an equally good case can be made for reading it without the *ezāfa* to mean 'Fannā Khosraw did / built it'.
6. See Christof Buergel and Roy Mottahedeh, "Azod al-Dawla', *EncIr*, III (New York: Routledge and Kegan Paul, 1989), 265–9.
7. Translation adapted from the excellent article by John J. Donohue, 'Three Buwayhid Inscriptions' *Arabica*, 20 (1) (1973), 74–80. Of philological interest in this inscription is the spelling of the second element in the ruler's name as 'Khosra'. Isfahan is written in the standard Arabic form, Isbahān.
8. Vesta S. Curtis, 'The Legacy of Ancient Persia' in *The Forgotten Empire: The World of Ancient Persia*, ed. by John Curtis and Nigel Tallis (London: The British Museum Press, 2005), 250–57, 252.
9. Clifford E. Bosworth, 'The Heritage of Rulership in Early Islamic Iran and the Search for Dynastic Connections with the Past', *Iranian Studies*, 11 (1/4) (1978), 7–34.
10. Donohue, *Inscriptions*, 78–80.
11. Al-Fāresi, *al-Masā'il al-shirāziyāt*, vol. I, ed. by Hasan Hindāwi (Riyadh: Konuz, 2004), 'h'.
12. Yāqut, *Ershād al-arib elā ma'refah al-adib,* vol. III, (Beirut: Dār al-Kutub al-'Ilmiyah, 1991), 479.
13. Richard N. Frye, 'Die Wiedergeburt Persiens um die Jahrtausendwende', *Der Islam* 35 (1960), 42–51.
14. Ebn Hawqal, *Ketāb surat al-ard*, ed. by Johannes H. Kramers and Gaston Wiet (Leiden: Brill, 1939), 289.
15. Mohammad Awfi, *Lobāb al-albāb* (Tehran: Ettehād, 1335 AH), 254–6.
16. See the outstanding thesis of my student Erez Naaman, 'Literature and Literary People at the Court of Al-Sāhib Ibn 'Abbād', Harvard University dissertation (2009), 8–9.
17. On the flourishing Arabic-language culture of the Buyid courts, see the classic study by Joel L. Kraemer, *Humanism in the Renaissance of Islam: the Cultural Revival during the Buyid Age* (Leiden and New York, Brill: 1992).
18. Estakhri, *Ketāb masālek al-mamālek* (Leiden: Brill, 1927), 4.
19. Maqdisi, *Ketāb al-bad' wa'l-ta'rikh*, vol. IV, ed. by Clément Huart (Paris: Ernest Leroux,1899–1919), 97–8.
20. Qazvini, 'Moqaddama-ye qadim-i Shāhnāma, *Bist Maqālah* , 2 (Tehran: Adab, 1332 AH), 49. I thank Professor Touraj Daryaee for calling my attention to this introduction by Tusi.

21. Qazvini, 'Moqaddama', 38.
22. The forthcoming work of my student Sarah Savant discusses the genealogical claims of the Iranians exhaustively.
23. Biruni, *Tahdid nehāyāt al-amāken* (Ankara: Dogus, 1962), 105–6; *The Determination of the Coordinates of Positions for the Correct of Distances between Cities*, trans. by Jamil Ali (Beirut: American University of Beirut Press, 1967), 101–2.
24. Awfi, *Lubāb*, 255.
25. Māfarrokhi, *Mahāsen-e Esfahān* (Isfahan: Markaz-e Esfahān-Shenāsi, 1385 AH), 119. I thank my student Alexander Key for drawing my attention to this passage.
26. The classic article on the subject is by Ahmad Tafazzoli, 'Fahlaviyat' *EncIr*, online. He quotes only one example of *fahlavihyāt* from Fars province.
27. Asadi Tusi, *Loghat-e Fors*, ed. by M. Dabir-e Siyāqi (Tehran: Tahuri, 1977), 1.
28. See now the learned work of Andrew C.S. Peacock, *Mediaeval Islamic Historiography and Political Legitimacy: Bal'amī's* Tārīkhnāma (London: Routledge, 2007).
29. Samarqandi, *Tarjumeh-e al-savād al-a'Zam* (Tehran: Enteshārāt-e Bonyād-e Farhang-e Erān, 1969).

Abbreviations

BEO	Bulletin d'Études Orientales
BSOAS	Bulletin of the School of Oriental and African Studies
EI^2	Encyclopaedia of Islam, 2nd edn.
EncIr	Encyclopaedia Iranica
Iran	Journal of the British Institute of Persian Studies
JAOS	Journal of the American Oriental Society
JSS	Journal of Semitic Studies
RAAD	Revue de l'Académie Arabe de Damas (= Majalla Majma' al-Lugha al-Arabiyya bi-Dimashq)
SPA	Survey of Persian Art
ZDMG	Zeitschrift der deutschen morgenländischen Gesellschaft

Bibliography

Abbas, I. (1977). 'Nazra jadida fi ba'd al-kotob al-mansuba l'Ebn-al-Moqaffa'', *RAAD* 52: 538–80.

Abel, A. (1955). *Le roman d'Alexandre, légendaire médiéval*, Brussels.

Abu'l-Ma'āli, Mohammad al-Hosayni al-'Alawi. (1964). *Bayān al-adyān*, Razi, H. (ed.), Tehran.

Afshāri, M. (1379/2000). 'Pari' in *Dāneshnāma-ye jahān-e Eslām*, 5, Tehran, 593–7.

Ahd Ardashir (1387 / 1967). Abbas, I. (ed.), Beirut.

Ahmad, Fo'ād Abd al-Mon'em (1988), 'Introduction' in Ahmad, F. (ed.), *Nasihat al-moluk al-mansub elā Abi'l-Hasan al-Māwardi*, Alexandria.

Ali, S.M. (2006). 'Reinterpreting al-Buhturī's Īwān Kisrā Ode: Tears of Affection for the Cycles of History', *Journal of Arabic Literature* 37 (1): 46–67.

Amanat, A. (1997). *Pivot of the Universe: Nasir al-Din Shah and the Iranian Monarchy, 1831–1896*, Berkeley.

Asmussen, J.P. (1966). 'Der Manichäismus als Vermittler literarischen Gutes', *Temenos* 2: 5-21.

— (1989). 'Barlaam and Iosaph', *EncIr* III: 801.

Atil, E. (1973). *Ceramics from the World of Islam*, Washington, DC.

Awfi, M. (1335 / 1957). *Lobāb al-albāb*, Tehran.

— (1335 / 1957). *Pānzdah bāb-e Javāme' al-hekāyāt*, Ramazani, M. (ed.), Tehran.

Āzarnūsh, A. (1370 AH). 'Āyā tarjuma-ye tafsīr-i Tabarī be-rāstī tarjuma-ye tafsīr-i Tabarī ast?' in Tafaaoli, A. (ed.), *Yekī qatra-ye bārān (Jashnnāma-ye ostād doktor 'Abbās Zaryāb Khū'ī)*, Tehran: 551–60.

Azarpay, G. (1981). 'The Islamic Tomb Tower: A Note on its Genesis and Significance' in Daneshvari, A. (ed.), *Essays in Islamic Art and Architecture in Honor of Katharina Otto-Dorn*, Malibu: 9–12.

Bäcker, J. (2007). 'Schwanjungfrau' in *Enzyklopädie des Märchens*, 13, Berlin, cols 311–8.

Baer, E. (1983). *Metalwork in Medieval Islamic Art*, Albany.

Bagley, F.R.C. (1964). *Ghazālī's Book of Counsel for Kings (Nasīhat al-mulūk)*, London.

Bahār, M.T. (ed.), (1381 AH). *Tārikh-e Sistān*, Tehran: 214–16.

Bahrami, M. (1952). 'A Gold Medal in the Freer Gallery of Art' in Miles, G.C. (ed.), *Archaeologica Orientalia in Memoriam Ernst Herzfeld*, Locust Valley, NY: 5–20.

Bal'ami, Abu Ali Mohammad (1999). *Tārikhnāma-ye Tabari gardānida-ye mansub be-Bal'ami*, Rawshan, M. (ed.), Tehran.

Balkhi, Abdallāh Mohammad b. Hosayn, (1350 / 1971). *Fazā'el-e Balkh*, Habibi, A. (ed.), Tehran.

Barthold, W. (1958). *Turkestan Down to the Mongol Invasion*, 2nd edition, London.
— (1977). *Turkestan Down to the Mongol Invasion*, 4th edition, London.
Baulo, A.V. (2002). 'A Sasanian Silver Plate from the Synya', *Archaeology, Ethnology and Anthropology of Eurasia* 1 (9): 142–8.
Bayhaqi, Zahir al-Din (1966). *Tārikh hokamā' al-Eslām*, Mohammad, M.H. (ed.), Beirut.
Benfey, T. (1876). 'Einleitung' in *Kalilag und Damnag. Alte syrische Übersetzung des indischen Fürstenspiegels. Text und deutsche Übersetzung von Gustav Bickell. Mit einer Einleitung von Theodor Benfey*, Leipzig: V– CXLVII.
Bernus, M., Marchal, H. and Vial, G. (1971). 'Le suaire de Saint-Josse', *Bulletin de Liaison du Centre International d'Études des Textiles Anciens* 33: 1–57.
Bianchi, U. (1980). 'The Category of Dualism in the Historical Phenomenology of Religion', *Temenos* 16: 10–25.
Bier, L. (1986). *Sarvistan: Study in Early Iranian Architecture*. University Park, PA.
Biesterfeldt, H.H. (1990). 'Ibn Farīgūn's Chapter on Arabic Grammar in his *Compendium of the Sciences*' in Versteegh, K. and Carter, M.G. (eds), *Studies in the History of Arabic Grammar II. Proceedings of the 2nd Symposium on the History of Arabic Grammar, Nijmegen, 27 April–1 May 1987*, Amsterdam / Philadelphia: 49–56.
al-Biruni, Abu Rayhān (1923). *al-Āthār al-bāqiya an al-qorun al-khāliya*, Sachau, C.E. (ed.), Leipzig; (1879) trans. Sachau, C.E, as *The Chronology of Ancient Nations*, London; repr. 1969, Frankfurt.
— (1377 / 1958). *Tahqiq mā lil-hend*, Hyderabad; (1964) trans Sauchau, C.E. as *Alberuni's India: An Account of the Religion, Philosophy, Literature, Geography, Chronology, Astronomy, Customs, Laws and Astrology of India about A. D. 1030*, London; repr. 1964, Dehli.
— (1962). *Tahdīd nehāyāt al-amāken*, Ankara.
Blair, S. (1992). *The Monumental Inscriptions from Early Islamic Iran and Transoxiana*, Supplements to *Muqarnas*, Leiden.
— (1983) 'The Octagonal Pavilion at Natanz: A Reexamination of Early Islamic Architecture in Iran', *Muqarnas* 1: 69–94.
— and Bloom, J. (2003). 'The Mirage of Islamic Art': Reflections on the Study of an Unwieldy Field, *The Art Bulletin*, 85, 152–84.
— and Bloom, J.M. (2006). *Cosmophilia: Islamic Art from the David Collection, Copenhagen*, with essays by von Folsach, K., Netzer, N. and Cernuschi, C., Chestnut Hill, MA.
— Bloom, J.M. and Wardwell, A.E. (1992). 'Reevaluating the Date of the "Buyid" Silks by Epigraphic and Radiocarbon Analysis', *Ars Orientalis* 22: 1–42.
Blois, F. de (1998). 'Epics', *EncIr*, VIII(5): 474–7.

— (1990). *Burzōy's Voyage to India and the Origin of the Book of Kalīlah wa Dimnah*, London.

— (1996). 'Shuhayd al-Balkhī, a Poet and Philosopher of the Time of Rāzī', *BSOAS* 59: 333–7.

Bloom, J. (1989). *Minaret:Symbol of Islam*, Oxford Studies in Islamic Art, Oxford.

— (2004). 'Fact and Fantasy in Buyid Art', *Oriente Moderno* XXIII (LXXXIV), n.s.: 387–400.

— and Blair, S. (2009). (eds), *The Grove Encyclopedia of Islamic Art and Architecture*, New York.

Boissel, J. (1993). *Gobineau. Biographie, mythes et réalité*, Paris.

Bombaci, A. (1966). *The Kufic Inscription in Persian Verses in the Court of the Royal Palace of Mas'ud III at Ghazni*, Rome.

Bosworth, C.E. (1962). 'On Mithra in the Manichaean Pantheon' in Henning, W.B. and Yarshater, E. (eds), *A Locust's Leg: Studies in Honour of S.H. Taqizadeh*, London: 44–54.

— (1965). 'On the Chronology of the Ziyarids in Gurgan and Tabaristan', *Der Islam* XL: 25–34.

— (1969). 'An Alleged Embassy from the Emperor of China to the Amir Nasr b. Ahmad: A Contribution to Samanid Military History' in Minovi, M. and Afshar, I. (eds), *Yād-nāmé-ye īrānī-ye Minorsky*: 17–29.

— 'The Tahirids and Arabic Culture', *JSS* 14 (1): 45–79.

— 'The Tahirids and Persian Literature', *Iran* 7: 103–6.

— (1973). 'The Heritage of Rulership in Early Islamic Iran and the Search for Dynastic Connections with the Past', *Iranian Studies* 11: 51–62.

— (1981). 'The Rulers of Chaghāniyān in Early Islamic Times', *Iran*, 19, 1–20.

— (1989). 'Balkh II: History from the Arab Conquest to the Mongols', *EncIr* III: 588–91.

— (1996). *The New Islamic Dynasties: A Chronological and Genealogical Manual*, Edinburgh.

— (2000). 'al-Thaʿālibī, Abu Mansūr,' *EI*² 10: 425–6.

Boyce, M. (1962). 'On Mithra in the Manichaean Pantheon' in Henning, W.B. and Yarshater, E. (eds), *A Locust's Leg: Studies in Honour of S.H. Taqizadeh*, London: 44–54.

— (1975). *A Reader in Manichaean Middle Persian and Parthian: Texts with Notes*, Leiden.

— (1992). *Zoroastrianism Its Antiquity and Constant Vigour*, Columbia Lectures on Iranian Studies, 7, Costa Mesa and New York.

Bozdoğan, S. and Necipoğlu, G. (2007). 'Entangled Discourses: Scrutinizing Orientalist and Nationalist Legacies in the Architectural Historiography of the "Lands of the Rum"', *Muqarnas* 24, 1–6.

Bray, J. (2010). 'Al-Thaʿalibi's *Adab al-muluk*, a Local Mirror for Princes' in Suleiman, Y. (ed.), *Living Islamic History. Studies in Honour of Professor Carole Hillenbrand*, Edinburgh: 32–46.

Browne, E.G. (1928). *A Literary History of Persia,* Cambridge.

Buenzod, J. (1967). *La Formation de la pensée de Gobineau et l'essai sur l'inégalité des races humaines*, Paris.

Buergel, C. and Mottahedeh, R. (1989). "Azod al-Dawla', *EncIr*, III: 265–9.

Bulliet, R.W. (1976). 'Naw Bahār and the Survival of Iranian Buddhism', *Iran* XIV: 140–45.

— (1979). *Conversion to Islam in the Medieval Period: An Essay in Quantitative History*, Cambridge, MA.

— (1994). *Islam: The View from the Edge,* New York.

Čačava, M. (1981). 'Dev' in *Enzyklopädie des Märchens* 3, Berlin, cols 569–73.

Chanom, M.G., (narrated) (1994). *Wenn er Esel singt, tanzt das Kamel. Persische Märchen und Schwänke*, Elwell-Sutton, E.P. (collected) and Marzolph, U. (trans. and ed.), Munich.

Chavannes, É. (1910–62). *Cinq cents contes et apologues extraits du Tripitaka chinois*, 3 vols, Paris.

Chraïbi, A. (2008). *Les Mille et une nuits. Histoire du texte et classification des contes*, Paris.

Christensen, A. (1941). *Essai sur la démonologie iranienne*, Copenhagen.

— (1944). *L'Iran sous les Sassanides*, Copenhagen.

Creswell, K.A.C. (1940). *Early Muslim Architecture,* vol. II. Oxford.

Curtis, V.S. (2005). 'The Legacy of Ancient Persia' in Curtis, J. and Tallis, N. (eds), *The Forgotten Empire: The World of Ancient Persia*, London: 250–57.

Dabiri, G. (2010). 'The *Shahnama*: between the Samanids and the Ghaznavids', *Iranian Studies* 43 (1): 13–28.

Daniel, E.L. (1979). *The Political and Social History of Khurasan under Abbasid Rule 747–820*, Minneapolis and Chicago.

— (2004). 'Historiography III: Early Islamic Period', *EncIr* VIII: 330–48.

Dankoff, R. (1983). *Wisdom of Royal Glory (Kutadgu bilig): a Turko-Islamic Mirror for Princes*, Chicago and London.

Darke, H.S.G. (1978). *The Book of Government or Rules for Kings*, revised edition, London.

Daryaee, T. (1998). 'Apocalypse Now: Zoroastrian Reflections on the Early Islamic Centuries', *Medieval Encounters* 4 (3): 188–202.

— (ed. and trans.) (2002). *Shahrestānīhā ī Ērānshahr: A Middle Persian Text on Late Antique Geography, Epic, and History*, Costa Mesa.

Davidovich, E.A. (1954). 'Vtoraia moneta Samanida Nukha b. Asada', *Epigrafika Vostoka,* 9: 38–9.

Day, F.E. (1951). 'Review of *Soieries Persanes* by Gaston Wiet', *Ars Islamica* 15–16: 231–44.

Demange, F. (2006) (ed.). *Les Perses Sassanides: fastes d'un empire oublié, (224–642)*, Paris.

Deschner, G. (1967). 'Gobineau und Deutschland. Der Einfluß von J.A. de Gobineaus *Essai sur l'inégalité des races humaines* auf die deutsche Geistesgeschichte 1853–1917', Ph.D. diss. Erlangen-Nürnberg.

Dickie, J. (1978). 'Allah and Eternity: Mosques, Madrasas and Tombs' in Michell, G. (ed.), *Architecture of the Islamic World,* London: 15–47.

Diez, E. (1915). *Die Kunst der Islamischen Völker,* Berlin.

— (1918). *Churāsānische Baudenkmäler,* Berlin.

— (1923). *Persien: Islamische Baukunst in Churāsān,* Hagen.

Al-Dinawari (1888). *Ketāb al-akhbār al-tewāl,* Guirgass, V. (ed.), Leiden.

Donohue, J.J. (1973). 'Three Buwayhid Inscriptions', *Arabica* 20 (1): 74–80.

Durand-Guédy, D. (2006). 'Mémoires d'exilés: lecture de la chronique des Saljuqides de 'Imād al-Dīn al-Isfahānī', *Studia Iranica* 35: 181–202.

Ebn Abd-Rabbeh, Ahmad b. Mohammad, (1951–5). *al-'Eqd al-farid,* al-Bustani, K. (ed.), 31 vols, Beirut.

Ebn Abi-Dharr, Abu'l-Hasan (1957–8). *al-Sa'āda wa-l-es'ād,* Minovi, M. (ed.), Wiesbaden.

Ebn al-Athir (1402 / 1982). *al-Kāmel fī al-ta'rīkh.* Beirut; (1996). *al-Kāmil fī al-ta'rīkh,* Tornberg, C.J. (ed.), vol. 8, (reprint), Beirut.

Ebn al-Balkhi (1921). *The* Fársnáma *of Ibnu'l-Balkhí,* Le Strange, G. and Nicholson, R.A. (eds), London.

Ebn Esfandiyār, M.b.H. (1941–2). *Ta'rikh-e Tabarestān,* Eqbāl, A. (ed.), 2 vols, Tehran.

Ebn Hajar al-'Asqalāni, Ahmad b. 'Ali (1416 / 1996). *Lesān al-mizān,* Ghanem, G.b.A. (ed.), Cairo.

Ebn Hawqal (1939). *Kitāb sūrat al-ard,* Kramers, J.H. and Wiet, G. (eds), Leiden; (1964). *Configuration de la terre (kitab surat al-ard),* Kramers, J.H. and Wiet, G. (trans.) Paris.

Ebn Khallikān, (1948). *Wafayāt al-a'yān,* Abd al-Hamīd, M. (ed.), vol. 4, Cairo.

Ebn al-Moqaffa', (1966). *Āthār Ebn-al-Moqaffa',* Abu'l-Nasr, O. (ed.), Beirut.

— (1816). S. de Sacy, *Calila et Dimna, ou Fables de Bidpai, en arabe,* Paris.

Ebn al-Nadim, Mohammad b. Eshāq (1991). *al-Fehrest,* Khalifa, S. and al-'Awza, W.M., (eds), 2 vols, Cairo; (1970); *The Fihrist of al-Nadīm: a Tenth-century Survey of Muslim Culture,* 1–2, Dodge, B., (trans. and ed.), New York; (1971). *Kitāb al-Fihrist,* Tajaddud, R. (ed.), Tehran.

Ebn Qotayba, 'A.b.M. (1343–8 / 1925–30). *'Oyun al-akhbār,* 4 vols, Cairo.

Ebn al-Zubayr, Rashīd (1959). *Ketāb al-dhakhā'er wa'l-tuhaf,* Hamīd Allāh, M. (ed.), Kuwait.

al-Esfahāni, Hamza b. al-Hasan (n.d.). *Ta'rikh seni moluk al-arz wa-al-anbiyā',* Beirut; (1922). *Ta'rīkh sinī mulūk al-ard wa'l-anbiyā',* Gottwald, I.M.E. (ed.), Petropolis.

Esin, E. (1967). 'Al Qubbah al-Turkiyya: An Essay on the Architectonic Forms of the Islamic Turkish Funerary Monument' in *Atti del Terzo Congresso di Studi Arabi e Islamici,* Naples: 281–313.

al-Estakhri, Abu Eshāq Ebrāhim b. Mohammad (1870). *Kitāb masālik al-mamālik,* de Goeje, M.J. (ed.), Lugduni Batavorum; (1927) 2nd edition, Leiden; (1967) 3rd edition, Leiden.

Ettinghausen, R. and Grabar, O. (1987). *The Art and Architecture of Islam 650–1250,* New Haven and London.

al-Fāresi, (2004). *al-Masā'el al-Shirāziyāt*, vol. I, Hendāwi, H. (ed.), Riyadh.

Fedorov, M.N. (2000). 'The Khwarazmshahs of the Banū 'Irāq (Fourth / Tenth Century)', *Iran* 38: 71–5.

Ferdowsi, Abu'l-Qāsem (1876–8). *Shāhnāma*, Mohl, J. (ed. and trans.), *Le livre des rois*, 7 vols, Paris.

— (2006). *Shahnameh. The Persian Book of Kings*, trans. Davis, D., New York.

Ferrier, R.W. (1989). (ed.) *The Arts of Persia*, New Haven.

Finster, B. (1994). *Frühe iranische Moscheen, vom Beginn des Islam bis zur Zeit salguqischer Herrschaft*. Archaeologische Mitteilungen Aus Iran: vol. 19, Berlin.

Flügel, G. (1868). 'Zur Frage über die Romane und Erzählungen der mohammedanischen Völkerschaften', *ZDMG* 22: 731–7.

Fouchécour, C.H. de (1986). *Moralia. Les notions morales dans la littérature persane du 3e / 9e au 7e / 13e siècle*, Paris.

Fragner, B. (2001). 'The Concept of Regionalism in Historical Research on Central Asia and Iran: a Macro Historical Explanation' in DeWeese, D. (ed.), *Studies on Central Asian History in Honor of Yuri Bregel*, Bloomington: 341–54.

— (2006). 'Das Persische als Hegemonialsprache in der islamischen Geschichte' in Johanson, L. and Bulut, C. (eds), *Turkic-Iranian Contact Areas: Historical and Linguistic aspects*, Wiesbaden, 39–48.

Frye, R.N. (1960). 'Die Wiedergeburt Persiens um die Jahrtausendwende', *Der Islam* (35): 42–51.

— (1966). *The Heritage of Central Asia: From Antiquity to the Turkish Expansion,* Princeton.

Fück, J. (1952). 'Sechs Ergänzungen zu Sachaus Ausgabe von al-Bīrūnīs "Chronologie Orientalischer Völker"', *Documenta Islamica Inedita*, Berlin: 69–98.

Gaillard, M. (1987). *Le Livre de Samak-e 'Ayyār. Structure et idéologie du roman persan médiéval*, Paris.

Galdieri, E. (1984). *Isfahan: Masgid-i Jum'a*, III, Rome.

Gardizi, Abd al-Hayy (1347 AH). *Zayn al-akhbār,* Habibi, A.H. (ed.), Tehran; (1384 / 2005). *Zayn al-akbār*, Mālek, R.R. (ed.), Tehran.

Gaudefroy-Demombynes, M. (1954). 'Le Voile de la Ka'ba', *Studia Islamica* 2: 5–21.

Gettens, R.J. (1971). 'Andarz Nama. Preliminary Technical Examination' in Pope, A.U. (ed.), Ackerman, P. (asst. ed.), *A Survey of Persian Art from Prehistoric Times to the Present*, vol. XIII-Fascicle. Addendum A – The Andarz Nama, A/53–A/63, London.

al-Ghazāli, Abu Hāmed (1351 / 1972). *Nasihat al-moluk*, Homā'i, J. (ed.), Tehran; (1964). Bagley, F.R.C. trans. as *Ghazālī's Book of Counsel for Kings (Nasīhat al-mulūk)*, London.

Ghirshman, R. (1962). *Iran, Parthes et Sassanides*, Paris.

Gignoux, P. 'Dēnkard', *EncIr*, online.

Gimaret, D. (1971). 'Traces et parallèles du *Kitāb Bilawhar wa Būdhāsf* dans la tradition arabe', *BEO* 24, 97–133.

Glassen, E. (1981). *Der mittlere Weg: Studien zur Religionspolitik und Religiosität der späteren Abbasiden-Zeit*, Wiesbaden.

Gobineau, A. Comte de (1922). *Trois ans en Asie (de 1855 à 1858)*, vols. 1–2. Paris.

— (1967). *Essai sur l'inégalité des races humaines.* Paris.

— (1999) [1915]. *The Inequality of Human Races.* New York.

Godard, A. (1949). 'Voûtes Iraniennes', *Athar-é Iran,* 4: 187–368.

Goldberg, C. (2002). 'Pars pro toto' in *Enzyklopädie des Märchens* 10, Berlin, cols 590–95.

Golombek, L. (1969). 'The Abbasid Mosque at Balkh', *Oriental Art* 15: 173–89.

Gonzalez, V. (2002). *Le piège de Salomon: la pensée de l'art dans le Coran,* Paris.

Gorgani, F. (2008). (trans.) Davis, D., *Vis & Ramin,* Washington.

Grabar, O. (1966). 'The Earliest Islamic Commemorative Structures, Notes and Documents', *Ars Orientalis* 4: 7–46.

— (1967). *Sasanian Silver: Late Antique and Early Mediaeval Arts of Luxury from Iran: August–September 1967, the University of Michigan Museum of Art,* Ann Arbor.

— (1969). 'Notes on the Iconography of the "Demotte" Shahname' in Pinder-Wilson, R. (ed.), *Paintings in Islamic Lands*, London, reprinted in Grabar, O. (2006). *Constructing the Study of Islamic Art*, vol. II, Hampshire: 115–66.

Grenet, F. (2005). 'Découverte d'un relief sassanide dans le nord de l'Afghanistan', *Comptes-rendus des séances de l'Académie des Inscriptions et Belles-Lettres,* 149 (1): 115–34.

— and Marshak, B. (1998). 'L'art soghdien' in Chuvin, P., *Les Arts de l'Asie Centrale*, Paris.

Grotzfeld, H., Grotzfeld, S. and Marzolph, U. (1993). 'Kalīla und Dimna' in *Enzyklopädie des Märchens*, 7, Berlin, cols 888–95.

Guidi, I. (1873). *Studii sul testo arabo del libro di Calila e Dimna,* Rome.

Gulacsi, Z. (2005). *Medieval Manichean Book Art: a Codicological Study of Iranian and Turkic Illuminated Book Fragments from 8th–11th Century East Central Asia,* Leiden.

Gutas, D. (1998). *Greek Thought, Arabic Culture: The Graeco-Arabic Translation Movement in Baghdad and Early 'Abbāsid Society (2nd–4th / 8th–10th centuries),* London.

Hanaway, W.L. (1987). ''Ayyār. 2: 'Ayyār in Persian Sources', in *EncIr* 2: 161–3.

Harper, P.O. (with a technical study by P. Meyers) (1981). *Silver Vessels of the Sasanian Period.* New York.

Hasuri, A. (1386 / 2007). 'Ezhdehā' in *Dāneshnāme-ye Irān*, vol. 2, Tehran: 777–86.

Henning, W.B. (1936). 'Zwei Fehler in der arabisch-manichäischen Überlieferung', *Orientalia* 5: 84–7.

— (1940). 'Sogdian Loan-words in New Persian', *BSOAS* 10: 93–106.

— (1962). 'Persian Poetical Manuscripts from the Time of Rūdakī' in Henning, W.B. and Yarshater, E. (eds), *A Locust's Leg: Studies in Honour of S.H. Taqizadeh*, London: 89–104.

Herrenschmidt, C. and Kellens, J. (1993). '*Daiva' in *EncIr*, 6: 599–602.

Herzfeld, E. (1920). 'Der Thron des Khusrô. Quellenkritische und Ikonographische Studien über Grensgebiete der Kunstgeschichte des Morgen-und Abendlandes' in *Jahrbuch der preussischen Kunstsammlungen*, 41.

Hillenbrand, C. (1988). 'Islamic Orthodoxy or Realpolitik? Al-Ghazālī's Views on Government', *Iran* 26: 81–94.

Hillenbrand, R. (1989). 'Architecture' in Ferrier, R. (ed.), *The Arts of Persia,* New Haven and London: 81–108.

— (1994). *Islamic Architecture: Form, Function and Meaning,* Edinburgh.

— (1999). *Islamic Art and Architecture,* London.

Hoffenck-De Graaf, J.H. (1973). 'Dyestuff Analysis of the Buyid Silk Fabrics of the Abegg Foundation, Bern', *Bulletin de Liaison du Centre International d'Études des Textiles Anciens* 37: 120–33.

Homā'i, Jalal al-Din, 'Dibācha' see al-Ghazāli, *Nasihat al-moluk*, i–cxcvi.

Huart, C. (1901). 'Annexe au procès-verbal', *Journal Asiatique*, 18: 16–21.

Hutt, A. (1978). 'Iran', in Michell, G. (ed.), *Architecture of the Islamic World,* New York: 251–7.

For names beginning Ibn see Ebn above

Insler, S. (1975). *The Gāthās of Zarathustra*, Leiden.

Irving, T.B. (1980). *Kalilah and Dimnah*, Newark.

al-Isfahānī – see al-Esfahāni above.

al-Istakhrī – see al-Estakhri above.

Ja'fari (Qanavāti), M. (1387 / 2008). *Do revāyat az 'Salim-e Javāheri',* Tehran.

Jafri, S.R. (1961). 'Description of India (Hind and Sind) in the works of al-Istakhrī, Ibn Hawqal, and al-Maqdisī', *Bulletin of the Institute of Islamic Studies* 5: 1–67.

al-Jahshiyari (1938). *Kitab al-wuzarā',* Cairo.

The Jātaka or Stories of the Buddha's Former Births (1957). Cowell, E.B. (ed.), 6 vols, London.

Jeroussalimskaja, A. (1978). 'Le cafetan aux simourghs du tombeau de Mochtchevaja Balka (Caucase Septentrional), *Studia Iranica* 7: 183–211.

Jones, D., Michell, G., Arts Council of Great Britain Staff, World of Islam Festival Trust Staff, Hayward Gallery Staff, (1976) *The Arts of Islam: Hayward Gallery 8 April–4 July 1976*, London.

Kaykāvus ebn Eskandar ebn Qābus, Onsor al-Ma'āli (1972). *Qābusnāma,* Tehran; (1368 / 1989). *Qābusnāma*, Yusofi, G.H. (ed.); (1951). Levy, R.

trans. as *A Mirror for Princes: The Qābūsnāma by Kai Kā'ūs ibn Iskandar Prince of Gurgan*, London.

Keith, A.B. (1920). *A History of Sanskrit Literature*, London.

Keith-Falconer, I.G.N. (1885). *Kalīlah and Dimnah or the Fables of Bidpai being an account of their literary history, with an English translation of the later Syriac version of the same, and notes*, Cambridge.

Khaleghi-Motlagh, J. (1989). 'Aždahā. 2: In Persian Literature' in *EncIr*, 3: 199–202.

Khalidi, T. (1975). *Islamic Historiography: The Histories of Mas'ūdī*, Albany.

— (1994). *Arabic Historical Thought in the Classical Period*, Cambridge.

Khānom, M.G. (1386 / 2007). *Qessahā-ye Mashdi Galin Khānom. 110 qessa-ye 'āmiyāna-ye irāni*. gerd-āvarda-ye L.P. Elwell-Sutton, virāyesh Ulrich Marzolph, Azar Amirhosseini-Nithammer, Ahmad Vakiliyān, 5th edn, Tehran.

Kiani, M.Y. (1984). *The Islamic City of Gurgan,* Berlin.

Kinberg, L. (1985). 'What is meant by *zuhd*', SI 61: 27–44.

Köhler-Zülch, I. (1996). 'Kristallisationsgestalten' in *Enzyklopädie des Märchens*, 8, Berlin: cols. 460–66.

Komaroff, L. (1998). *Islamic Art at the Los Angeles County Museum of Art,* Los Angeles.

Kraemer, J.L. (1992). *Humanism in the Renaissance of Islam: the Cultural Revival during the Buyid Age*, Leiden and New York.

Lakoff, G. and Johnson, M. (eds) (1980). *Metaphors We Live By*, Chicago.

Lang, D.M. (1957). *The Wisdom of Balahvar: A Christian Legend of the Buddha*, London.

Latham, J.D. 'Ebn al-Moqaffa', Abu Mohammad 'Abdollāh Rōzbeh' *EncIr* online.

— (1986). 'Bilawhar wa-Yūdāsaf', *EI²*, I: 1215–17.

— (1990). 'Ibn al-Muqaffa and Early Abbasid Prose' in Ashtiany, J., Johnstone, T.M., Latham, J.D., Serjeant, R.B, and Smith, G.R. (eds.), *The Cambridge History of Arabic Literature. 'Abbāsid Belles-lettres*, Cambridge: 48–77.

Laveille, J.-L. (1998). *Le Thème de voyage dans Les Mille et une Nuits: Du Maghreb à la Chine*. Paris.

Lawrence, B.B. (1976). *Shahrastānī on the Indian Religions*, The Hague and Paris.

Lazard, G. et al. (1964). *Anthologie de la Poésie Persane, XIe–Xème siècles*, Paris.

— (1975). 'The Rise of the New Persian Language' in Frye, R. (ed.), *The Cambridge History of Iran*, IV: *The Period from the Arab Invasion to the Saljuqs,* Cambridge.

Lecomte, G. et al. (1965). *Ibn Qutayba (mort en 276 / 889). L'homme, son oeuvre, ses idées*, 2 vols, Damascus.

Leisten, T. (1998). *Architektur für Tote: Bestattung in architektonischem Kontext in den Kernländern der islamischen Welt zwischen 3. / 9. und 6. / 12. Jahrhundert*. Materialien zur Iranischen Archäologie, Berlin.

Lemberg, M. (1973). 'The Buyid Silks of the Abegg Foundation, Berne', *Bulletin de Liaison du Centre International d'Études des Textiles Anciens* 37: 28–43.

Levy, R., see Kaykāvus.

Loghatnāma (1325– AH), Dehkhodā, A.-A. (ed.), Tehran; also electronic resource.

Lowry, G.D. (1989). 'On the Gold Jug Inscribed to Abu Mansur al-Amir Bakhtiyar Ibn Mu'izz al-Dawla in the Freer Gallery of Art', *Ars Orientalis* 19: 103–15.

Madelung, W. (1969). 'The Assumption of the Title Shāhānshāh by the Buyids and "The Reign of the Daylam (Dawlat Al-Daylam)"', *Journal of Near Eastern Studies* 28 (2): 84–108.

— (1975). 'The Minor Dynasties of Northern Iran' in Frye, R. (ed.), *Cambridge History of Iran, vol. 4: From the Arab Invasion to the Saljuqs,* Cambridge: 198–249.

Māfarrokhi, (1385 AH). *Mahāsen-e Esfahān,* Isfahan.

Mahmoodi-Bakhtiari, B. (2003). 'Planning the Persian Language in the Samanid period', *Iran and the Caucasus* 7/1–2: 251–60.

Majumdar, R.C. (1971). *Ancient India,* 6th revised edition, Delhi.

Maqbul Ahmad, S. (1960). 'Al-Mas'ūdī on the Kings of India' in Maqbul Ahmad, S. And Rahman, A, (eds), *Al-Mas'ūdī: Millenary Commemoration Volume,* Aligarh: 97–112.

Maqdesi (1899–1919). *Ketāb al–bad' wa'l-ta'rikh,* Huart, C. (ed.), 6 vols, Paris.

Marlow, L. (2007). 'A Samanid Work of Counsel and Commentary: The *Nasīhat al-mulūk* of Pseudo-Māwardī', *Iran* 44: 181–92.

Marshak, B. (1986). *Silberschätze des Orients,* Leipzig.

— (1997). 'Persian Silver and Gold' in Marshak, B. et al., *The Treasures of Khan Kubrat,* St. Petersburg.

— (2002). *Legends, Tales, and Fables in the Art of Soghdiana,* New York.

— and Darkevich, V.P. (1974). 'O tak nazyvaemom siriiskom bliude', *Sovetskaia Arkheologiia.*

Marzolph, U. (1984). *Typologie des persischen Volksmärchens,* Beirut.

— (1994). 'Social Values in the Persian Popular Romance "Salīm-i Javāhirī"', *Edebiyat,* n.s. 51: 77–98.

— (2001). *Narrative Illustration in Persian Lithographed Books,* Leiden.

— (2007). 'The Persian "Nights": Links between the "Arabian Nights" and Iranian Culture' in Marzolph, U. (ed.), *The 'Arabian Nights' in Transnational Perspective,* Detroit: 221–43.

Marzolph, U. and Amirhosseini-Nithammer, A. (trans. and eds) (1994). 'Wenn der Esel singt, tanzt das Kamel. Persische Märchen und Schwänke' in *Erzählt von Maschdi Galin Chanom. Aufgezeichnet von L.P. Elwell,* Wiesbaden: 112–27.

— and van Leeuwen, R. (2004). *The Arabian Nights Encyclopedia,* 1–2, Santa Barbara.

Massé, H. (1951). 'Les versions persanes des contes d'animaux' in Contenau, G. et al, *L'Âme de l'Iran*. Paris: 129–49.

Mas'udi, 'Ali b. al-Hosayn, (1861–77). (eds) Barbier de Maynard, C.A. and Pavet de Courteille, A.J., *Moruj al-zahab wa-ma'āden al-jawhar*, 9 vols, Paris; (1404 / 1984) 4 vols, Beirut; (1965); de Meynard, B. and Pavet de Courteille, P. trans. as *Les prairies d'or*, 2 vols, Paris.

al-Māwardi, see *Nasihat al-moluk*.

Meier, F. (1974), 'Orientalische belege für das motiv, nur einmal zuschlagen' in Salmon, P. (ed.), *Mélanges d'Islamologie. Volume dédié à la mémoire d'Armand Abel*, 1, Leiden, 207–23.

Meisami, J.S. (1999). *Persian Historiography to the End of the Twelfth Century*, Edinburgh.

— (2000). 'Why Write History in Persian? Historical Writing in the Samanid Period' in Hillenbrand, C. (ed.), *Studies in Honour of Clifford Edmund Bosworth*, vol. II, Leiden: 348–74.

Melikian-Chirvani, A.S. (1971). 'Royaume de Salomon', *Le Monde Iranien et l'Islam* I: 1–41.

— (1990). 'Buddhism II: In Islamic Times', *EncIr*, 4: 496–9.

— (1995). '*Rekāb*: The Polylobed Wine Boat from Sasanian to Saljuq Times' in *Au carrefour des religions: mélanges offerts à Philippe Gignoux*, Bures-sur-Yvette: 187–204.

— (1997). 'The Wine-Birds of Iran from Pre-Achaemenid to Islamic Times', *Bulletin of the Asia Institute* 9: 41–97.

Menasce, J. de (1958). *Une Encyclopédie Mazdéenne Le Dēnkart: quatre conférences données à l'Université de Paris sous les auspices de la Fondation Ratanbai Katrak*, Paris.

— (1973). *Le troisième livre du Dēnkart*, Paris.

Michailidis, M. (forthcoming 2011). 'In the Footsteps of the Sasanians: Funerary Architecture and Bavandid Legitimacy' in Babaie, S. and Grigor, T. (eds.), *Persian Architecture and Kingship: Displays of Power and Politics in Iran from the Achaemenids to the Pahlavis*, London.

Minorsky, V. (1932). *La Domination des Daylamites*, Paris.

— (1942). *Sharaf al-Zamān Tāhir Marvazi on China, the Turks and India*, London.

— (1953). 'The Iranian Intermezzo' in *Studies in Caucasian History*, Cambridge.

— (1964). 'The Older Preface to the Shāh-nāma' in Minorsky, V., *Iranica: Twenty Articles*, Tehran: 268–9.

Moayyad, H. (1988). 'Lyric Poetry' in Yarshater, E. (ed), *Persian Literature*, Albany, New York: 120–46.

Mohammadi, M. (1964). *Tarjama wa al-naql 'an al-fāresiya*, Beirut.

Mojmal al-Tawārikh wa'l-Qesas (1381 AH). Bahār, M.T. (ed.), Tehran.

Moqaddasi, Muhammad b. Ahmad (1906). *Ahsan al-taqāsim fi ma'refat al-aqālim*, de Goeje, M.J. (ed.), Bibliotheca geographorum arabicorum, vol. 3,

Leiden; (1994). Collins, B.A. (trans.), *The Best Divisions for Knowledge of the Regions,* Reading.

Müller, A. (1880). 'Arabische Quellen zur Geschichte der indischen Medizin', *ZDMG* 34: 465–556.

Naaman, E. (2009). 'Literature and Literary People at the Court of Al-Sāhib Ibn 'Abbād', Harvard University dissertation.

Nainar, S.M.H. (1942). *Arab Geographers' Knowledge of Southern India,* Madras.

Narshakhi, Abu Bakr Mohammad b. Ja'far (1351 / 1972). *Tārikh-e Bokhārā,* Razavi, M. (ed.), Tehran.

al-Nasafi, Najm al-Din Omar b. Mohammad (1999). *al-Qand fi zekr olamā' Samarqand,* al-Hādi, Y. (ed.), Tehran.

Nasihat al-moluk al-mansub ilā Abi'l-Hasan al-Māwardi (1988). Ahmad, F.A.M., (ed.), Alexandria; (1403 / 1983). Kedr, K.M., (ed.), Kuwait.

Nāzim, M. (1931). *The Life and Times of Sultān Mahmūd of Ghazna,* Cambridge.

Nezām al-Molk (1347 / 1960). *Siyar al-moluk,* Darke, H. (ed.), Tehran.

O'Kane, B. (2005). 'The Origin, Development and Meaning of the Nine-Bay Plan in Islamic Architecture' in Daneshvari A. (ed.), *A Survey of Persian Art: Vol XVIII: From the End of the Sasanian Empire to the Present, Studies in Honor of Arthur Upham Pope,* Costa Mesa: 189–244.

Omidsalar, M. (1989). 'Aždahā. 3: In Iranian Folktales' in *EncIr* 3: 203–4.

— (1996).'Dīv' in *EncIr* 7: 428–31.

— (2002).'Peri (Pari)' in *Enzyklopädie des Märchens,* 10, Berlin: cols 743–6.

— and Omidsalar, T. (1999). 'Narrating Epics in Iran' in Macdonald, M.R. (ed.), *Traditional Storytelling Today. An International Sourcebook.* Detroit: 326–40.

Otto-Dorn, K. (1964). *L'art de l'Islam,* Paris.

Pancaroğlu, O. (2002). 'Serving Wisdom: The Contents of Samanid Epigraphic Pottery' in *Studies in Islamic and Later Indian Art from the Arthur M. Sackler Museum, Harvard University Art Museums,* Cambridge, MA: 59–75.

Paul, J. (1993). 'The Histories of Samarqand', *Studia Iranica* 22: 69–92.

Peacock, A.C.S. (2007). *Mediaeval Islamic Historiography and Political Legitimacy: Bal'amī's* Tārīkhnāma, London.

— (2010). *Early Seljūq History: a New Interpretation,* London.

Pellat, C. (1993). 'al-Nadr b. al-Hārith' in EI², 7: 872–3.

Perry, B.E. (1960). *The Origin of the Book of Sinbad,* Berlin.

Pingree, D. (1968). *The Thousands of Abū Ma'shar,* London.

Pope, A.U. (ed.) (1964). *Survey of Persian Art, Vol. III: The Architecture of the Islamic Period,* Ashiya.

— and Ackerman, P. (9 January 1943). 'The Most Important Textile Ever Found in Persia', *Illustrated London News*: 48–9.

— and Ackerman, P. (eds) (1977). *A Survey of Persian Art from Prehistoric Times to the Present.* 1938–39, Tehran.

Pourshariati, P. (2008). *Decline and Fall of the Sasanian Empire: The Sasanian-Parthian Confederacy and the Arab Conquest of Iran*, London.

Pritsak, O. (1951). 'Von den Karluk zu den Karachaniden', *ZDMG* 101: 270–300.

Qazvini, M. M.(1332 / 1943). 'Moqaddama-ye qadim-e Shāhnāma' in Qazvini, M.M., *Bist maqāla*, 2 vols, Tehran.

Rāfe'i, 'Abd al-Karim b. Mohammad. (1374 AH). *al-Tadwin fi akhbār Qazwin*, Tehran.

Ramaswamy, T.N. (1962). *Essentials of Indian Statecraft. Kautilya's Arthaśāstra for Contemporary Readers*, New York.

Rekaya, M. (1978). 'Kārinids', *EI²*: 644–7.

Rhys Davids, T.W. and Oldenberg, H. (1882). *Vinaya Texts*, translated from the Pali, in the series *The Sacred Books of the East*, Müller, F.M. (ed.), vol. 17, Oxford; (1982). reprinted Delhi.

Richter, G. (1932). *Studien zur Geschichte der älteren arabischen Fürstenspiegel*, Leipzig.

Richter-Bernberg, L. (1974). 'Linguistic Shuʻūbīya and Early Neo-Persian Prose', *JAOS* 94 (1): 55–64.

— (1980). *'Amir-Mālik-Shāhānshāh:* 'Adud ad-Daula's Titulature Re-examined', *Iran* 18: 83–102.

Robinson, C.F. (2003). *Islamic Historiography*, Cambridge.

Röhrich, L. (1981). 'Drache, Drachenkampf, Drachentöter in *Enzyklopädie des Märchens*, Berlin, 3: cols 787–820.

Rosenthal, F. (1968). *A History of Muslim Historiography*, 2nd revised edition, Leiden.

— (1989). 'Abū Zayd al-Balkhī on Politics' in Bosworth, C.E. et al (eds), *Essays in Honor of Bernard Lewis. The Islamic World from Classical to Modern Times*, Princeton: 287–301.

Rowson, E.K. (1988) *A Muslim Philosopher on the Soul and its Fate: al-ʿĀmirī's Kitāb al-Amad ʿalā 'l-abad*, New Haven.

— (1990). 'The Philosopher as Littérateur: al-Tawhīdī and his Predecessors', *Zeitschrift für Geschichte der Arabisch-Islamischen Wissenschaften* 6: 50–92.

— (2011). 'al-Thaʻālibī, Abu Mansūr ʻAbd al-Malik b. Muhammad', *EI²*, 10: 426–8.

Safadi, Salāh-al-Din Khalil b. Aybak, (1962–). *al-Wāfi be 'l-wafayāt*, Wiesbaden.

'The Saint-Josse Shroud'
http://www.louvre.fr/llv/oeuvres/detail_notice.jsp?CONTENT%3C%3Ecnt_id=10134198673226262&CURRENT_LLV_NOTICE%3C%3Ecnt_id=10134198673226262&FOLDER%3C%3Efolder_id=9852723696500781&bmLocale=en, accessed June 29, 2010.

Samʻāni, Abū Saʻd Abd al-Karim b. Mohammad (1382–1403 / 1962–82). *Ketāb al-ansāb*, al-Yamani, A.R.b.Y.a-M., (ed.), 13 vols, Hyderabad.

Samarqandi (1969). *Tarjoma-ye al-Savād al-aʻzam*, Tehran.

al-Samarqandi, Mohammad b. Ali al-Zahiri (1949). *Sindbād-nāma*, Ateş, A. (ed.), Istanbul.

Sarakhsī, Muhammad b. Ahmad, (1324 AH). *Ketāb al-Mabsūt,* vol. 1, al-Hanafī, M.R. (ed.), Cairo.

Sarkārāti, B. (1350 / 1971). 'Pari. Tahqiqi dar hāshiya-ye ostura-shenāsi-ye tatbiqi' in *Nashriya-ye Dāneshkada-ye adabiyāt va olum-e ensāni-ye Tabriz,* 23: 1–32.

Sarkhosh Curtis, V. and Stewart, S. (eds) (2008). *The Sasanian Era*, The Idea of Iran, vol. 3, London.

Sauvaget, J. (1940). 'Remarques sur les monuments omeyyades II: Argenteries "sassanides"', *Mélanges asiatiques* [*Journal Asiatique*] 222 (1940–41), 19–57.

Schaeder, H. (1930). *Iranische Beiträge* I, *Schriften der Königsberger Gelehrten Gesellschaft,* 6 vol. 5, Halle.

Schiefner, A. (1875). *Mahkâtjâjana und König Tshannda-Pradjota. Ein Cyklus buddhistischer Erzählungen,* Mémoires de l'Académie Impériale des Sciences de St Pétersbourg, VIIe série, XXII, 7.

Semenov, A.A. (1954). 'K voprosu o proiskhozhdenii Samanidov', *Sbornik statei, posviashchennykh istorii i kul'tura perioda formirovaniia tadzhikskogo naroda i ego gosudarstvennosti* (Trudy akademii nauk Tadzhikskoi SSR*),* 27, Stalinabad, 3–11.

Sezgin, F. (1967–2000). *Geschichte des arabischen Schrifttums,* Leiden and Frankfurt.

Shahbazi, A.S., 'Bahrām vi. Bahrām Čubin', *EIr* online.

— (1990). 'On the *Xʷadāy-nāmag',* *Varia Iranica: Papers in Honor of Professor Ehsan Yarshater,* Leiden = *Acta Iranica* 30: 208–29.

Shahrazuri, Mohammad b. Mahmud (1396 / 1976). *Nozhat al-arwāh wa rawdat al-afrāh fi ta'rikh al-hokamā' wa'l-falāsefa,* Ahmad, K. (ed.), Hyderabad.

Shaked, S. (ed. and trans.) (1979). *The Wisdom of the Sasanian Sages (Dēnkard VI) by Āturpāt ī Ēmētān,* Boulder, Co.

— (1984). 'From Iran to Islam: Notes on Some Themes in Transmission', *Jerusalem Studies in Arabic and Islam* IV: 31–67. Repr. (1995) *From Zoroastrian Iran to Islam,* London.

Shepherd, D.G. (1973). 'In Defence of the Persian Silks', *Bulletin de Liason du Centre International d'Études des Textiles Anciens* 37: 143–45.

— (1974). 'Medieval Persian Silks in Fact and Fancy (A Refutation of the Riggisberg Report)', *Bulletin de Liaison Du Centre International d'Étude Des Textiles Anciens* 39–40, nos i–ii.

Shojaei Kawan, C. (2002). 'Schwester: Die treulose S. (AaTh/ATU 315)' in *Enzyklopädie des Märchens,* Berlin, 12: cols 434–9.

Skjærvø, P.O. (1989). 'Aždahā. 1. In Old and Middle Iranian', *EncIr* 3: 191–9.

Smirnov, I.I. (1909). *Vostochnoe Serebro,* St Petersburg.

Soroudi, S. (1980). 'Islamization of the Iranian National Hero Rustam as Reflected in Persian Folktales', *Jerusalem Studies in Arabic and Islam* 2: 365–83.

Soudavar, A. (2003). *The Aura of Kings: Legitimacy and Divine Sanction in Iranian Kingship*, Costa Mesa.

Sourdel, D. (1947–8). 'Le "Livre des secretaries" de 'Abdallāh al-Baghdādī', *Bulletin d'études orientales* 12: 115–53.

Sourdel-Thomine, J. and Spuler, B. (1973). *Die Kunst Des Islam.* Propyläen Kunstgeschichte, Berlin.

Soyuti, Jalāl-al-Din (2004). *Boghyat al-wo'āt fi tabaqāt al-loghawiyin wa-l-nohāt*, Ata, M.A.Q. (ed.), Beirut.

Steinschneider, M. (1870). 'Zur Geschichte der Übersetzungen aus dem Indischen in's Arabische und ihres Einflusses auf die arabische Literatur', *ZDMG* 24: 325–92.

Sundermann, W. (1999). '*Fehrest* III: The Representation of Manicheism in the *Fehrest*', *EncIr* 9: 479–83.

Tabari, Ali b. Sahl b. Rabban, (2002). *Ferdaws al-hekma fi l-tebb*, al-Jondi, A.K.S., (ed.), Beirut.

Tabari, Mohammad b. Jarir, (1960–[1977]). *Ta'rikh al-Tabari: Ta'rikh al-rosul wa-l-moluk*, Ebrāhim, M.A.F. (ed.), Cairo.

Tafazzoli, A., 'Fahlaviyat', *EncIr*, online.

Talbot-Rice, D. (1965). *Islamic Art,* London.

Tā'rikh-e Sistān. (1381 AH). Bahār, M.T. (ed.), Tehran.

Tawhidi, Abu Hayyān (1939–44). *al-Emtā' wa 'l-mo'ānasa*, Amīn, A. and al-Zayn, A. (eds), Cairo.

Tha'ālebi, Abd al Malek (1381 / 1961). *al-Tamthil wa 'l-mohādara*, al-Helw, 'A.F.M., (ed.), Cairo.

— (1990). *Ādāb al-moluk*, 'Atiya, J. (ed.), Beirut.

al-Tha'ālebi, *Ghorar akhbār moluk al-fors wa siyarehem*, first volume published as Aboû Mansoûr 'Abd al-Malik ibn Mohammad ibn Ismâ'îl al-Tha'âlibî (1900). *Histoire des Rois des Perses*, Zotenberg, H. (ed. and trans.), Paris; both first and second volumes in MS Süleymaniye Library, Istanbul, Damad Ibrahim 916; (1963). *Ta'rikh ghorar al-siyar al-ma'ruf be-Ketāb ghorar akhbār moluk al-fors wa siyarehem li Abi Mansur al-Tha'ālebi,* Tehran.

— (1968). (trans.) Bosworth, C.E., *The Book of Curious and Entertaining Information: The Lata'if al-Ma'arif of Tha'alibi,* Edinburgh.

[Pseudo-]Tha'ālebi, (1977). *Tohfat al-wozarā' al-mansub elā Abi Mansur 'Abd al-Malek b. Mohammad b. Esmā'il al-Tha'ālebi*, al-Rawi, H.'A. and al-Saffar, I.M., Baghdad.

Thapar, R. (1966, reprinted 1990). *A History of India.* vol. 1, London.

Thompson, D. (1976). *Stucco from Chal Tarkhan-Eshqabad Near Rayy*, Warminster.

Tor, D.G. (2009). 'The Islamization of Central Asia in the Samanid Era and the Reshaping of the Muslim World', *BSOAS,* 72 (3).

Trautmann, T.R. (1971). *Kautilya and the Arthaśāstra: A Statistical Investigation of the Authorship and Evolution of the Text*, Leiden.

Treadwell, W.L. (1991). 'The Political History of the Sāmānid State', Unpublished D. Phil. Thesis, University of Oxford.

— (2000). 'Ibn Zafir al-Azdi's Account of the Murder of Ahmad b. Isma'il al-Samani and the Succession of his Son Nasr' in *Studies in Honour of Clifford Edmund Bosworth*, vol. 2, Leiden: 397–419.

— (2003). '*Shāhanshāh* and *al-Malik al-Mu'ayyad*: the Legitimation of Power in Samanid and Buyid Iran' in Daftary, F. and Meri, J.W. (eds), *Culture and Memory in Medieval Islam: Essays in Honour of Wilferd Madelung*, London: 318–37.

— (2007). 'The Monetary History of the Bukharkhuda Drachm ("Black Dirham") in Samanid Transoxiania (204–395 / 819–1005)', *Coinage and History in the Seventh Century Near East* (Supplement to the Oriental Numismatic Society Journal, 193, Autumn): 25–40.

Turtushi, Abu Bakr Mohammad b. al-Walid, (1414 / 1994). *Serāj al-moluk*, Fathi Abu-Bakr, M. (ed.), 2 vols, Cairo.

Tusi, A. (1977). *Loghat-e Fors*, Dabir-e Siyāqi, M. (ed.), Tehran.

Vial, G. (1973). 'Technical Studies on the Buyid Silk Fabrics of the Abegg Foundation – Berne', *Bulletin de Liason du Centre International d'Études de Textiles Anciens* 37: 70–80.

Volov (Golombek), L. (1966). 'Plaited Kufic on Samanid Epigraphic Pottery', *Ars Orientalis* 6: 107–34.

Wagle, N.K. (1995). *Society at the Time of the Buddha*, 2nd revised edition, Bombay.

Weber, A. (1878). *The History of Indian Literature*, Mann, J., and Zachariae, T. (eds), (translated from the second German edition), Boston.

Werkmeister, W. (1983). *Quellenuntersuchungen zum Kitāb al-'Iqd al-farīd des Andalusiers Ibn 'Abdrabbih (246 / 860–328 / 940)*, Berlin.

Wiet, G. (1948). *Soieries Persanes*, Cairo.

Wilkinson, C.K. (1973). *Nishapur: Pottery of the Early Islamic Period*, New York.

Williams, A.V. (1989).'The Body and the Boundaries of Zoroastrian Spirituality', *Religion* 19: 227–39.

— (1990). The *Pahlavi Rivāyat Accompanying the Dādestān ī Dēnīg*, Copenhagen.

— (1994). 'Zoroastrian and Jewish Purity Laws: Reflections on the Viability of Sociological Interpretation' in Shaked, S. and Netzer, A. (eds), *Irano-Judaica III*, Jerusalem: 72–89.

— (1997). 'Zoroastrianism and the Body' in Coakley, S. (ed.), *Religion and the Body*, Cambridge: 155–66.

— (2005). 'Lexicography and Zoroastrian Meanings in the Pahlavi Books' in Cereti, C.G. and Maggi, M. (eds), *Middle Iranian Lexicography*, Serie Orientale Roma XCVIII, Orientalia Romana 8, Roma: 387–98.

— (2009). *The Zoroastrian Myth of Migration from Iran and Settlement in the Indian Diaspora: Text Translation and Analysis of the 16th Century Qesse-ye Sanjān 'The Story of Sanjan*, Numen Book Series, Studies in the History of Religions, Texts and Sources in the History of Religions, vol. 124, Leiden and Boston.

— (forthcoming 2012). 'Purity, Pollution and the Body' in Stausberg, M. and Vevaina, Y.S.D. (eds), *The Blackwell Companion to the Study of Zoroastrianism*, London.

Ya'qubi, Ahmad b. Abi Ya'qub (1400 / 1980). *Ta'rikh al-Ya'qubi*, 2 vols, Beirut.

Yāqut b. 'Abd Allāh al-Hamawi, (1923-31). *Ershād al–arib elā ma'refat al–adib al-ma'ruf be-Mo'jam al-odabā'*, Margoliouth, D.S. (ed.), London; (1991). *Ershād al-arib elā ma'refah al-adīb*, vol. III, Beirut.

— (1957). *Mu'jam al-buldān,* vol. 3, Beirut.

Yarshater, E. (1983). 'Iranian National History' in Yarshater, E. (ed.), *The Cambridge History of Iran* III/i: *The Seleucid, Parthian and Sasanian Periods*, Cambridge.

Yücesoy, H. (2007). 'Ancient Imperial Heritage and Islamic Universalist Historiography: al-Dīnawarī's Secular Perspective', *Journal of Global History* 2: 135–55.

Yusuf, S.M. (1955). 'The Early Contacts between Islam and Buddhism', *University of Ceylon Review* 13: 1–28.

Zaehner, R.C. (1955). *Zurvan: A Zoroastrian Dilemma*, Oxford.

Zakeri, M. (1995). *Sāsānid Soldiers in Early Muslim Society. The Origins of 'Ayyārān and Futuwwa*, Wiesbaden.

— (2007). *Persian Wisdom in Arabic Garb: 'Alī b. 'Ubayda al-Rayhānī and his* Jawāhir al-kilam wa-farā'id al-hikam, 1–2, Leiden.

Zimmermann, F.W. (1990). 'Al-Kindī' in Young, M.L.J., Latham, J.D., and Serjeant, R.B. (eds), *The Cambridge History of Arabic Literature. Religion, Learning and Science in the 'Abbāsid Period*, Cambridge: 364–9.